PUBLIC SERVICES AND CITIZENSHIP IN EUROPEAN LAW

PUBLIC SERVICES AND CITIZENSHIP IN EUROPEAN LAW

Public and Labour Law Perspectives

Edited by

MARK FREEDLAND

and

SILVANA SCIARRA

CLARENDON PRESS · OXFORD
1998

Oxford University Press, Great Clarendon Street, Oxford OX2 6DP
Oxford New York
Athens Auckland Bangkok Bogotá Buenos Aires Calcutta
Cape Town Chennai Dar es Salaam Delhi Florence Hong Kong Istanbul
Karachi Kuala Lumpur Madras Madrid Melbourne Mexico City Mumbai
Nairobi Paris São Paulo Singapore Taipei Tokyo Toronto Warsaw
and associated companies in
Berlin Ibadan

Oxford is a registered trade mark of Oxford University Press

Published in the United States
by Oxford University Press Inc., New York

First published 1998

British Library Cataloguing in Publication Data
Data available

Library of Congress Cataloging in Publication Data
Data available
ISBN 0–19–826575–1

1 3 5 7 9 10 8 6 4 2

Typeset by Hope Services (Abingdon) Ltd.
Printed in Great Britain
on acid-free paper by
Bookcraft Ltd., Midsomer Norton, Somerset

Contents

Preface

As we explain more fully at the beginning of the first chapter, this book, whatever its shortcomings, can at least claim to be a symposium work in the full and classical sense, the product of the shared enthusiasm and intellectual collaboration of all those who have contributed to it. Most of us took part in the Workshop which took place on February 2 and 3, 1996 at the Villa Schifanoia of the European University Institute in Florence as part of the annual Forum, in that year on the subject of Citizenship, directed by Klaus Eder, Steven Lukes and Massimo La Torre. We have taken time, as Editors, to assemble further contributions and to organise the chapters in relation to each other, so that the book which results is a more fully fashioned piece of work than the mere publication of the proceedings of the workshop would have been. This is not to under-rate the importance of the contributions to the workshop which are not directly reflected in the chapters of this book, especially those of Steven Lukes, Antonio Baylos and, last but by no means least, Robert Villeneuve of CEEP, the Centre Européen des Entreprises à Participation Publique, of which more below.

There are some costs of allowing this relatively long period of gestation. We are conscious that some contributors might have changed and developed their own positions more extensively than the exigencies of book production allow us to reflect. Moreover, some technical problems were created. There was, for instance, the issue of how to respond to the making of the Treaty of Amsterdam in October 1997. We decided to adapt to it in substance, but to leave references to articles of the earlier Treaties unchanged. We hope that both contributors and readers will be tolerant of our editorial stance in this, as in other, respects.

Of one part of our editorial approach at least, we can feel quite confident. Given that the contributors are from different EU Member States, it seemed to us extremely important to ensure that the composite work was produced in high quality and continuous English. If this, as we hope, has been achieved, that is entirely to the credit of the remarkable skills as a translator and linguistic reviser of Rita Inston, to whose profound grasp of the subtleties of legal language we pay most heartfelt tribute.

Several other acknowledgments are due. First of all, we record our gratitude for the intellectual, organisational and financial support we received from the Annual Forum of the EUI, to Yves Mény as the Director of the Robert Schuman Centre and of the European Forum Centre for Advanced

Legal Studies at the EUI, and to the administrator of the annual Forum, Katinka Espana, whose great managerial talents have been fully called upon. Invaluable secretarial and information technology support have been provided by Susan Garvin, research assistant in the Law Department of the EUI, and by Ruth Toureau, and Matthew Jennings, respectively Deputy College Secretary and Computing Officer at St. John's College, Oxford. Robert Villeneuve of CEEP, whom we mentioned earlier, provided a most useful set of notes of the proceedings of the workshop, and a body of background documentation, which were of great assistance in preparing this work.

We are also extremely grateful to the Delegates of the Oxford University Press for agreeing to publish our work, and to their Editorial staff for law books, especially Myfanwy Milton and John Louth, for the effort and imagination which they have contributed to the development of the project. They and we were ably supported by the copy-editing work of Kate Elliot and the indexing work of Robert Spicer. If the mountainous labours of all those contributors and collaborators have brought forth only a mouse, it is we as Editors who are to blame for its smallness. If the outcome is judged to have any larger dimension, the credit for that is due to those we have acknowledged in the Preface, and those who have helped them in our shared task.

Mark Freedland
and
Silvana Sciarra

Oxford and Florence
St. John the Baptist Day 1998

List of Contributors

Professor Giuliano AMATO (until the end of 1997 President of the Italian Anti-trust Authority), Professor of Law, Robert Schuman Center and Department of Law, European University Institute, Florence

Professor Mark FREEDLAND, Professor of Employment Law, University of Oxford

David FAULKNER, Fellow of St John's College Oxford

Professor Carol HARLOW, Professor of Public Law, London School of Economics

Professor Elisenda MALARET GARCIA, Professor of Administrative Law, University of Barcelona

Professor Alessandro PETRETTO, Professor of Public Economics, Faculty of Economics, University of Florence

Professor Etienne PICARD, Professor of Public Law, University of Paris I (Panthéon-Sorbonne)

Professor Wolf SAUTER, Professor of Economic Law, University of Groningen and Research Fellow, Centre for European Law and Policy (ZERP), Bremen

Professor Silvana SCIARRA, Professor of European Labour and Social Law, European University Institute, and University of Florence

Professor Alain SUPIOT, Professor of Law, University of Nantes, and Fellow (1997–8) of Wissenschaftskolleg zu Berlin

Table of Abbreviations

AJDA	Actualité Juridique—Droit Administratif
CDE	Cahiers des Droit Europénne
CEEP	European Centre for Enterprises with Public Participation
CNRS	Centre National de la recherche scientifique (National Centre for Scientific Research)
EC	European Community
ECJ	European Court of Justice
ECLR	European Competition Law Review
ECR	European Court Reports
EDF	Electricité de France
EEC	European Economic Community
ESCR	Economic and Social Research Unit
ETUC	European Trade Union Congress
ETUI	European Trade Union Institute
EU	European Union
FCC	Federal Communications Commission
FS	Italian State Railways
GATS	General Agreement on Trade in Services
GATT	General Agreement on Tariffs and Trade
GDP	Gross domestic product
HMSO	Her Majesty's Stationery Office
IGC	Inter-Governmental Conference
ILO	International Labour Office
ISO	International Standards Organisation
MIT	Massachusetts Institute of Technology
NPM	New Public Management
NRAs	National Regulatory Authorities
OECD	Organisation for Economic Cooperation and Development
OFTEL	Office of Telecommunications
OFWAT	Office of Water Services
OJ	Official Journal [of the EC]
ONP	Open Network Provision
PTTs	Post, Telegraph and Telephone Ministries
RDP	Revue de Droit Public
SNCF	Société nationale des chemins de fer (French State Railways)
TENs	Trans European Networks
TOs	Telecommunications Operators
WLR	Weekly Law Reports
WTO	World Trade Organization

1

Law, Public Services, and Citizenship—New Domains, New Regimes?

MARK FREEDLAND

1. The General Thesis—a Public Service Sector

In the academic year 1995–6, the European University Institute devoted its annual Forum to the subject of citizenship, the principal focus being on European Community citizenship; this created the opportunity to organize workshops on topics relevant to the subject of citizenship. It was decided to organize a workshop which had the purpose of exploring the idea of citizenship in labour law and public law, especially in relation to public services. The notion that this was a useful and coherent subject for discussion was a matter far more of intuition than of evidence; and the group of people we invited to participate in this workshop was decidedly heterogeneous in terms of their interests and intellectual backgrounds.

Nevertheless, the symposium which resulted produced a powerful feeling of excitement among the participants, and a stimulating sense of convergence upon an interesting theme from a variety of very different starting points. So much was this the case that it was decided to treat the papers which had been given as the basis for a symposium book. However, the gathering together of those papers, even with the addition of one or two more contributions, did not in itself resolve the question, what was the exact relationship between them, or, in other words, what was the thesis which would link them together, which they between them would sustain and elaborate. It has required a further period of reflection and discussion to establish that synthesis; the purpose of this chapter is to indicate the results of those deliberations.

The central thesis may be boldly stated as follows.[1] We are witnessing,

[1] Since proposing this thesis, I have had the great benefit of reading Wade MacLauchlan's chapter on 'Public Service Law and the New Public Management' in the symposium edited by Michael Taggart, *The Province of Administrative Law* (Hart Publishing, Oxford, 1997) (ch. 6). His paper, by 'evok[ing] a discipline of public-service law *en emergence*' (*ibid.*, 119) engages in a project which is similar to the one which I attempt in this chapter, with the difference, perhaps, that I am less inclined than he is to construct public-service law as a distinct discipline, in that I prefer to see the discourse about the law applicable to the public-service sector as remaining within the disciplines of public law and employment law (and, for that

in the law and practice of European countries, quite a rapid evolution of a third sector which we might call the public-service sector, which we have to distinguish from, on the one hand, the state sector and, on the other hand, the wholly private sector. In this third sector, ideas about citizenship (both at State level and at European Community level) are particularly significant and influential, especially in the way that they inform the shape and application of public law and labour law. That is how we arrive at the title of this symposium. So the central and unifying argument of this work is that it is useful to envisage a distinct and distinctive body of law for public services, and to expound that body of law in a way which draws on notions of citizenship. But we should not be deceived, by the high-sounding references to notions of public service and of citizenship, into thinking that this is a sector in which there is a particular consensus as to values and policies which should determine the shape of the legal regime. On the contrary, by identifying this third sector, we actually concentrate attention upon a set of conflicts and tensions which occur, certainly, in the other sectors, but which are experienced especially acutely in this sector. There is reason to think, and the papers in this symposium point towards the conclusion, that the existing discourse both of public law and of labour law needs to be re-aligned towards the problems of this rapidly growing third sector.

However, before those conclusions, so boldly stated, can be regarded as having been substantiated, quite a long intellectual journey has to be undertaken. This involves travelling through less than fully explored territory, in which the terrain is at times extremely difficult. In particular, it will be necessary to spend quite a lot of time in the field of public law before going into the field of labour law. In fact, the chapters fall into two groups, in a way which reflects this. There is a general group, which is mainly about public law (chapters 1–8); and there is a special group which is directly concerned with labour law (chapters 9–10). Between them, they construct and explore the idea of a third, public-service, sector both in relation to public law and in relation to labour law.

2. The Growth of a Distinct Public-service Sector in the Political Economy

The central thesis of this chapter is the assertion of the extreme transformative significance, in relation both to public law and to labour law, of the growth of a public-service sector as a third sector distinct both from the

matter, competition law), albeit as the subject of distinct treatment within those disciplines. This is in no way to disparage his argument, which seems to me to have great force and usefulness.

public and the private sectors. The purpose of this section is to define that development, and in particular to identify it as primarily an economic and political development, and only secondarily a development in legal doctrine and legal reasoning. We have to begin, therefore, by defining this phenomenon, which we allege to be not just authentic but also profoundly important, of the growth of a third, public-service, sector of the political economies of European countries.

For the purposes of our argument, then, we offer the following working definition of the third, public-service, sector. It is the sector of the economy in which services or activities, recognized as public in the sense that the State is seen as ultimately responsible for the provision of them, are nevertheless not provided by the State itself but by institutions which are intermediate between the market and the State. These institutions are, on the one hand, too independent of the State to be regarded as part of the State, but are, on the other hand, too closely and distinctively associated with the goals, activities, and responsibilities of the State to be thought of as simply part of the private sector of the political economy.

We will, of course, have to justify and defend various aspects of this purportedly definitive assertion. Indeed, the first thing we have to do is show that this phenomenon exists outside our own imagination, our abstract mental constructions. It is important, for this purpose, to realize that the existence of this distinctive third intermediate sector is not asserted as a matter of existing political, economic, or legal theory. In fact, the point will be made that the assertion of the distinctness of the public-service sector cuts across and challenges much conventional legal analysis, which is of an essentially binary character, insisting on a straightforward dichotomy between the public and the private sectors, between the realms of public and of private law.

Perhaps the best way of arguing for the distinctive existence of our third, public-service, sector as a matter of practical reality is to point to the political dynamics which have so greatly increased its significance in recent years. We can confidently assert that there has been a great political fashion in the 1980s and 1990s for attempting to transfer to the private sector many of the service-providing functions which had been assumed by the State in most European countries. This push has varied in its intensity between those countries, but has produced a large measure of privatization of state enterprises, dissolution of state monopolies, and contracting-out by the State of many of its previous activities.

Note that we described these initiatives as *attempts* to transfer to the private sector rather than actual transfers to the private sector. This is the key to understanding why these initiatives in fact create or augment the intermediate third sector which we have postulated. That is to say, we suggest that these initiatives, these exercises in hollowing-out the State, often amount to an incomplete or partial transfer to the private sector, leaving the activity in question perched between the public and private sectors in a genuinely distinctive situation, which should be regarded as constituting a third sector. We now need to explain in what sense we assert that the transfer to the private sector is incomplete in the situations to which we refer.

The point is that in relation to many of these exercises in privatization (using that word in its broadest and loosest sense), we find that the State is left not just with that ultimate regulatory responsibility which we might regard it as having for *all* activity occurring within its political economy, but with a higher level of responsibility which, although reduced from primary to secondary level, nevertheless still ascribes a partly public character to the activity in question. Is this, however, simply a re-statement in slightly different terms of our theoretical construction of a third sector, or can we demonstrate the existence of this kind of intermediate level of responsibility in practical terms?

We can do this most effectively by pointing to the many situations in which even the most extreme proponents of total privatization have had to accept that there are a number of services and utilities which governments cannot transfer completely to the private sector, however much they may wish to do so. They have at least to leave in place a special apparatus of regulation of the economic and social functioning of the activity concerned, as where they 'privatize' utilities such as the supply of water, gas, or electricity, or transport systems such as railways, or as where they contract out governmental services such as the prison service. Or they may have to content themselves with going no further than creating market analogues or 'internal markets' in the service or activity in question, as (at one stage, at least) in health and education services in the United Kingdom, though in that case it may be highly debatable whether the activity has even been moved out of the pure public sector. So privatized but regulated public utilities and contracted-out custodial services probably provide the best and purest practical examples of transfer of activities to an intermediate public-service sector.

All this is not to say that it is only by means of partial privatization that activities become located in the intermediate public-service sector. There was a long period during which European countries were as much or more engaged in various forms of nationalization or partial socialization as they have recently been engaged in privatization; in many cases, the latter movement is largely a reversal of an earlier, in its time no less radical, movement in the opposite direction. And, although that kind of partial socialization seems to be out of fashion among the nation States of Europe, there are some stirrings in this direction at Community level, for instance in the form of recognition of 'services of general interest', with which we shall be extensively concerned in the present work. So transfer of an activity into the public-service sector can occur on more than one trajectory; it is not purely and necessarily the product of neo-liberal marketization of the political economy.

If, as we shall hope to argue, it is thus possible to construct a useful tri-partite theoretical model from these practical realities, it is at the same time also important to acknowledge the limitations of that model. Above all, it is essential to acknowledge that the intermediate public-service sector, which is of course the critical and novel feature of our model, is nevertheless not homogeneous in character. Indeed, that is evident from the variety of the arrangements to which we have referred. That is to say, the secondary responsibility of the State which is the distinguishing feature of this sector will be embodied in various different kinds of regulatory arrangements, such as the institution of a regulator, or on the other hand a process of enforcement of compliance with extra-commercial standards in contracts, or even the use of a 'golden share' in an otherwise purely commercial company.

Moreover, because these arrangements for implementing the secondary responsibility of the State vary considerably, the boundaries of this sector cannot be regarded as precise. It will often be a matter for difficult debate whether the particular set of arrangements places the activity fully in the public sector, where the responsibility of the State is primary, or fully in the private sector where the responsibility of the State is purely residual. However, these imprecisions are not so great as to discredit the whole model; the tri-partite scheme still improves on the precision of the bi-partite model, and does so without simply descending to compiling lists of species of flora and fauna in the garden of political economy. It does seem to be useful to think of a new *genus*, distinct from the accepted two. Perhaps we are now in a position to consider the implications of this analysis for legal doctrine and legal regulation in the fields of public law and labour law.

3. The Public Service Sector in Relation to Public Law

The recognition of a distinct public-service sector, between the public and the private sectors of the political economy, in which, as a defining and distinguishing feature, the responsibility for an activity or service is shared between the State (at a secondary level), and a separate service provider (at a primary level), permits some important analytical refinements to the way we think about the regulation of public-service provision as a matter of public law. We shall find that the insights which these analyses seem to provide also turn out to be helpful in relation to labour law;

but the process of re-casting the legal analysis of public-service provision has to begin in relation to public law.

One good reason for beginning, in that sense, with public law is that the recent growth of the intermediate public-service sector, even if not recognized as such—or, perhaps, *because* not recognized as such—has produced a kind of crisis in legal analysis which has been far more obvious in relation to public law than it has been in relation to labour law—though we shall argue that the crisis, in reality, extends to labour law as well. This crisis, manifested in several of the papers in this symposium, is produced by, indeed consists of, the enormous difficulty of sustaining and applying the accepted and traditional division between public law and private law in the current situation, in which, as we have argued, so much of the activity of the political economy now occurs in a zone which is truly intermediate between its public and private sectors.

The recognition of that zone as a distinct sector does not simply sidestep that problem; it actually addresses the problem, and helps to resolve the crisis associated with that problem, in two main ways. First, by breaking away from a monolithic statist analysis of public-service provision, it enables us to recognize two distinct though complementary roles, in our public law analysis, for, on the one hand, the public-service provider and, on the other hand, the State as the bearer of secondary responsibility in the public-service sector. Secondly, by identifying a conceptual state between the public and private sectors, it enables us to consider at a profound level the tangential relationship between public law and private law at a point where they intersect, and where their different approaches come into contestation with each other.

Each of those two themes or analyses will obviously require substantial elaboration. In the elaboration of these arguments, it will be suggested that ideas about citizenship play a crucial role. First, it will be argued that in this intermediate sector it is a distinctive feature that separate relationships exist between the State and the citizen on the one hand, and, on the other hand, between the citizen and the public-service provider. Those two relationships differ in character in a way which is concealed by a perspective in which a single simple relationship exists between the State and the citizen.

Secondly, and even more centrally to the project of this book, we shall seek to show that it is in the public-service sector that we find revealed most clearly a contestation between rival conceptions of citizenship. For, although there exist many versions and accounts of citizenship, they can usefully be grouped into two types which correspond respectively to the values and concerns of public law and of private law. We can think of these two types as constitutional citizenship on the one hand and market citizenship on the other hand. This proposition challenges a widespread assumption that the discourse about citizenship is one which takes place wholly or mainly in the public sphere, and which is therefore associated with public law *rather than* with private law. This ambiguity or equivocality of citizenship as between the public and the private spheres can be brought out into the open more effectively in a framework of analysis which asserts, precisely, the existence of an intermediate sector poised between the two domains.

We should first, then, revert to and expand upon the suggestion that our analysis in terms of a third distinct public-service sector is useful in exposing the separation of roles as between the State and the public-service provider, and the further suggestion that this can best be understood by reference to their distinct relationships with citizens. We shall suggest shortly why it is legitimate, and indeed helpful, to speak here in terms of *citizens*, rather than simply in terms of *individual persons*; for the moment, it is the relationships between the institutions on the one hand, that is the State and the public-service provider, and the citizen on the other hand with which we are concerned.

The crucial point about these relationships is that they are multiple ones, and that it is the separation between the State and the public-service provider which brings about that multiplicity, by contrast with the situation where the service in question is provided directly by the State itself. In the public-service sector, the citizen has relationships both with the public-service provider (as the bearer of the primary immediate responsibility for the service) and with the State (as the bearer of the secondary but still very significant responsibility in relation to the service concerned). The bilateral relationship between State and citizen in the purely public sector, and for that matter the bilateral relationship between the citizen and the private service provider in the purely private sector, are transformed into trilateral relationships between State, citizen, and public-service provider in the intermediate public-service sector.

It is very important to be able to recognize that this trilateral structure is, from the perspective of public law, really a reorganization of the direct relationship between the State and the citizen into a more complex form, a redistribution of the responsibility of the State so that it is located in two places instead of one. This recognition is important for public law because otherwise public law may easily lose the sharpness of its focus in the public-service sector. That is to say, in the public-service sector, the State on the one hand and the public-service provider on the other might each be able to escape its responsibility in public law by referring to the other as the proper bearer of that responsibility.

This risk, that the control exerted by public law might be mutually deflected and jointly or severally evaded by the State and the public-service provider, is greatly reduced by the analysis in terms of a public-service sector (especially when the analysis is conducted by reference to the idea of citizenship). That is because this analysis recognizes that the trilateral set of relationships, so far from being a marginal and unimportant deviation from a normal public-sector pattern, is on the contrary an entirely stereotypical feature of a different sectoral pattern, namely that of the public-service sector. It thus becomes apparent that if public law is to maintain its vigour, indeed its very integrity, in this sector, it is necessary to make sure that each of the divided parts of public responsibility is maintained in a state where it can be effectively asserted by the citizen—in other words, that it is not possible, *vis-à-vis* the citizen, to 'play both ends off against the middle' in three-sided public-service situations.

This, however, by no means represents the full extent of the problems of applying or interpreting public law in the public-service sector. There is a further and more profound sense in which, if we argue for the distinctiveness of a third, intermediate, public-service sector, we have to accept that the application of public law to it becomes more deeply contestable and contested than if we were content merely to operate on the margins of the traditionally accepted territory of public law. That is to say, it comes into question whether and how far this whole zone is within the province of public law. In other words, has the enterprise of 'privatizing' the activity in question been successful to the point where it has been taken out of the territory of public law, even though described as part of a public-service sector? This is a problem which our second line of argument seeks to address; and, even more so than with the first line of argument, we shall find that reference to ideas of citizenship is helpful. This justifies a section of its own, to which we now turn.

4. Rival Conceptions of Citizenship in Relation to the Public Service Sector

We have argued earlier that the distinctive public-service sector is often enlarged, sometimes even created, by projects of 'privatization' in the broadest sense, whereby governments seek to limit, by deflecting towards public-service providers (who are not, or who can be represented as not being, part of the machinery of the State), their responsibility for activities which would otherwise be viewed as wholly or largely a matter of the public responsibility of the State. But it is of the essence of this intermediate sector that the State retains, whether as a matter of choice and design or despite the best endeavours of governments to the contrary, a secondary public responsibility, of a more than residual kind, for the activity in question. As a result, this third intermediate sector is one which is shared between, or contested as between, the frameworks of public and of private law. One important way in which this sharing or contestation takes place, or at least can be better understood, consists in an interplay between rival versions of citizenship, some of which fit into or form part of a public law framework, others of which promote or sustain a private law approach.

What, then, characterizes these rival versions of citizenship? It might be thought that there was only one obvious basic version of the idea of citizenship, which we shall call constitutional citizenship. On this view, citizenship is the conception we have of full individual membership of the society, State, or community in question. In a democratic society, it implies a claim to participate in the processes of democracy; more generally, it implies a set of links between the State and the individual which it is the very business of public law to maintain in a meaningful and coherent condition.

A very significant component—possibly, it could be argued, the defining feature, of this conception, and certainly the dimension of it with which public law is centrally concerned—consists in the obligation which it imposes upon the institutions which have a relationship of a public character with the citizen to behave in a constitutional, principled, and non-arbitrary fashion *vis-à-vis* the citizen. Increasingly, we tend to think of this as an obligation to refrain from unjustifiably *discriminatory* behaviour towards the citizen, either generally, or particularly in respect of the citizen's membership of a sub-group of the community in question—such as a sub-group distinguished by race, ethnicity, religion, gender, family status, age, or disability.

It is that set of obligations which we tend to think of as creating the 'rights' which this conception of citizenship is seen as giving rise to. From this, as it were 'constitutional', perspective, those rights will tend to be seen as inalienable; and in so far as those rights admit of qualification by reference to the behaviour of the citizen, that will tend to be by reference to the willingness of the citizen to be law-abiding, or, in more exacting variants, by reference to the extent of the citizen's positive contribution to the social or political goals of the community ('active citizenship'). It will be reasonably clear how closely these ideas correspond to the broad notions and approaches of public law (allowing, of course, for the diversity of those approaches as between different European legal systems).

One might imagine that all the versions of citizenship which one would encounter in present-day European societies would conform to this conception; and perhaps we could say that this is in some basic sense the case. However, it is suggested that recent neo-liberal political fashions have tended to involve or evolve a different set of conceptions of citizenship, which we can think about as 'market citizenship' or 'consumer citizenship'. This rival set of conceptions is especially associated with the public-service sector; protagonists of neo-liberal policies of 'privatization' tend to see it as the very *raison d'être* of that sector, to the limited extent to which they are willing to admit of that sector as distinct from the purely private sector. This obviously needs some more explanation.

The expanded explanation runs as follows. A simplistic view of neo-liberal projects of 'privatization' would assess their feasibility, or success if attempted, in terms of their ability to accomplish the complete transfer of a given activity from the public to the private sector. Governments engaged in such projects, however, have on the whole needed to arrive at a less simplistic view, if only because the scope for absolute privatization in that simple sense turns out to be rather limited. That is mainly because such governments perceive, or at least are driven by trial and error to accept, that their electorates will expect and exact of them that they continue to accept a secondary responsibility in relation to most of the services or activities which they seek to privatize. This amounts to a political demand that the service or activity remains to some extent within the domain of public law, and within the framework of constitutional citizenship.

The sophisticated neo-liberal response to this problem or demand is a highly interesting one (and incidentally one which is inherent in much of the school of thought of 'law and economics'). It consists of reconceptualizing the citizen as primarily an economic rather than a social or political actor, in other words of promoting a notion of market citizenship rather than of constitutional citizenship, thus drawing on and developing a different philosophical tradition. On this view, the individual person is accounted a full member of the community, is identified as a citizen, more by reference to that person's role in its economy than by reference to his or her role in its political society.

It is quite striking to what an extent the governments which have espoused this approach have experienced and responded to incentives to identify and interpret the citizen, not just as a market citizen, but more particularly as a consumer citizen. That is to say, the citizen is especially valued as the maker of choices about consumption of goods and services by which alone the market economy can be disciplined into the condition of 'efficiency' which is necessary to its prosperity in an internationally competitive environment. Emphasis is placed on the role of the citizen as the discriminating purchaser of goods and services, as the maker and enforcer of economically sound and rational consumer contracts.

Note how well this approach equips governments engaged in neo-liberal projects of privatization to respond to the difficulties of absolute privatization. Instead of simply denying the responsibility of the State for the activity in question, they can transform it into a responsibility for creating and maintaining consumer choice, and for policing the quality of service afforded to the consumer, in relation to the activity in question. Instead of formally severing the link between the citizen and the State in relation to a given service generally regarded as a public service, governments can maintain that they have actually re-affirmed those links in a different form. Moreover, they can and do assert the superiority of that form, by contrasting it to the monopolistic form of service provision in the purely public sector.

This, then, is the sort of approach to citizenship which jockeys for position with the constitutional approach to citizenship; and the public-service sector is precisely the arena in which that contest occurs—we might almost say that it is the arena which is created by that contest. It will be apparent that the rights and claims attributed to market citizens, being especially contractual rights and claims associated with contracts, are of the kind which private law, rather than public law, recognizes and protects. Again we find that there is a major challenge for public law; it has to redefine itself in relation to the distinctive public-service sector if it is to resist a highly sophisticated project of transferring that sector largely into the domain of private law. However, rather than pursuing further that set of issues about the role of public law, our present purpose is to use this discussion to tease out the parallel, and no less weighty, implications for the development of labour law in relation to the public-service sector. But before doing so, we need to sketch in one more piece of the relevant background, this consisting of the identification of a public-service sector in the context of the European Union.

5. The Public Service Sector in the Law and Policy of the European Union

In this section, it will be argued that it is helpful, for the purpose of acquiring a general understanding of the issues of law, public services and citizenship, to consider the evolution towards the recognition of a distinct public-service sector in the law and policy of the European Union. This argument will be developed in three stages. At the first of those stages, the reasons for this emergent recognition will be identified. At the second stage, the fact of this occurrence—limited enough, but nevertheless clearly discernible—will be described, while at the third and final stage we shall canvass the consequences of this phenomenon and begin to consider its implications for public law and labour law.

If, then, we first consider the reasons why there might be expected to be an impetus towards recognizing a public-service sector in the law and policy of the EU, we find, I suggest, that there are two sets or kinds of reasons for such a development. One set of reasons is directly comparable to and parallel with the rationale for recognition of a public-service sector within each Member State. In relation to that set of reasons, the EU is in the situation of being a macrocosm of its Member States. However, it will also be argued that the EU has another and further set of reasons for recognizing a public-service sector which is peculiar to its situation as a community of States. In relation to that set of reasons, the EU is pursuing concerns which are distinct from those of its Member States, even, it might be said, in competition with those of the Member States. The two sets of reasons will be explained in turn.

The first set of reasons for the tentative emergence of a distinct public-service sector in the law and policy of the EU, which replicates the situation within Member States, has to do with changes in the patterns and structures of economic and social organization and activity. Essentially, the regulatory structures of at first the EEC and then the EC were predicated upon a certain set of assumptions about the division of economic and social activities into the public and private sectors of the economies of the Member States. This is not to say that the allocation of economic and social activities between those sectors was entirely uniform as between the Member States. Nor is it to say that the extent and kind of regulatory differentiation between the two sectors was the same as between the Member States. But for about the first twenty-five years of the existence of the Community, there was enough convergence of patterns as between the Member States to make it coherent and sustainable to construct Community regulation and policy around a binary system, recognizing a mixed-economy paradigm in which most Member States had placed a wide range of public services and public utilities squarely within their state or public sectors. There was a certain amount of argument about what counted as an emanation of the State, but the logic seemed broadly sustainable.

From the early 1980s, however, this picture began to change, and the division of the economy into sectors started to need to be re-conceptualized. There were two main movements at work. One was the movement towards privatization and liberalization of enterprises and activities hitherto conducted within the public sector or dominated by the public sector. This produced (in varying degrees as between Member States) a momentum from the public sector towards the private sector. There was, however, a countervailing movement towards a recognition and vindication of the public interest, often expressed as the interests of consumers or of citizens, in various kinds of public interest regulation of these privatized or liberalized activities. This resulted in a reverse momentum back towards the public sector. These two pressures upon the boundary between the public and the private sectors caused the boundary in effect to disintegrate, to the point where it became necessary, or at least important, to conceive of a third, intermediate, public-service sector in which the kind and degree of regulation could be different from those applying to the fully public sector on the one hand and the fully private sector on the other. This was a rationale for recognition of a public-service sector both at Member State and at Community level.

There was also, as we have said, a further set of reasons for such an evolution at Community level, which was distinctive to the EU in the sense that it did not have an obvious parallel at Member State level. In fact, this set of reasons derives precisely from the (changing) nature of the relationship between the Community and its Member States. In the law and policy of the EU, the binary division of the economy, and of the society, of Europe into a public and a private sector is even more complicated and mutating than it is within the Member States, not only because the Community has to reconcile different approaches to that division as between Member States, but also because the Community as an entity, or as a set of institutions, has a complex relationship with its Member States. That complex relationship alters the way that the division is made between the public and the private sectors or spheres, so much so as to create a special impetus towards the recognition of a third, intermediate, public-service sector at Community level. This thesis obviously requires expansion in greater detail.

The complexity of the relationship between the institutions of the Community on the one hand and the Member States on the other, when it comes to making the division between the public and private sectors at Community level, consists in the particular way in which the mission of the Community was formulated. That is to say, the Community was formally dedicated to, indeed constructed around, the notion of the free and competitive market; the conceptual pillars upon which it was rested were explicitly identified in those terms. The public sector of this liberal European economy and society was that of the Member States; the Community was concerned, in theory at least, not with creating a supranational public sector, but, on the contrary, with putting in place an integrated European private sector characterized by free and undistorted competition. There was, of course, a considerable measure of artificiality and not a little irony in this formulation, as the normative or regulatory structures, and the institutional and bureaucratic apparatus to support them, grew ever more elaborate in ostensible pursuit of the free and single market; but there was at the same time an apparently coherent rationale for a Community which defined its private sector in expansive and inclusive terms, and its public sector in narrow and constrained terms (for example by subjecting public authority contracting or procurement to requirements of compulsory competitive tendering).

From the mid-1980s onwards, the tensions which had always been present within and around this mode of Community self-definition were heightened. On the one hand, as we have said, the stereotype of social welfarist Member States started to disintegrate, and there was an evolution towards neo-liberalism at national level. This threatened to create private sectors of de-regulated trade competition which would be more fiercely neo-liberal than was readily compatible with the Community model. On the other hand, for the Community itself, the nearing of its goal of realizing the Single Market accentuated its own need for further and other bases of self-legitimation than that of free trade alone. For both those reasons, it was important for the institutions of the Community to acquire an enhanced capacity for public interest regulation of the provision of services to the Community public or citizenry.

The acquisition of this new or enhanced capacity would inevitably, however, run up against the sensibilities of various Member States, concerned sometimes with maintaining the integrity of their sovereign national public sectors, sometimes with protecting their liberalized private sectors from the encroachment of Community normativity. The path between these sets of constraints has, of course, been a narrow one; but it has afforded enough space for a limited evolution of a Community concern with what is, in reality, an intermediate public-service sector identified under the title of Services of General Interest.

It is only very recently that there has been the political will in the Community institutions to begin to concretize these policies and treat them as the basis for legislative measures. It was early in 1996, during the process of preparation for the Intergovernmental Conference leading to the 1997 Amsterdam Treaty, that the Commission began to stake out the territory of Services of General Interest as one of the main areas in which the new political expansionism of the Community would be manifested. Thus the Commission makes the following pronouncement in February of 1996:

> 'Europe is built on a set of values shared by all its societies and combines the characteristics of democracy—human rights and institutions based on the rule of law—with those of an open economy underpinned by market forces, internal solidarity and cohesion. *These values include access for all members of society to universal services or to services of general benefit, thus contributing to solidarity and equal treatment*' (emphasis added).[2]

It was that strand in the thinking of the Commission about the then forthcoming Intergovernmental Conference which was fashioned into their Communication of September 1996 on *Services of General Interest in Europe*.[3] This Communication is in effect the White Paper or definitive pol-

[2] *Reinforcing Political Union and Preparing for Enlargement—Commission Opinion for the Intergovernmental Conference*, COM(96)90 final, 28 Feb. 1996.

[3] COM(96)443 final of 11 Sept. 1996.

icy document for the development of a Community public-service sector, or services of general interest sector; as such, the details of its formulation deserve some attention. It proceeds in three stages: the first is that of purposive analysis of the *status quo*; the second is that of identifying aims for future development; the third is that of recommending legislation. Each stage will be considered in turn.

In this Communication, the Commission is extremely cautious in its legislative proposals, so that its purposive evaluation of the present position, with its identification of future objectives, is probably the most significant part of the policy document. The purpose and effect of the descriptive analysis are to indicate that the Community, both as a group of nation-States and through its central institutions, is already engaged in recognizing and conducting a general interest services sector in which, it is asserted, the Member States and the central institutions of the Community share a responsibility for vindicating the public interest and the set of values associated with that interest.[4]

The Communication pursues an interesting and important argument as to the way in which the general interest services sector is to be identified or defined. It is a two-part argument, the first part of which is general, and the second part of which is specific to certain sectors of the European economy. In the general part of the argument, it is asserted that this general interest services sector is and should be identified by reference to a European consensus as to the need for a certain set of services to be provided as essentially public services. It explicitly rejects a contrary approach, which would confine the general interest service sector to the services provided by institutions which are in their nature public or state authorities or enterprises. So the general interest services sector, as envisaged by the Commission in this Communication, is functionally defined, and extends into the provision of public services by private sector enterprises.[5]

Those who formulated this Communication seem to have been aware that an attempt to identify a European general interest sector solely by reference to this rather abstract mode of functional definition would have lacked any sharpness of focus or sense of concrete reality. So they go on to

[4] That set of values is specified thus:
'The roles assigned to general interest services and the special rights which may ensue reflect considerations inherent in the concept of serving the public, such as ensuring that needs are met, protecting the environment, economic and social cohesion, land-use planning and promotion of consumer interests' (COM(96)443, para. 7).

[5] The point is put thus:
'It is all too easy to treat public sector and public-service as synonymous and fail to distinguish the legal status of a service provider from the nature of the service being provided. . . . European policy is concerned with general interest, with what services are provided and on what terms, not with the status of the body providing them' (COM(96)443, para. 11).

argue that we can also identify this European general interest services sector by pointing to those specific areas of economic activity in which the Community has in some sense or other recognized and asserted an important public interest concern. The sectors which are so identified in the Communication are those of telecommunications, postal services, transport, electricity, and broadcasting.[6] It is very important to observe exactly how that selection is reasoned in the Communication.

The significance of this sector-specific approach in the Communication is very great, because it enables the Communication to identify a multiplicity of models for the services which it can claim to treat as general interest services. The models vary both in the way that the general or public interest is defined in relation to them, and in the intensity with which that general or public interest is pursued. It would be fair to say that the central or most influential model is derived from the areas of telecommunications and postal services. That is because there is a long and important history of imposing so-called universal service obligations on providers of telephone and postal services. That means to say that European States and societies have recognized at least some degree of need to impose on providers of those services a set of obligations to offer their services to all those wishing to have access to them on an affordable basis.

As the Communication argues, the Community has been able to assert a capacity to pursue universal service obligations on a cross-border basis between the Member States in relation to postal services and, especially, in relation to telecommunications services; and it has been able to do that irrespective of whether the service providers are within the public sectors or the private sectors of the Member States, or are on the move between the two sectors.[7] The Communication goes on to argue that the Community has shown a concern to secure analogous obligations upon the providers of electricity,[8] and of transport services, whether air, maritime, or inland, in relation to which the Commission has canvassed the

[6] 'The principles and approach outlined above [i.e. the functional definition of general interest services] combine the dynamism of opening up markets with general interest requirements at European and national levels. The Commission has already taken steps in this directions in several areas, such as telecommunications, postal services, transport and energy.' 'In most Member States, television and radio have a general interest dimension, despite the structural and technological changes affecting those markets' (COM(96)443, paras. 33, 52).

[7] 'The opening up of markets and infrastructures [for telecommunications] goes hand in hand with the definition of universal service obligations, which the Community has asked Member States to impose on operators to ensure the provision of a wide range of basic services.' 'The basis of the proposal [made by the Commission in July 1995 for common rules for the postal sector] is to safeguard the postal service as a universal service in the long term. Universal postal service means providing a high-quality service country-wide with regular guaranteed deliveries at prices everyone can afford. . . . It . . . would apply to both domestic and cross-border deliveries' (COM(96)443, paras. 35, 38).

[8] See COM(96)443, paras. 47–50.

creation of a 'Citizen's Network' at Community level.[9] Finally, in its enumeration of sectoral models, the Communication identifies a parallel Community set of general interests in broadcasting, the general interests being defined in this context by reference more to social than to economic considerations.[10]

In the analysis of general interest services which is offered in this Communication, the Commission is at pains to stress one particular theme, both at the general level and at the sector-specific level of its description. That is to say, it is recognized and asserted that there is a potential tension, and often various sorts of actual tension, between market forces and general interest considerations.[11] Moreover, it is seen as self-evidently part of the function of public authorities in general to concern themselves with the resolution of such tensions.[12] Indeed, the Community is depicted as recognizing the freedom of Member States to do that; it is said that the Community's approach to general interest services is underpinned by two basic principles, one of which is neutrality as regards the public or private status of companies an their employees, and the other of which is:

> 'Member States' *freedom* to define what are general interest services, to grant the special or exclusive rights that are necessary to the companies responsible for providing them, regulate their management and, where appropriate, fund them, in accordance with Article 90 of the Treaty'.[13]

The establishing of this description of a general interest services sector within the Community provided a strong theoretical base upon which the Commission could build a set of objectives for the role of the Community institutions in relation to that sector. The description conveys the messages, first, that the Commission believes that a general interest services sector exists and should be recognized as existing within the Community; secondly, that the central institutions of the Community have a legitimate and important existing function in relation to that sector of balancing general or public interest goals against the goals of free market competition; but, thirdly, that the central Community institutions have hitherto been

[9] COM(96)443, paras. 41–6, referring to the Green Paper, *The Citizens' Network*, COM(95)601 final of 1995.

[10] 'The general interest considerations [relating to broadcasting] basically concern the content of broadcasts, being linked to moral and democratic values, such as pluralism, information ethics and protection of the individual' (COM(96)443, para. 51).

[11] 'Market forces produce a better allocation of resources and greater effectiveness in the supply of services, the principal beneficiary being the consumer, who gets better quality at a lower price. However, these mechanisms sometimes have their limits; as a result the potential benefits might not extend to the entire population and the objective of promoting social and territorial cohesion may not be attained' (COM(96)443, para. 15).

[12] 'The public authority must then ensure that the general interest is taken into account' (*ibid.*).

[13] COM(96)443, para. 16.

confined to recognizing that general or public interest in the rather passive form of condoning Member State activities which would conflict with the Community requirements of free competition if they were not recognized as coming within the exception afforded by Article 90 of the EC Treaty.

In the Communication, the Commission goes on from those starting points to declare its objectives. The aims are to acquire what is, in effect, a more positive capacity to identify its own, supra-national, general interest services sector,[14] to apply to that sector its own concept of universal service or other public-service obligations,[15] and to be ultimately responsible for striking the balance between those public-service obligations and the demands of free competition in the internal market.[16] There are those who are apt to see in all this nothing more than an aim to protect the vested interests of public-sector undertakings in Member States in the face of increasingly harsh and direct intra-European and extra-European competition, but the foregoing analysis of this Communication suggests that it reveals aims which are at once more ambitious and less concessionary than a simple rearguard state public-sector protectionism would be.

All this said, the Commission was, as we indicated earlier, very cautious as to the nature of the legal measures which it recommended in pursuit of these objectives. In the Communication, it did recommend going beyond the option of simply leaving Article 90 in place as it stood, relying on it as a sufficient basis for the development of a Community general interest services sector. But the Commission was not prepared to recommend the actual creation of a new legal base, preferring instead to suggest an addition to Article 3 of the Treaty, that is to say a new paragraph which would have added to the list of the tasks of the institutions of the community that of making 'a contribution to the promotion of services of general interest'.[17]

The framers of the Treaty of Amsterdam preferred to proceed in a slightly different way; it is hard to be sure whether they achieved less or more than the Commission had recommended. They enacted an addi-

[14] 'The opening up of markets on a sector-by-sector basis for economic services and, in particular, networked services, and the introduction of universal service obligations should be continued . . .' 'There are several sectors that have a cross-border dimension . . . which means that the general interest role is not necessarily best fulfilled at national level' (COM(96)443, paras. 60, 63).

[15] '[The criteria of universal service] are not always all met at national level, but where they have been introduced using the concept of European universal service, there have been positive effects for the development of general interest services' (COM(96)443, para. 28).

[16] 'The Community's aim is to support the competitiveness of the European economy in an increasingly competitive world and to give consumers more choice, better quality and lower prices, at the same time as helping, through its policies, to strengthen economic and social cohesion between the Members States and reduce inequalities. . . . General interest services have a key role to play here' (COM(96)443, para. 57).

[17] COM(96)443, paras. 70–4.

tional Treaty Article, to be added to the Article 7 group which between them specify what is meant by the completion of the Community's internal market. The new Article 7d provides that:

> 'Without prejudice to Articles 77, 90 and 92 and given the place occupied by services of general economic interest in the shared values of the Union as well as their role in promoting social and territorial cohesion, the Community and the Members Sates, each within their respective powers and within the scope of application of this Treaty, shall take care that such services operate on the basis of principles and conditions which enable them to fulfil their missions.'

This is accompanied by a Declaration to the Final Act which will, if and when made, provide that:

> 'The provisions of Article 7d on public services shall be implemented with full respect for the jurisprudence of the Court of Justice, inter alia as regards the principles of equality of treatment, quality and continuity of such services.'

It will be interesting and crucially important to see how much significance these provisions will have in the event. They may provide a vehicle by which the Commission can move the ideas set out in its Communication into its body of law and policy. The possibility that this will turn out to be the case has real implications for the subject which is being discussed in the present symposium, and we should turn to the task of teasing out what those implications might be.

I advance the bold suggestion that we may be witnessing the evolution of a general-interest sector or public-service sector at Community level, which is characterized by a recognition, on the part of the institutions of the Community, that it is necessarily and fundamentally a contested zone as between the economic objective of market efficiency and the social objectives of cohesion and inclusion, and that it is part of the task of the Community institutions to find the right way to reconcile those objectives. We could say, and we hope that it will emerge in the course of this book, that this is the way in which discussion of the law and policy relating to public services becomes linked with the discussion of labour law. That is because this dilemma between economic objectives and social objectives is one which permeates labour law as we currently understand it, and which has to be resolved partly by reference to labour law. We pursue this theme in the next section of this Chapter.

6. Labour Law in Relation to the Public Service Sector

In this section it will be argued that the evolution and enlargement of the public-service sector is if anything an even more significant development in relation to labour law than in relation to public law. The transfer of services or activities from the purely public sector into the public-service sector has effects upon labour law which are parallel with its effects upon public law, but which may be even stronger and more decisive. In order to develop this argument, it will be necessary to show how labour law contains its own public law as well as private law sectors and how the balance between those sectors is altered by the growth of the public-service sector.

If we say that labour law contains its own public law as well as private law sectors we are in fact advancing a complex proposition which it is useful to disentangle into various aspects. Systems of labour law generally identify two broad types of employment regime, which we can think of as those of public and private employment. Under the private law regime, employment is conceived of as a market transaction, basically governed by the private law of the contract of employment. Under the public law regime, the employment relationship is differently conceived of, so that it exists between public institutions and public functionaries, and is basically governed by the principles of public law.

The matter becomes very complex, however, when we consider whether we can therefore say that there is a public sector of labour law in which the public law regime obtains, and a private sector in which the private law regime prevails. It is in fact difficult to enforce such a distinction too strongly, because systems of labour law vary considerably in the rigidity with which they separate the two regimes, and the ways in which they allocate employment relationships as between the two regimes. Nor can we resolve that problem simply by asking which employees are 'employees of the State', because different systems approach that question in ways which vary greatly.

Despite these difficulties, we could still, let us say twenty years ago, have asserted that the labour law systems of European countries generally contained a public sector of which the core consisted of employees of the State, and which was at least to some extent governed by public law. That public sector was, to that extent, in a contrasting situation to a private sector governed by private law, pivoting upon the private law contract of employment. Very broadly speaking, the public-sector employment law regimes were characterized by the fact that they imposed greater obligations of loyalty upon employees, but conferred a greater degree of integration and security upon them, than the corresponding private sector employment law regimes.

More recently, however—and this is the key point in the present argument—the evolution and growth in importance of the intermediate public-service sector has fundamentally impinged upon, we might say has de-stabilized, that sort of dual-sector, dual-regime structure of labour law systems to the point where that kind of bi-polar analysis has become extremely difficult to sustain. For not only have we seen the evolution of what is, in effect, a third typology of labour law which is poised between the public law and private law regimes, but we can also observe that this typology is becoming so important and influential as to influence and encroach upon what happens in the original two sectors.

In order to understand why that is the case, we have to reconsider in the context of labour law the two features of the public-service sector which were seen to be so significant in the public law context, that is to say, first, the interposition of the public-service provider between the State and those who would otherwise have a direct relationship with the State, and, secondly, the augmenting of the role of the market citizen. We proceed, as previously in relation to public law, to elaborate on both those features, but especially the second one because of our special preoccupation with issues about citizenship—which do turn out to be particularly relevant to this discussion.

It has been argued earlier that when governments engaged on neo-liberal projects of privatization transfer activities from the purely public sector into the public-service sector, there nevertheless remains in place a significant secondary relationship between the citizen and the State in relation to that activity. In the context of labour law, however, we find that such transfers result in a much more complete severance of relationships between the employee and the State. In particular, the interposition of the public-service provider between the employee and the State operates to exclude the perception that the employee is a functionary of the State with a resulting special set of expectations about security of employment and the protection of a high standard of terms and conditions of employment. That is one of the main reasons why transfers of activities from the pure public sector to the public-service sector are often so controversial, especially in labour law systems where the public-sector regime is very distinct, and very strongly ring-fenced from the private sector.

In fact we can say that, for this set of reasons, transfers of activities into the public-service sector tend to be seen, both by their protagonists and their opponents, as paradigms for the achievement of gains in 'efficiency' because of the opportunities they provide for the introduction and development of more flexible employment regimes than are legally or practically available in the purely public sector. Given the extent of economic incentives currently operating upon governments of European countries to engage in this kind of flexibilization of employment in the provision of services for which they are politically responsible, it is not surprising that we find the public-service sector not only generally gaining in size and importance, but also becoming a model for the development of the other sectors of the labour market and the labour law system, especially of course the purely public sector.

There are important structural reasons why the public-service sector should be such an important location for the development of flexibility of employment, and by identifying these reasons we can understand better the meaning and implications of flexibilization for labour law as a whole, especially for the labour law of the public sector, and for the labour law of the individual employment relationship more generally. These structural reasons can best be understood by considering the nature of the public-service provider as an employer, and by contrasting that with the very different nature of the State as an employer.

This contrast originates in the general contrast which exists between the institutions of executive government on the one hand, and on the other hand the institutions which are public-service providers in the public-service sector. At least as a broad generalization, we can say that, both in principle and practice, the goals, objectives, or tasks of executive government and its institutions tend to be more diverse and diffuse, a more complex bundle of political, social, and economic factors than the corresponding goals, objectives, or tasks of public-service providers.

That is not to say that the goals, objectives, or tasks of public-service providers are in themselves simple or uni-directional ones. They are normally not simple, if only because we may regard it as one of the features which distinguish the public-service sector from the private sector that in the public-service sector, governments will have acquired or retained the power to some degree to shape and determine those goals, objectives, or tasks. Nevertheless, it is normally the case that the very rationale for the transfer of an activity from the purely public sector into the public-service sector is to ensure that there will be a unit of delivery of the service in question whose goals, tasks, and objectives will be more clearly and tightly defined than would be the case if that activity were being conducted directly by one of the institutions of executive government.

Much of the discourse of new public management turns on precisely this contrast; the essence of new public management is to bring about the formation of specific units of management or of delivery of services, with precisely defined goals and objectives by reference to which efficiency can be measured, and gains in efficiency can be sought. This, moreover, links up very closely with the flexibilization of employment, which consists (in all but its crudest forms, at least), not simply of making the legal and contractual norms of employment looser and more malleable, but, particularly, of making them more responsive to the specific (and changing) goals, objectives, and tasks of the employing institution.

The public-service provider constitutes, and is created or chosen because it constitutes, the best vehicle for this kind of new public management and this kind of flexibilization of employment. That is to say, it can be endowed with tightly defined (yet controllable) goals, objectives, and task definitions; and the legal and contractual norms of employment within that institution can be made flexible by reference to those controllable goals, objectives, and task definitions, as regards both tenure of employment (especially by means of fixed-term contracts of employment or contracts of employment the duration of which is task-defined) and terms and conditions of employment (especially by means of performance-related remuneration, where the criteria of assessment can be tied to the immediate objectives of the public-service provider).

We can argue about whether this represents the triumph of managerialism over professionalism in the public-service sector, and whether, if so, that is a good or a bad thing. Without resolving those questions, we can accept that it is unsurprising, given the current interest in this kind of development both in employment practice and in labour law, that the public-service sector becomes a central arena for the contest between 'traditional' and 'flexible' labour law. We also find that the public-service sector acquires this paradigmatic or flagship status in terms of the role which ideas about citizenship play within it, and it is worth devoting a separate section to exploring the sense in which that occurs.

7. Labour Law, the Public-service Sector, and Citizenship

We saw in an earlier section that one of the most significant attributes of the intermediate public-service sector was the way in which it provided fertile ground for the establishment and growth of a market or consumerist conception of citizenship. The importance of that in relation to public law was, we saw, considerable; in relation to labour law, especially that of the traditional public sector, it is positively transformative. We shall seek to show that this is true in more than one dimension of labour law.

One such dimension is that of the flexibilization of employment in the public-service sector, as described in the previous section. In relation to the public-service sector, it proves to be especially attractive, and perhaps effective, for governments, when demanding and requiring efficiency, and in particular flexibility of employment in pursuit of efficiency, to do so in the name of the market citizen or the consumer citizen. One could almost say that they sometimes create the consumer citizen precisely in order to perform this task, to fulfil this disciplinary role.

This is more than mere rhetoric; it amounts to the promotion of a consumerist conception of citizenship as a major force, the focus of a major set of interests, in the formulation of the labour law of the public-service sector. Thus far, we have conducted that argument in terms mainly of the flexibilization of individual employment relationships, though no doubt with implicit reference to collective labour law. It will be useful to develop this analysis further in terms directly of collective labour law, in which dimension also the role and conception of citizenship turn out to be extremely and increasingly important.

The importance of the role and conception of citizenship to the collective labour law of the public-service sector comes about in the following way. The growth of the public-service sector in general effects a degree of re-alignment of the law and practice of collective bargaining and industrial disputes, especially as compared with the traditional public sector. Quite a lot of this is to the advantage of the State or government. For example, by transferring activities from the public sector into the public-service sector, governments can hope to fragment the previous patterns of collective bargaining and industrial action; and the public-service provider may be relatively free of the expectations placed upon the State itself to behave as a good or 'model' employer.

However, governments or public-sector employers may, upon transfer of an activity to the public-service sector, lose the benefit of specific legal restrictions upon industrial action applying to public-sector employees, either generally or in particular occupations. More generally, they may lose the benefit of a more general set of expectations, textured in a diffuse sense into the labour law system, that public-sector employees will feel and display greater loyalty and commitment to their duties of service provision than their private sector counterparts. Furthermore, they may, by transferring an activity into the public-service sector, have abandoned a state monopoly and so no longer be able to threaten the workforce with the loss of that monopoly as a sanction against major industrial action in the relevant occupation or activity.

One quite significant pattern of response on the part of governments to the loss of those positions of strength in labour law or public-sector employment practice is to introduce the consumer citizen as a countervailing actor. This, in effect, counter-poises the claims of the consumer citizen to continuity of provision of goods and especially services against the heightened claims of public-service sector employees (compared with their public-sector predecessors) to freedom to take industrial action and deploy their industrial power to full effect.

All this tends towards a recognition of the rights of consumer-citizens as rights of the private law type, but brought within the framework of labour law. And it is in the intermediate public-service sector that this effect occurs most strongly, because it is there that the citizenship claims coming from a public law tradition converge with the consumerist or contractualist claims coming from a private law tradition. Governments in effect invite and encourage the consumer-citizen to regard most or all of the services provided by the public-service sector as essential services, and present themselves as maintaining or pursuing the claims, thus conferred upon the market citizen, to limit or prohibit industrial action in those, to that extent 'essential', services. It is to be noted that the designation of services as 'services of general interest' is especially conducive to that analysis.

We thus see, from what has been discussed both in this section and the previous one, that there is quite a significant tendency for a new kind of labour law to evolve in and from the public-service sector. This new kind of labour law is characterized by a new conception of the balancing of interests. Historically labour law has primarily been seen as a balancing of the interests of employers and employees, with the State figuring in the role of employer in the public-sector. There has of course been a consideration of the public interest or the interest of the community; but this has on the whole played a secondary role. In this new kind of labour law, that third set of interests, newly conceptualized as the interests of the market or consumer citizen, become part of the central balancing process, sometimes even coming into a direct theoretical and practical opposition to the interests of the workforce, especially in the arena of the public-service sector.

This section concludes by pointing to some concerns about and problems relating to this new kind of labour law which seems to be developing particularly in the public-service sector. It is suggested that, in the balancing of competing interests in relation to the labour market generally and the public-service sector in particular, the analysis in terms of an antithesis between the interests of the citizen and those of the employee is far from being inevitable and may well indeed be suspect. It is an idea of antithesis which is generated or encouraged from within the perspective of the market or consumer citizen. The notion of antithesis is weakened or may even be dispelled if one examines the issues from a perspective of constitutional citizenship. Those arguments are very briefly enlarged upon in the ensuing paragraphs.

It follows from arguments which have been advanced in earlier sections that the notions of the public-service sector and of market citizenship go closely together and are in a sense mutually supportive. That is to say, the provision of public services by intermediate providers takes place in what is consciously designed as a market context or a market-like context. That market context is in effect created by the organizing of service provision either on a competitive basis, or on a basis where the pressures and incentives of competition are sought to be introduced by other means. In that kind of structure, the competition is identified as consumer demand, and it is the citizen-consumer who is regarded as making the demands, and the choices associated with the demand. This is regarded as a virtuous role for the citizen because of the importance of a keenly discriminating demand in ensuring rigorous competition.

In this context, the sense of opposition between the interests of the citizen and those of the public-service worker tends to be maximized. Whereas in the provision of goods, the workers who manufacture the goods are generally anonymous, so that there is little or no sense of presence between them and the consumers of the goods, the reverse is the case for public-service sector workers, who are typically the very embodiment and presence of the institutions by which services are provided to the public. Shortcomings in the quality or completeness of service provision present themselves as public-service sector workers acting directly to the detriment of citizens, especially when those shortcomings are the result of concerted industrial action.

This can all too readily come to appear as such a compelling account of the relationship between citizens and public-service sector workers as to appear totally inevitable and irrefutable. If, however, the citizen is regarded not so much as a consumer or market citizen but rather as a constitutional citizen, a rather wider set of possibilities opens up. The constitutional citizen is conceived of as having a wider role or set of roles, as having a more complex participation in the working of the democratic process. In this conception, it is more manifest that citizens include workers, that workers are also citizens, and that the two sets of interests cannot be satisfactorily separated from each other. In the remaining part of this Chapter, we shall be concerned to show how the particular contributions to this symposium relate to those central themes.

8. Public Services, the State, and Citizenship: Welfare State, Post-welfare State, or European Social State?

In the earlier sections of this chapter, it has been argued that it is legitimate and useful to identify a distinct public-service sector, located between the public and the private sectors, for the purpose of improving our analysis and understanding of the current development of public law and policy, labour law and policy, and of the interaction between them. It has also been argued that this analysis, and this identification of a distinct public service sector, has to take place both at the level of the Member States and at the level of the European Community. At the former level, it is a matter of comparing and contrasting the development of different legal and political traditions and configurations. At the latter level, it is a matter of considering also the nature and extent of development of the European Union as a community, or as a federal state or meta-state. In this concluding section, I shall seek to show how this analysis involves a number of different but interlocking discussions or debates, which can be identified by reference to groups of chapters in this book, and to which those chapters make contributions which I regard as highly significant.

The succeeding chapters, and these groups of chapters, interrelate in the following way. The public-service sector, as identified earlier in the present chapter, is the forum for and the focus of a set of changes in the nature of the modern European state, its public law, and its labour law. This is true both in the sense that the public-service sector is the central arena for these changes, and in the sense that the emergence of an analytically distinct public-service sector is itself a product and an index of those changes. The ensuing chapters show how this is a change occurring both at state level and at Community level and by way of interaction between those two levels. They also show how these changes are taking place both in public law and policy and in labour law and policy, and by way of interaction between those legal topics or disciplines.

There is an underlying reason for the complexity of these interactions. It is that we are seeing in the public-service sector, and indeed in the very fact of the evolution of a distinct public-service sector, an evolution, not just in the public law and policy and in the labour law and policy of the European nation-state, but in the very nature of the European nation-state itself. The point about this evolution is that it is occurring not just at nation-state level but also at Community or meta-state level and by way of reaction between those levels. We can understand this by invoking the idea of an evolution away from the welfare-state model of the European nation-state. That evolution seems to involve movement both towards various kinds of post-welfare model for the nation-state, and also towards a certain kind of meta-state model at Community level. Much of that movement takes place in and around the public-service sector; that is the sense in which and the reason why that sector, and its distinct analytical existence, are of such transformative significance.

The above argument clearly needs further explanation. Let me begin by explaining what I mean by the evolution from the welfare state to the post-welfare state. Within the framework of Western Europe in the decades after 1945, we can say that the welfare state, which became a dominant model, was characterized by its relatively strong interventionism in guaranteeing high levels of social protection to its citizens. This was typically achieved by the direct assumption, by the State, of a high level of responsibility for the provision of services affecting the quality of life for citizens in the community, for sustaining guarantees of social security, and for underpinning minimum labour standards both of a substantive and of a procedural kind. Starting in the later 1970s, and gathering momentum in the 1980s and 1990s, was an evolution towards the post-welfare state, characterized by a scepticism as to whether those goals could effectively be pursued by means of public activity or close public regulation, and a systemic preference for seeking to achieve those goals by relying on free enterprise and the operation of the product market (to some extent in goods, but more particularly in services) and of the flexible labour market to do so as efficiently as was possible. Whether as part of this transformation or as a result of it, there emerges a public-service sector, now distinct from the public sector in a way that it previously was not, which is a zone of contestation between the values and approaches of the welfare state on the one hand, and of the neo-liberal state on the other. It is here, and in this, that the rather fragile self-definition of the post-welfare state is to be found.

This kind of transition from welfare state to post-welfare state also had a very important set of implications for the development of the European Community and of its role *vis-à-vis* its Member States. As the Member States began to move, in different ways and at different speeds, from being welfare states to being post-welfare states, it was probably predictable, and certainly became evident in the event, that the policy-makers who wished to retain, at least as ideals, the social goals of the welfare state would look to the Community itself as the residual guardian of those welfarist ideals, in however diluted a practical form. To this extent, there was an impetus towards an ironical reversal of the original role of the Community as the guardian of liberal free trade against national protectionism, often of a statist or welfarist kind, practised by the Member States.

There are particular reasons why this should result in the evolution of a Community public-service sector, and a Community concern with that sector, such as we have identified earlier in this chapter. The move from the welfare state to the post-welfare state involves, as we have seen, the retreat of the state from the role of primary provider of many services or primary undertaker of many service activities. In the post-welfare state, there is a corresponding expansion of the state or public role of regulating in the public interest the provision of public services which is increasingly being entrusted to private or semi-private undertakings. That regulatory role is identified in various different ways, but is generally envisaged as one of vindicating various kinds of public social and economic rights. There tends to be, as we have observed, a contest as to what kind of social and economic claims are being vindicated, indeed a contest as to whether it is social rights or economic arguments which are primarily at stake.

As the contest thus develops, in various ways, as to the sorts of policies which are to shape and inform the regulation of the emerging public-service sector, so the European Community becomes necessarily implicated in that contest. That is because it becomes apparent to all concerned that the Community has a very important actual role, and a still more important potential role, as a regulator of that sector. So the various policy makers and interest groups whose activities bear upon the central institutions of the Community become more and more strongly motivated to develop that Community role on their own terms. In varying degrees, they encourage the central Community to identify a public-service sector and a role in the regulation of that sector, in order to maximize the chances that this regulation will be according to their own conceptions of social and economic rights and claims. This is one of the ways, indeed one of the most important ways, in which the Community becomes implicated in the transition from the welfare state to the post-welfare state.

Hence it becomes apparent why this symposium, by focusing itself upon the public-service sector, takes place within an area of not yet fully articulated debates about the nature of the post-welfare state, and about the respective roles in relation to the post-welfare state of European nation-states and the European Community itself. It is extremely interesting and informative to try to locate the different contributions to this symposium within that arena. Although the contributors can all, I suggest, be regarded as having moderate centrist positions within this area of discussion, although moreover a high level of consensus pervaded our exchanges at our workshop, nevertheless highly revealing divergences of position about the public-service sector, law and citizenship started to emerge during those exchanges, and can be observed even more clearly in the written contributions. It would be a crude over-simplification to portray the chapters as a series of antitheses between opposite positions. Nevertheless, by grouping the chapters together, we can identify a series of debates, or sub-themes, within our general discussion; and we can see how the participants take up positions which reflect the set of interests, indeed the intellectual and experiential base, on which each person is constructing his or her contribution.

The first group of chapters which can usefully be considered as relating closely to each other is made up of this chapter, that of David Faulkner, and that of Carol Harlow. Our contributions are derived from the British experience of a relatively rapid and far-reaching move from the welfare state to a prominent, perhaps even the dominant, model of the post-welfare state in which the quest for economic efficiency by means of transfer of public-service activity away from the state has been pursued with particular ferocity. In that British context, the challenge has been more to the political system and ideology than to the legal system and ideology. In my chapter, writing from the point of intersection between public law and labour law, I have sought to show how this challenge has resulted in the need to recognize a new analytical paradigm, both for the political system and for the legal system, which recognizes that the post-welfare state is typified by a third intermediate public-service sector in which the regulatory system is in various ways distinct from that of either the public (state) sector or the wholly private sector. I have been more concerned to develop this analytical framework than to discuss how far I welcome or how far I deplore the set of changes which are the subject of that analysis.

This is not to suggest that the other two chapters in this group are in any way less analytical or more judgmental than my own. Nevertheless, one can discern some degree of interesting divergence between them in the evaluations which they imply. David Faulkner writes from a base of public administration, from a deep experience of the working of British government over the last forty years, and from a strong personal commitment to the values which the British Civil Service brought to bear upon the British welfare state. He might be said to be specially concerned to point up the risks and dangers of too headlong a rush from the welfare state to the particularly commercially oriented version of the post-welfare state which was promoted in Britain during and after the 'Thatcher years'. At all events, he proposes a course of public discussion designed to ensure that concerns about community and about citizenship are not downgraded, or reduced to the level of lip-service, in current social, political, and ideological development.

Carol Harlow writes from a somewhat different perspective, and to interestingly different effect. Her perspective is from the standpoint of public law, rather than from the standpoint of public administration. She is anxious to remind us that the ways in which legal systems bear upon public services are multifarious and complex, so that we should not assume that they express a single ideal of public service which is an obviously superior basis for the regulation of public services than other ideals emerging from other dimensions of legal systems. Thus, she points, in effect, to divergent traditions within public law—in particular, a French tradition which focuses upon the State itself is contrasted with an Anglo-Saxon tradition which focuses upon the individual or private citizen and his or her process rights against public authorities. Although in her view these and other relevant traditions are on the whole fairly convergent, she is nevertheless conscious of spaces between and around them, within which she thinks that the values and concerns of 'new public management' may have an important and legitimate place—at least to the extent that they should not be regarded as inherently and necessarily repugnant or threatening to the ideals of public service in public law. That is to say, the criticisms one may have of 'new public management' ideology may also be in some measure applicable to older ideologies of public-service—there is as yet no clearly identifiable moral high ground in this debate.

For writers such as David Faulkner and Carol Harlow, reflecting British experience, the concerns are more with the ideology of public service and public law than with the delineation of the proper sphere of public service and public law. The experience to which they are relating is one in which the public sphere and public law are not set strongly and clearly apart from the private sphere and private law. The theoretical construction of a third intermediate public-service sector, for which I have argued, would, I imagine, raise questions for them as to the administrative and legal ideology which ought to apply within it, but would not, I suspect, be specially controversial as a classificatory or taxonomical proposition. It is quite otherwise, I think, for the writers of the following two chapters, Elisenda Malaret and Etienne Picard, for whom the relevant administrative and legal traditions make a much sharper division between the public and the private sphere, and correspondingly between public and private law. So, for them, the set of issues about the ideology of public service and public law is crucially linked with very important questions about the proper *boundaries* of public service and public law.

The direction of Elisenda Malaret's chapter is towards a loosening of the boundaries of public law. She wants to challenge the idea that public law is constructed solely upon the State and public authorities. She wishes the idea of public-service, or of service to the public, to operate not solely as an obligation upon the State and bodies designated as public authorities, but rather as a way of both identifying and regulating a set of functions which may be carried out by private actors as well as by the State or other public authorities. This approach is seen as according a fluid boundary to the scope of public law. This is combined with a multi-tiered structure as to the kind of regulation which public law represents. That is to say, there is a top tier in which public law addresses the State as a primary and exclusive or monopolistic executant of a public function, and lower tiers in which public law addresses a wider range of executants of public-service functions, who may be operating in a market or market-like situation. So, in the terms of my argument, she wishes public law to be understood as extending beyond the traditional public sector into the intermediate public-service sector.

Etienne Picard, though speaking from within the same legal tradition as Elisenda Malaret and sharing with her a set of concerns for the fundamental and human rights of citizens, nevertheless takes a somewhat different position with regard to the extension of public law into the realm where public services are provided by private actors. His concern is that if public law, and indeed the public realm itself, are viewed in too open-ended a way, we may risk overwhelming and subsuming the values of the private realm of society, and the liberal rights enshrined in private law. Perhaps we could say that his stance in relation to the intermediate public-service sector is analogous, albeit taken up in a rather different idiom, to that of Carol Harlow. They share a view that we should not take our enthusiasm for the public-service values of public law to the lengths of embracing public law, especially in its more statist versions, as the dominant or exclusive discourse for the public-service sector. So real debates begin to emerge within an area of apparent consensus between generally like-minded jurists.

The succeeding three chapters, those of Alessandro Petretto, Wolf Sauter, and Giuliano Amato, indicate that there is in a sense a parallel set of debates among those working in the field of law and economics, whether as economists such as Petretto, or as lawyers specially interested in the regulation of competition, such as Sauter or Amato. If we can regard these three chapters as a group, we find that they converge, even more obviously than the previous two groups, upon the notion that there is an intermediate public-service sector to which a special set of regulatory considerations applies (as compared with the fully public sector on the one hand, and with the purely private sector on the other hand). They diverge, however, in their conceptions of what those regulatory considerations are, and of how those considerations are most effectively taken into account.

In the first of these three chapters, that of Alessandro Petretto, a considerable measure of confidence is displayed in the capacity of the European nation-state to invent and implement new patterns of effective regulation in the public-service sector, and in particular in relation to public utilities in a liberalized regime. He attaches great importance to the flexibility and adaptability of the forms of governance which become available once the State has defined its role in relation to public utilities in terms of regulation rather than of primary service provision. In particular, he sees great potential for various ways of separating regulatory responsibilities from planning responsibilities on the one hand and from control responsibilities on the other, with the regulatory responsibilities being entrusted to distinct regulatory authorities. Such hierarchies, moreover, can also be made more responsive, it is argued, by decentralizing them to subnational levels. He reviews in this light some Italian and some British institutional examples of actually or potentially positive development.

In the second of this group of chapters, that of Wolf Sauter, the focus is on the central institutions of the European Community, rather than upon the Member States, as the location of development of new and promising approaches to the regulation of the intermediate public service sector. Taking as his case in point the telecommunications sector, he shows how the EC Commission has started to transform and build upon the idea of the universal service obligation, which has often been a rather general rationale for the intransigent defence of public monopolies, so that a more refined notion of universal or general service obligation becomes a basis for public interest regulation and sustains moves towards liberalization. This is an example of the way in which, it has been argued earlier in the present chapter, there is the emergence of a public-service sector at Community level as well as at nation-state level.

Of the three chapters in this group, it is the third, that of Giuliano Amato, which offers the most general overview of the developments which are occurring in this field, so much so that this chapter almost constitutes a kind of synthesis of the previous ones. He argues that, both at Community and at Member-State level, if I understand it correctly, we are witnessing in the third, intermediate, public-service sector a convergence of two legal or regulatory traditions. The one is a continental civilian legal tradition in which the identification of a public interest in a type of service resulted in its generally being subjected to an essentially statist regime of public law. The other is an Anglo-Saxon common law tradition in which the identification of a public interest in a type of service might but did not necessarily result in its being placed within a statutory regime, but in any case could leave that service basically in the realm of private law but subject to special public interest liabilities or requirements, of which the paradigm examples are those of the common carrier and common innkeeper.

For Giuliano Amato, the systemic outcome of this convergence is best understood in terms of competition law. What starts to emerge is not so much a new type of competition law, to be contrasted with a more traditional type, but rather a combination of parallel types of competition law—the one primarily concerned with the creation and maintenance of free competition and a free market, the other more concerned with the regulation of that competition in the public interest. I would add that it is perhaps in EC law that we can most clearly see those two interwoven strands of competition law, though we might argue that this tension between the two types is also inherent in Member-State legal systems of market regulation, and that it is also an identifying feature of the third, intermediate, public-service sector. We could also say that this is or can become a tension between Member-State legal systems on the one hand, and the Community legal system on the other. There is, moreover, a similar set of tensions within labour law in relation to the public-service sector, and it is with the consideration of that tension that the final group of chapters in this book, those of Alain Supiot and Silvana Sciarra, is concerned.

It will become apparent to the readers of this book how fully and effectively those two chapters succeed in transposing the themes of the earlier chapters into the discourse of labour law; I shall not, at this stage, attempt to summarize their arguments, beyond what is necessary to draw attention to certain nuances as between their respective approaches to the topic, nuances which are quite fine ones but which express the potential, and in a real sense the need, for serious debate among labour lawyers about the role of their discipline in the public-service sector. Alain Supiot writes from a position of concern about the way in which the legal regime for public employment in Member States of the Community such as France may have become too rigid to serve the needs of the public-service sector. He welcomes the chance to recognize a new European conception of services of general interest, which will form an important element in a developing idea of European social citizenship. Like Etienne Picard, he emphasizes the complexity of the relationship between such a conception of social citizenship on the one hand and, on the other hand, the set of fundamental individual human rights which he conceives it to be the task of a legal system to vindicate; but, at the same time, he sees a real opportunity to integrate the needs and legitimate expectations of the public-service workforce into that concept of social citizenship.

In the final, and summatory, chapter of the book, Silvana Sciarra completes the accomplishment of the task of linking the earlier discussions of issues of public law and administration, and of economic and competition law, into the particular discussion of labour law; she can justly indicate, as she does in its title, that the chapter has a bridge-building function. In her analysis of the issues for and from labour law, she is as willing as Alain Supiot to be enthusiastic about the possibilities for, as she puts it, constructing a new paradigm for the public-service sector and adopting it as a frame of reference for new citizenship rights. At the same time, she is much concerned with the need to secure, in the new situation and through those new conceptions of citizenship, the collective and representative protections which the public-service workforce enjoyed under the welfare-state paradigm, and she wishes to alert us to the risks that the rights and claims of consumer citizens may encroach upon the rights to collective bargaining and the freedom to take industrial action which are accorded to public-service workers, also to be regarded as citizens in that capacity. She reviews some extremely interesting legislative developments in Italian labour and public law from that perspective. However, to engage in further description and analysis of the chapters which follow would be improperly to pre-empt the role of the readers and reviewers. Enough has been said to suggest the way in which this symposium is meant to have structure and coherence. It is for others to judge whether that has in fact been achieved.

2

Public Services, Citizenship and the State—the British Experience 1967–97

DAVID FAULKNER

This chapter traces the changes which have taken place in the structure, management, and culture of public services in Britain from the mid-1960s to the present time. It relates those developments to wider changes in social and economic conditions, in public and political attitudes to society and citizenship, and in views of the nature and role of communities and the State. It speculates about the direction which further developments might take in the future, and draws some conclusions for issues which government and public services ought to consider over the coming years and the approach they might take to them.

1. Political and Administrative Change 1967–79

The period from the 1960s to the present can reasonably be described as a time of uncertainty and declining confidence, both nationally and among individuals. Early indications are to be found not only in changing patterns of social behaviour and attitudes to authority and personal and working relationships, but also in the period of economic weakness in the late 1960s, including the effects of the devaluation of sterling in 1967; the gradual reaction against the so-called 'permissive society' of the 1960s; and—especially relevant to this chapter—the decline in political confidence in the civil service, particularly the administrative civil service, exemplified by the setting up of the Fulton Committee and its Report published in 1968.[1]

Changes resulting from the Fulton Report included the creation within government of a separate Civil Service Department, responsible for the central management of the civil service, which had previously been a responsibility of the Treasury; new procedures for recruitment and promotion to the civil service 'fast stream'; the formation within the Cabinet Office of the Central Policy Review Staff, charged with taking an

[1] The Fulton Report, *The Civil Service*, Cmnd 3638 (HMSO, London, 1968).

independent and long-term view of issues of government policy; and the process known as 'Programme Analysis and Review', which all departments were required to apply to the programmes for which they were responsible. The changes themselves are now for the most part a matter of history, but they brought about (or coincided with) a change in the culture and attitudes of public servants, who became less complacent and elitist, more sensitive to public and political opinion, and often more dynamic and systematic in their approach. Ministers themselves became increasingly concerned with handling the media, as the media's influence gathered strength through television and investigative journalism. They also became more concerned with the management of their departments. But the country's underlying economic weakness continued, and public and political confidence were further damaged by the period of rapid inflation and industrial disputes at the end of the 1970s.

2. Economic and Social Change 1980–97

The Conservative government which was elected in 1979 made a determined and single-minded attempt to tackle the problems of economic weakness as they were perceived at that time. Central to its policies were the control of inflation; the reform of industrial relations including a reduction in the power of organized labour; and reductions or more rigorous control of public expenditure to be achieved by reducing the cost and increasing the efficiency of public services. An early element in the last of these was the Financial Management Initiative (1982); a theme of the later initiatives was the separation of the 'purchasing' from the 'providing' or 'producing' functions, whether by privatization, contracting-out, or the creation of executive agencies to operate in a competitive or 'internal' market. A further development was the Citizen's Charter (1991). The resulting changes came to be known as the 'New Public Management' or 'Government by Contract'.[2] Similar developments were taking place in other countries.[3]

[2] The extensive literature, published by the Government, by the Treasury and Civil Service (later the Public Service) Committee of the House of Commons, and by various commentators, includes: *Improving Management in Government*: *The Next Steps*: *A Report to the Prime Minister* (the Ibbs Report) (HMSO, London, 1988); *The Citizen's Charter*, Cm 1599 (HMSO, London, 1991); *Competing for Quality*, Cm 1730 (HMSO, London, 1991); *The Civil Service*: *Continuity and Change*, Cm 2627 (HMSO, London, 1994); *The Citizen's Charter 5 Years On*, Cm 3370 (HMSO, London, 1996); *Next Steps Agencies in Government: Review 1996*, Cm 3579 (London, Stationery Office, 1997) (also contains a fuller reading list of relevant government publications); House of Commons, Session 1995–6, *Ministerial Accountability and Responsibility*, Second Report from the Public Service Committee (HMSO, London, 1996); House of Commons, Session 1996–7, *Ministerial Accountability and Responsibility*, Second Report from the Public Service Committee (three volumes) (Stationery Office, London, 1997);

The driving force came partly from public frustration at the perceived inefficiency of public services and the industrial action which had been taken in some of them during the 1970s, and a natural political wish to exploit that frustration. But an equally powerful influence, affecting all the major political parties, was the sense that in a world of global markets the country could not afford to sustain public services and a public bureaucracy, paid for from taxation, on the scale that it had in the past.[4] Those on the political right were ready to go further and argue that economic survival, or at least individual and national prosperity, required a major reconstruction of the apparatus of the State, a re-ordering of the relationship between the State and the individual, and a major redistribution of political and economic power in the country as a whole.

3. New Public Management

Characteristics of the New Public Management included its emphasis on the discipline of competition and market forces; the threat of redundancy or dismissal; individual, often short-term contracts; a top-down structure of output measures and performance indicators; compliance with rules; and material rewards, especially through performance-related pay. Not much was made of such notions as equity, personal loyalty, or mutual confidence. It was essentially the 'low trust' view of management which had been described by Alan Fox twenty years previously.[5]

A contrasting 'high trust' view would emphasize a participative style of management, based on negotiation, consultation, and communication. It would reward teams rather than individuals, and seek to improve and recognize good performance rather than punish failure. It would value equity, discretion, and trust. Partnerships and contracts would be between equals, not between superiors and inferiors or the more or less powerful. This view would acknowledge that an organization's internal style must

House of Commons, Session 1996–7, *The Citizen's Charter*, Third Report from the Public Service Committee (Stationery Office, London, 1997); A. Barron and C. Scott, 'The Citizen's Charter Programme' (1992) 55, *Modern Law Review*, 526; I. Bynoe, *Beyond the Citizen's Charter* (Institute for Public Policy Research, London, 1996); C. Foster and F. Plowden *The State Under Stress* (Open University Press, Buckingham, 1996); M. Freedland 'Government by Contract and Public Law' [1994] *Public Law* 86; I. Harden, *The Contracting State* (Open University Press, Buckingham, 1996); C. Hood, 'A Public Management for All Services?' 69 *Public Administration*, 3–19; D. Osborne and T. Gaebler, *Reinventing Government* (Addison-Wesley, Reading); J. Stewart and R. Walsh, 'Change in the Management of Public Services' 70, *Public Administration*, 499–518.

[3] For an account of a similar experience in Australia under the Hawke administration, see M. Pusey, *Economic Rationalisation in Canberra* (Cambridge University Press, Sydney, 1991).

[4] See e.g. Foster and Plowden, n. 2 above; also Pusey, n. 2 above.

[5] A. Fox, *Beyond Contract*: *Work, Power and Trust Relations* (Faber and Faber, London, 1974).

match the functions it has to perform: if public servants, especially those in positions of authority over their fellow citizens, do not feel respected by Ministers, their employing organizations or others to whom they feel accountable, they will not easily show respect for others or receive it in return.

4. Social Conditions and Attitudes

The application of the policies and practices associated with the New Public Management coincided with, and itself contributed to, a number of wider social developments—changes in patterns of employment and the formation of careers, in the expectations and relative prospects of men and women, in personal relationships and the formation of families, and the transition to a more diverse and plural society. It also coincided with increasing uncertainty, and controversy, over the country's position in Europe and, less prominently, over its own constitutional arrangements and the relationship between the different parts of the United Kingdom.

The New Public Management has coincided with the emergence of an 'exclusive' view of society and social and working relationships. This view shares some of the characteristics of a 'low trust' view of management and organizations, and is reflected in some of the policies and attitudes of both the main political parties. It emphasizes personal freedom and responsibility, and is inclined to disregard the influence of situations and circumstances. It distinguishes between a deserving majority who are self-reliant and law-abiding and entitled to benefit themselves and those around them without interference from others; and an undeserving, feckless, welfare-dependent, and potentially criminal minority—or under-class—from whom they need to be protected. The benefits of citizenship, or membership of a community, are confined to those who conform to accepted standards or who can afford to pay for them. Human behaviour is thought to be motivated mainly by a desire for material gain or by fear of punishment or disgrace. There is not much interest in, or respect for, notions of equity or social justice, or of public duty or service.

A society which adopts this view is likely to be unsure of itself, suspicious of strangers, hostile towards foreigners and fearful of those who do not conform to its assumptions and stereotypes. It will favour such measures as the carrying of identity cards, the maintenance of personal records—including any criminal convictions—with access to them by those in authority, the reporting of suspicious persons or events, and the large-scale use of imprisonment. Its criminal justice processes will concentrate on controlling and punishing crime, and on speed and certainty of conviction, rather than due process and justice for its own sake.[6] Its decision-making processes will be cautious, closed, and secretive.[7] It is likely to be vulnerable to corruption in public life. Many of these characteristics were to be found in Great Britain in the mid-1990s.

The contrasting 'inclusive' view has been less commonly expressed. This view recognizes the capacity and will of individuals to change—to improve if they are given guidance, help, and encouragement; to be damaged if they are abused or humiliated. It emphasizes respect for human dignity and personal identity, and a sense of public duty and social responsibility. It looks more towards putting things right for the future than to allocating blame and awarding punishment, although the latter may sometimes be part of the former. Citizenship and membership of the community are seen as permanent attributes, not to be forfeited by misfortune or failure. The duty to conform to society's or the community's standards is matched by the community's own obligation to support its vulnerable and disadvantaged members.

Solutions to social problems or to crime have to be sought by inclusion within the community itself—among parents, in schools, by providing opportunities and hope for young people—and not by punishment or exclusion from it. Authority has to be accountable, and legitimate in the sense that respect for it has to be earned and justified. The 'inclusive' view is likely to be characteristic of a society which is open and compassionate, which accommodates and respects plurality, and which has some confidence in the future.

5. The Nature and Role of the State

Changes can also be found in attitudes to the nature and role of the State. During the period of (broadly speaking) political consensus after the Second World War, the State was mostly seen as a benevolent institution, not only securing the defence of the realm and the Queen's peace, but also providing essential services for the general population, specialized services for those who needed them, and protection and support for those who were vulnerable or disadvantaged. These functions were performed

[6] For accounts relating to the construction of the Criminal Justice Act 1991 and to the Report of the Royal Commission on Criminal Justice, see N. Lacey, 'Government as Manager, Citizen as Consumer' (1994) 57, *Modern Law Review*, 534–54; and also 'Missing the Wood . . . Pragmatism and Theory in the Royal Commission', in M. McConville and L. Bridges (eds.), *Criminal Justice in Crisis* (Edward Elgar, Aldershot, 1994).

[7] For an 'exclusive' view of society and human relationships, see American writer Charles Murray's articles on the underclass, 'The Emerging British Underclass' and 'The Underclass: The Crisis Deepens', published in London by the Institute for Economic Affairs in 1990 and 1994, also his articles in the *Sunday Times* on 5, 12, and 19 Jan. 1997. For an analysis of its dangers, see A. Rutherford, 'Criminal Policy and the Eliminative Ideal' (1998) 31(5) *Social Policy and Administration* 116–35.

with some regard to notions of equity and social justice, even though there might be different views of what those notions implied in particular situations or for certain individuals. In a more general sense, it was the duty of the State to protect its citizens' freedoms and guarantee their rights. That duty was enshrined in the United Nations Covenant on Civil and Political Rights and in the European Convention on Human Rights.

More recently, a view has come to be expressed which portrays the State not so much as protecting individual freedoms but as presenting a threat to them. The threat may take the form of an expensive and inefficient bureaucracy which consumes a disproportionate share of the country's wealth; of interference in matters of individual choice through excessive regulation or taxation; or of a corrupting influence which destroys individual initiative—or even moral integrity—by creating dependence on state benefits. The focus of debate has changed from one of promoting collective or national well-being through the agencies of the State to one of reducing the scale of state activity and to making the activities which remain more efficient, and in particular less expensive.[8] The political debate has been mostly dominated by the political right (or 'new right'); there is an alternative 'centre left' vision based on the notion of a 'stakeholding' society or economy, but it has not so far achieved the same political resonance or widespread public appeal.[9]

6. Rights and Citizenship

At the same time, it has been argued that the notion of 'rights' has been taken too far, especially if rights are to be interpreted and legally enforced by a 'foreign' court such as the European Court of Justice or the European Court of Human Rights; and that it is time to reassert the notion of duties and responsibilities. Often in the same context, there is an appeal to the values or social cohesion of the 'community', to which the individual owes some loyalty and a duty to conform to its expectations. Much of the argument is confused, and those who would deny a 'right' to be protected from, say, unfair dismissal or discrimination might use similar language to claim a 'right' to exercise freedom of action or choice in matters of individual or corporate behaviour (for example as employers). Those who argue for the recognition of duties and responsibilities are not usually

[8] See, e.g., the speech by the Prime Minister, John Major, to the Conservative Central Council on 15 Mar. 1997, and the views of Charles Murray, n. 7 above. For a more critical analysis, see Foster and Plowden, n. 2 above.

[9] See, e.g., W. Hutton, *The State We're In* (Jonathan Cape, London, 1995); and his later publication, *The State to Come* (Vintage, London, 1997). Also see J. Kay, *The Business of Economics* (Oxford University Press, Oxford, 1996).

specific about the means, if any, by which they might be enforced, but there is increasing political interest, in both main political parties, in measures to give parents statutory responsibility for the behaviour of their children, including criminal liability in some instances.[10]

'Citizenship' is not a word which is now much used in ordinary discourse. The dictionary definition of a citizen is a native or inhabitant of a state or city, often in the sense of possessing its 'freedom' or franchise. The notion of citizenship has thus come to imply both rights and obligations—a right to protection, and to consideration and respect; a right or qualification to participate in the running of the State; and an obligation to pay taxes or to perform military service if required. It may also imply a less formal willingness to contribute to charity, to help neighbours, or to undertake voluntary public service (for example as a magistrate). More recently, for example in the Citizen's Charter, the term has been used in a different sense. The citizen is there seen as a consumer of public services, entitled (in theory but not always able in practice) to make choices about which to use or whether or not to use them; to expect certain standards of service (but with little or no opportunity to say what those standards should be); and to complain if they are not met.[11]

7. Communities

A parallel discourse relates to the notion of the 'community' or 'communities'. The language it uses can be interpreted as an expression of the 'inclusive' approach, if it implies a spirit of mutual co-operation and a sense of obligation towards their weak and vulnerable members and the acceptance and reintegration of those who are disruptive or deviant. But communities can also be defined exclusively. Communities which are most easily recognized—such as those based on culture, religion, occupation, or geographical location—implicitly exclude those who do not qualify for membership or conform to their requirements. Emphasis on communities can be used positively to promote the notions of self-reliance and independence, but also a sense of separation from the State and the protection and support it might otherwise be expected to provide. Appeals to the community's interests can be used as populist opportunism to devalue the principles of respect for the individual and of procedural justice. Community sentences, care in the community and

[10] See, e.g., the relevant provisions in the Criminal Justice Act 1991, and more recent proposals in the Conservative and Labour Party manifestos for the 1997 General Election.

[11] For a discussion on different views of 'the community' see N. Lacey and L. Zedner, 'Discourses of Community in Criminal Justice' (1995) 22 *Journal of Law and Society*, 301–25. Also see A. Etzioni in the *Guardian*, 28 June 1997, and subsequent correspondence on 2 and 5 July.

community health are often defined negatively—by the fact that they are not served in prisons, or delivered in hospitals or other institutions—rather than by any positive reference to the energy, skills, services, and obligations which are to be found within communities, or to the means of mobilizing them for public purposes. The language of communities needs to be used with caution, and scrutinized with care.[12]

8. Citizenship, the State and Public Service

All notions of citizenship imply a structure of public services and a responsibility for the State to ensure that they are provided and perform to some acknowledged standard of efficiency. There are, however, important differences in the views which might be taken, not only about the scale on which they should operate and how they should be organized, but also about how they should perform, what should be expected from them, and what role the State, the Government, communities, or individual citizens should play in relation to them.

A change from the attitudes, outlook, and culture which had been characteristic of public services in the 1960s and 1970s was undoubtedly needed. Public funds were too easy to obtain for some purposes, and too difficult for others. They were often spent with too little regard for the cost-effectiveness of the service that was being provided. Too little attention was paid to the feelings, expectations, and reactions of those for whom services were provided or who came into contact with them. Most professionals were conscientious and (often supremely) hard-working as individuals, but collectively they could be secretive, complacent, and obstructive.[13] The change from a culture of performing a function to one of achieving a result was one which many public servants welcomed, at least so long as they were results to which they could feel personally committed and they had some part in deciding what the results should be. The change to agency status had in some instances an invigorating effect, transforming a troubled organization with low status and poor morale into a more dynamic, confident, and forward-looking enterprise. Separating the function of purchasing, or commissioning, services from the function of providing them has sometimes helped to generate and release the energy and imagination to develop new ideas and new ways of working. The Citizen's Charter and the charters associated with it have

[12] See I. Bynoe, n. 2 above, and the Third Report from the House of Commons Public Service Committee, Session 1996–7, n. 2 above.

[13] See, e.g., H. Young, 'The Department of Civil Liberties,' in R. Morris (ed.), *The Home Office: Perspectives on Policy and Administration*, a collection of essays to mark the bicentenary of the Department (Royal Institute of Public Administration, London, 1982).

encouraged greater sensitivity to the views and feelings of the public, and have provided avenues for explanation and, if necessary, apology or compensation for those not satisfied with the service they have received. They have also placed valuable information in the public domain and have made possible a more penetrating analysis of an organization's activities.

Against this background, the public service reforms described in this chapter are often described as if they were common sense, practical, and even inevitable in a world of global markets and constraints on resources, as uncontroversial and politically neutral. In fact they involve fundamental changes in public and public-service values, attitudes, and expectations. They have profound implications for civic values, the role of the State and the nature of its authority, and the rights and duties of citizenship, which are only now beginning to emerge.[14] Health, education, employment, and housing are treated as commodities to be purchased and traded on the most competitive available terms, not as obligations to be undertaken, and still less rights to be protected, by the State, provided by public services, and enjoyed by the citizen. Citizens are defined as individual consumers of public services, rather than as people who share a sense of common interest or identity or who are joined by any sense of mutual obligation or trust. Public service is defined by the achievement of internal targets and performance indicators, or as the accurate performance of an internal process (perhaps accredited to a national or international standard such as ISO 9001), rather than by reference to any social or economic outcomes. The values of public service become those of managerial efficiency, to be achieved for its own sake and not in pursuit of any wider purpose or obligation. The State, or rather the political administration of the day, becomes increasingly powerful, centralized, and remote, while divesting itself of its responsibilities towards its citizens and placing such responsibilities as remain in the hands of private or intermediate organizations with their own, often commercial or quasi-commercial, interests and objectives.

Some of the language of debate has portrayed the Government, explicitly or implicitly, in commercial terms as the main board of a company—'Great Britain PLC'. Members of the previous government have often spoken as if they see themselves in that role, trading and competing in domestic and global markets. National competitiveness and the national interest came to be seen as identical; those thought to be the Government's supporters were seen as its shareholders, to be rewarded accordingly. The purpose of economic and fiscal policy was seen as being to promote national competitiveness; social policy, and even justice itself, was

[14] Foster and Plowden, n. 2 above.

subordinate and might even be regarded as instrumental to it.[15] For example, a successful education policy was one which would create a flexible workforce able to supply the skills which employers require in order to compete with low-wage economies in the Far East. Appeals for rights to be recognized and protected in matters such as rates of pay, hours of work, unfair dismissal, or discrimination were dismissed with little or no evidence as a 'threat to jobs'. Increasing poverty, and social and economic inequality, could be tolerated, even promoted, if they contribute to economic competitiveness. Organizations, professions, and interest groups which sought to influence the political process on behalf of those whom they represent—at a time of increasing frustration with the working of the ordinary, democratic, parliamentary process—were seen as threatening the free operation of the market, and as needing to have their influence curtailed, or to be made more accountable. The criminal justice process was seen as having social control and public protection as its overriding purpose.

The role and authority of the State came increasingly to be assumed by the government of the day, and in effect by the political administration which controlled it. It is to the Government, rather than the State, that civil servants are considered to owe their loyalty;[16] it is the Government which, to a large extent, controls Parliament; and because it controls Parliament it has become—in normal language—the Government which claims to give

[15] See, e.g., N. Deakin and R. Parry, 'Images of the Treasury', a paper presented to a conference on the ESRC Whitehall Programme 'Understanding Central Government: Theory into Practice', University of Birmingham, 16–18 Sept. 1996. For an account of the instrumental view of justice, see Lacey, n. 6 above.

[16] The 'Armstrong Memorandum', issued by Sir Robert Armstrong as Head of the Home Civil Service and Secretary to the Cabinet in 1985, stated that:

> 'Civil Servants are servants of the Crown. For all practical purposes the Crown in this context means and is represented by the Government of the day . . .'

The memorandum was issued to rebut the claim, made by the civil servant, Clive Ponting, in his defence to a prosecution under the Official Secrets Act for disclosing secret information at the time of the Falklands War, that civil servants had a duty to the public interest which could take precedence over their duty to serve Ministers. In a Written Answer to Sir Geoffrey Johnson Smith, MP, the Prime Minister, Margaret Thatcher, described the memorandum as 'a note of guidance restating the duties and responsibilities of Civil Servants in relation to Ministers' (Hansard, Written Answers, 26 Feb. 1985). It was not regarded as introducing any new doctrine or principle and there was no written doctrine or principle for it to replace. The possibility that the public interest, or the interests of the Crown, could differ from those which Ministers might pursue for their own or their Party's advantage, had simply not been contemplated. Ministers had historically owed, and still owe, their own duty of loyalty to the Crown in their capacity as Privy Councillors, and Ministers and civil servants had both regarded themselves as working together in pursuit of a public or national interest which was in principle distinct from personal or party interests (even if they would usually be thought to coincide in practice). The increasing politicization of government placed Ministers and officials under increasing pressure from the early 1980s onwards, and the issues again came into prominence in the Scott Report in 1996. The Armstrong Memorandum has been amended and re-issued from time to time and it is reproduced in its present form in the Public Service Committee's First Report for Session 1996–7, n. 2 above.

the courts and the rest of the apparatus of the State their powers. It is to the Government, rather than to local communities or stakeholders, that public services are now held to be primarily responsible. All are required, not so much to serve the national, local, or public interest as they may perceive it, but to work in accordance with the centrally and politically determined policies of the Government, communicated to them through an increasingly elaborate structure of legislation, instructions, objectives, targets, performance indicators, league tables, contracts, and service-level agreements. It is ironic that a movement which had as its declared objective a reduction in the role and bureaucracy of the State has resulted in an increase in the power and influence of central government and in the bureaucracy needed to support it.[17]

9. Prospects and Conclusions

Public services in Britain are now at a critical stage. At least until the change of government in May 1997, the forces of exclusion and the harsher forms of managerialism seemed to be in the ascendant. The legislative programme for the last sessions of the 1992–7 Parliament was dominated by proposals for penalization, punishment, and social control. Similar proposals were prominent in the two main parties' manifestos for the 1997 General Election. There has been increasing demonization of unruly children, social misfits, and those who do not comply with what are portrayed as generally accepted social norms—single parents, the unemployed, the mentally disturbed, refugees, those with a criminal record. In public services, the skills which seemed to be most highly rewarded, and the values which seemed to be most highly respected, were those of accountancy and financial management and of cutting costs. Financial procedures and quantified, internal measures of performance seemed to take precedence over those concerned with quality or social outcomes. Public service was not so much seen as a career or a long-term commitment, but as an episode in an individual's personal advancement to be continued for as long as, but no longer than, it was the most financially rewarding option that was available. Preoccupation with the short term extended both forwards, with little interest in any longer term sense of direction or purpose, or recognition that it might be relevant; and backwards, with little or no corporate memory or sense that previous experience might be of use in understanding the present or foreseeing the future. 'De-layering' had removed many of those who might have contributed to a corporate memory, and their loss had weakened the services' capacity to think

[17] S. Jenkins, *Accountable to None: The Tory Nationalisation of Britain* (Hamish Hamilton, London, 1995); Foster and Plowden, n. 2 above.

strategically or to provide support for staff who might feel vulnerable or isolated. Policies and legislation were based on political judgement and supposed popular appeal, with no serious attempt to establish an empirical base, to take account of consultation, or even to make a responsible assessment of the costs and practical consequences.[18] On the other hand, there have been some signs of a revival of interest in ideas of citizenship, civic responsibility, and social inclusion. It was coming to be recognized that individualism and even competition were not necessarily efficient, and neglect of the public sphere could soon have consequences for individuals which the public would begin to resist.[19] The more extreme forms of market oriented managerialism are starting to be challenged.[20] Policies concentrating on exclusion and punishment without regard to their operational, financial, and social consequences were coming to be seen as inherently precarious, and as disproportionately expensive when set alongside other demands for public expenditure. Appeals to social inclusion and public duty, even to compassion, could still prompt a positive response; calls for prevention rather than punishment could increasingly be heard; and public servants looked for a sense of professional purpose which was based on something more than accountancy and cost effectiveness. It is too soon to say whether the defeat of the Conservative Party at the general election in May 1997 and the election of a Labour government reflect a significant change in public attitudes and opinion, or how far the previous government was mistaken in believing that its policies and approaches had widespread public support. It is also too soon to say how far the new government's policies represent a substantial departure from them. Some of its early decisions certainly do so—for example to accede to the Social Chapter of the Maastricht Treaty, and to incorporate the European Convention on Human Rights in domestic law. Social inclusion

[18] A conspicuous example is the Government's proposals on sentencing set out in the White Paper 'Protecting the Public: the Government's Strategy on Crime in England and Wales', Cm 3190 (HMSO, London, 1996), and subsequently enacted (with some modifications) in the Crime (Sentences) Act 1997. The proposals asserted a dogmatic view of the deterrent effect of sentencing which ignored the available evidence; made wholly unrealistic assumptions about their effect on sentencing practice, the consequences for the prison population, and the protection they would give to the public; and seriously under-estimated the financial cost. For the arguments see R. Hood and S. Shute, 'Protecting the Public: Automatic Life Sentences, Parole and High Risk Offenders' [1996] *Criminal Law Review* 788–800, and two papers by the Penal Affairs Consortium, *Protecting the Public: Comments on the White Paper*, and *The Crime (Sentences) Bill* (Penal Affairs Consortium, London, 1996 and 1997 respectively).

[19] See G. Mulgan, 'On the Brink of a Real Society', *Guardian*, 19 Feb. 1997.

[20] See Hutton, n. 9 above, and Foster and Plowden, n. 2 above. Also see J. Raine and M. Wilson, 'Beyond Managerialism in Criminal Justice' 36(1) *Howard Journal* 80–95. And from a different perspective, the report from the Council of Churches for Britain and Ireland, *Unemployment and the Future of Work: an Enquiry for the Churches* (Council of Churches for Britain and Ireland, London, 1997).

and public-service are themes in the policy-making process, although the actual policies to put them into effect have not yet been formulated in detail.

Whatever the new Government's intentions, it cannot attempt to return to the practices and assumptions of the past. Resource constraints, and pressure to do more with less, will always be present. Life-time public-service careers, whether or not they had value in sustaining integrity and professional standards, would simply not interest the ablest young people who are planning their careers today. Modern public servants need to be more aware of and responsive to the needs and feelings of their fellow citizens, and to be drawn from a wider range of backgrounds, than was the situation in the past. So do the public's elected representatives in Parliament and in local government, and those appointed as members of public bodies. Matters which could once be dealt with informally, on a basis of goodwill, mutual understanding, and respect for traditional sources of authority may now need more formal structures and procedures. There is an increasing role for intermediate regulatory, advisory, and facilitatory bodies in both the statutory and independent (often charitable) sectors.

The proliferation of such bodies over the last twenty-five years has been the subject of regular political and public criticism, with concern being expressed especially over their perceived lack of accountability and the disproportionate influence they are thought to give to the particular interests which are represented in their membership or which have access to them. Similar concern arises from the influence of interest groups and lobbying organizations. At the local level, people seem generally to have a high regard for the services provided in their areas, but to want a greater influence and a broader process of consultation on the outcomes to be sought and the methods of achieving them.[21] More representative, and more accountable, structures are therefore needed at both national and local level.[22]

Policies, practices, and approaches which are based on the principles of inclusion, trust, and public-service have not yet become as organizationally coherent as those which base their appeal on efficiency, safety, and self-interest. The arguments to support them are more complex, less easy to reduce to slogans, and harder to express in the spaces which are usually available in newspapers or on television. Their success is more difficult to

[21] Public Management Foundation, *Hitting Local Targets The Public Value of Public Services* (Public Management Foundation, London, 1997).

[22] For a discussion of the accountability, legal status, membership, and relationship with Parliament and Whitehall of its proposed 'Constitutional Watchdogs', see the Constitution Unit's briefing paper, *Constitutional Watchdogs* (Constitution Unit, London, 1997). On advisory bodies, see the Lord Chief Justice, Lord Bingham's call for a Royal Commission on crime and punishment and for a revival of the Advisory Council on the Penal System in an address to the Prison Reform Trust on 25 June (Lord Chancellor's Department, London, 1997).

prove in quantified or mechanical terms, especially when they seek outcomes whose achievement has to be judged by other means. There are fewer ready-made models or points of comparison, such as the 'market', and the language of 'rights', the 'State', and the 'public interest' in which the arguments were previously expressed can be corrupted or made to appear alien or out-dated.

The change in approach and outlook discussed in this chapter is not just a matter of adopting alternative policies on specific issues, although that would certainly be involved. Nor is it just a matter for central government, although leadership from central government, and from Parliament, would be important. It also involves the way in which public services are organized, managed, and delivered to the public; and in which professions are led and relate to their clients and others with whom they work. Themes should include:

—Greater openness and consultation in decision-making, with accessible structures for this purpose at central and regional level;
—Greater devolution of responsibility, and of the power to make decisions and commit resources, away from Westminster and Whitehall;
—Structures and procedures for effective local accountability, as well as accountability to central government;
—A culture of enquiry, analysis, and learning from experience, with the aim of anticipating and preventing problems rather than allocating blame and imposing punishment when things go wrong.

It should not be the Government's instinct to propose legislation as the means of dealing with every issue, but legislation which should be considered includes:

—a Public Service Act, specifying the responsibilities and duties of public servants and the mechanisms for their accountability, not only to Ministers but also to local communities and members of the public;
—similar Acts for particular services involving special relationships of authority, influence, or confidentiality, such as police, social services, health, education, and prisons;
—statutory structures for consultation and representation on the main areas of public policy and public-service;
—an independent, statutory Public Service Commission to oversee matters of appointment and professional conduct;
—a Freedom of Information Act;
—a Bill of Rights, probably achieved by incorporating the European Convention on Human Rights in domestic law.

The last two of these are already part of the new Government's programme: the remainder should also be included.

3

Public Service, Market Ideology, and Citizenship

CAROL HARLOW

The term 'public service' possesses two distinct meanings. The first is institutional, focusing on the personnel who operate state-run services. In legal systems where public and private law are strongly demarcated (such as France), this typically involves a special regime of employment law. Although this is the meaning on which the chapters of this book largely focus, as a public lawyer I have to admit that it is tangential to my concerns. True, the law of public service has come to occupy a significant space within public law. The jurisprudence on which it is largely founded has contributed many of the general principles of administrative law. Moreover, the cases, which occupy much of the time of administrative jurisdictions, tend to spill over from the separate, public-function sector, giving the impression that administrative justice is an important prerogative of the public service. Thus there has been continuous pressure, so far wisely resisted, to open up the British Ombudsmen's offices to personnel complaints; again, criminal injuries compensation is widely seen by the police and rescue services of the State as a means of topping up pension schemes[1] and so on.

A popular understanding (or misunderstanding) of a public service privileged with its own system of law, as exists in France in consequence of the law of 16–24 August 1790, and, to a lesser extent, in the European Community, may lead to demands for integration. Dicey's influential definition of the rule-of-law State as one in which everyone is subject to the 'ordinary courts of the land'[2] is founded on just such a perception of privilege. In modern English administrative law, staff cases mark the divide between public and private law for jurisdictional purposes,[3] and a wish to secure parity between public and private employees may help to explain

[1] See, e.g., *R.* v. *Home Secretary, ex p Fire Brigades Union* [1995] 2 WLR 464 and, for statistics, the *Annual Reports of the Criminal Injuries Compensation Board* (now the Criminal Injuries Compensation Authority).

[2] See A. V. Dicey, *Introduction to the Study of the Law of the Constitution* (10th edn. by E. C. S. Wade, Macmillan, London, 1959) and A. V. Dicey, '*Droit administratif* in Modern French Law' (1901) 18 *Law Quarterly Review* 302.

[3] S. Fredman and G. Morris, 'The Costs of Exclusivity: Public and Private Re-examined' [1994] *Public Law* 73.

some of the case law. The special position of European Community staff before the Court of Justice has also become a cause of complaint, giving rise to demands for a special but less prestigious staff tribunal.[4]

The second, functional, meaning treats 'public service' as an activity. More strongly developed in continental public law, an ideology of public-service has developed around this notion, emerging as a centrepiece of continental administrative law. Collective in character, this ideology can be traced at least as far back as the work of the French jurist, Léon Duguit (1859–1928).[5] For Duguit, the function of the State was merely to secure the provision of public services. These he defined as including 'any activity that has to be governmentally regulated and controlled because it is indispensable to the realisation and development of social solidarity . . . so long as it is of such a nature that it cannot be assured save by governmental intervention'. Duguit's theory anticipated and laid the theoretical foundation for the emergent welfare State and also for a State in which planning and the control of private economic activity in the interests of the collectivity are legitimate activities. He foresaw that transport and utilities (mining and electricity) would ultimately become public services, though not their subsequent re-privatization. The basis for an ideology of public service is laid in the single remark that '[t]he one governmental rule is the governmental obligation to organize and control public services in such a fashion as to avoid all dislocation. The basis of public law is therefore no longer command but organization . . . government has . . . a social function to fulfil'.

Following the French tradition, an important study made by the French Conseil d'Etat in 1994 reflects on the public service concept in a period which is described as one of 'economic, social, and ideological change'.[6] The study opens by affirming the link between the theory of public service and collectivism and notes its evolution during a period of political liberalism. 'The concept translates on to the legal plane political efforts to consolidate the republican contract, by founding it not only on universal suffrage and representative democracy, but also on the development of social solidarity and, at the same time, on a new relationship, or perhaps a new presentation of the relationship, between the State and law: a State where law is not only an instrument of public power, but also an instrument to bring to fulfilment the tasks laid on the State for the service of the community'.[7]

[4] See OJ 1978, C225/6 and 17th. Report of the House of Lords Select Committee on the European Communities, *Staff Administrative Tribunals*, HL 113 (1978–9).

[5] See L. Duguit, *Traité du droit constitutionnel* (5 vols, Paris, 1911) and *Les transformations du droit public* (Paris, 1913). The quotations are from the English translation by H. Laski, *Law in the Modern State* (Allen & Unwin, London, 1921), at 48–9.

[6] Conseil d'Etat, *Rapport Public* (La Documentation Française, Paris, 1994) (author's translation).

[7] At 15 (my approximate translation).

From this underlying conception of public service a number of fundamental public law principles flow. Thus it is the governmental obligation to keep the public service operative which forms the justification for special provisions about strikes in the public service. Again, it is the well-known principle that 'the State must act as an honest man' from which we derive special rules of administrative contract. (I shall return to this point.) The same principle underlies the idea that state employment law must be fair and equitable. Similar links could be traced through other areas of public law.

To summarize before moving forward, the idea of public service imbues public law with a strong set of values and morals. These ideas differ from those familiar to common lawyers, for whom the values of administrative law tend to be, on the one hand, individualistic and, on the other hand, procedural. To put this differently, with certain significant exceptions, Anglo-Saxon systems of public law prioritize process values (e.g. natural justice and fairness[8]) in the establishment of a public-service ethic.

But although these two sets of values may differ, they patently belong to the same family. Thus Hood[9] identifies three clusters or families of administrative values: the 'sigma' values of economy and parsimony ('keep it lean and purposeful'), 'lambda' values of security and reliability ('keep it robust and resilient') and 'theta' values of integrity and equity ('keep it honest and fair'). In Hood's categorization, classic theta values are protected by machinery and techniques which patently belong to public law:

(i) recall systems for removing public officials from office by popular vote (accountability);
(ii) 'notice and comment' and 'hard look' requirements in administrative law (participatory democracy);
(iii) independent anti-corruption investigatory bodies (integrity).

This listing could be extended.

Writing in 1991, Hood prophesied conflict between the three categories, and his prophecy helps to explain why supporters of 'public-service ideology' experienced shock at the rapid spread of 'New Public Management (NPM)', at first through the Anglophone world but also to a lesser extent in continental Europe, where stronger legal protection for the ideology of public-service helped to provide a counterweight. The rise of NPM was linked by Hood[10] with 'four other administrative mega-trends':

[8] See J. Mashaw, *Due Process in the Administrative State* (Yale University Press, New Haven, Conn., 1985); G. Richardson, 'The Legal Regulation of Process', in G. Richardson and H. Genn, *Administrative Law and Government Action* (Clarendon Press, Oxford, 1994).

[9] C. Hood, 'A Public Management for all Seasons' (1991) 69 *Public Administration* 3, 10–12. The protected values added in brackets are mine.

[10] At 3.

(i) attempts to slow down or reverse government growth in terms of overt public spending and staffing;
(ii) the shift towards privatization and quasi-privatization and away from core government institutions, with renewed emphasis on 'subsidiarity' in service provision;
(iii) the development of automation as a means for the production and distribution of public services; and
(iv) the development of a more international agenda, increasingly focused on general issues of public management, policy design, decision styles, and inter-governmental co-operation.

For different reasons all these trends have provoked alarm and resistance from inside the discipline of public law.[11] The first two hit at the public employment facet of public service. Downsizing, hiving-off to agencies, and privatization damage the public-service unions; indeed, in the United States and United Kingdom, the intention was to break their power. Internationalization may contain the seeds of further damage, in that the State, and with it the system of national public law, is weakened.[12] Rhodes devised the metaphor of 'hollowing out'[13] to explain the process as it has occurred in the United Kingdom. Internally, through downsizing, privatization, limitations on the scope and forms of public intervention, and loss of functions by central and local government to alternative service-delivery systems (such as agencies); externally, power has leached away to international organizations and multi-national corporations. Rhodes deplores the threat to public-service ideology, as public-service values are replaced by 'emphasis on managerial accountability, and clearer political control through a sharper distinction between politics and administration'.

We might now postulate that, during the nineteenth century, public law with its distinctive ideology developed so as to bring the extended state powers of sovereignty (*puissance publique*) under the rule of law: 'towards the end of the nineteenth century, doctrine and jurisprudence in administrative law were trying to limit the area inside which the sovereign power could set its seal on administrative action'.[14] During the twentieth century, after a long period in which the State extended its field of activity, expanded its personnel, became more centralized and increased in power,

[11] See especially the essays in C. Graham and T. Prosser (eds.), *Waiving the Rules, The Constitution under Thatcherism* (Open University Press, Milton Keynes, 1988).

[12] See W. Muller and V. Wright, 'The State in Western Europe: Retreat or Redefinition?' (1994) 17 *W. European Politics* 6; S. Strange, *The Retreat of the State, The Diffusion of Power in the World Economy* (Cambridge University Press, Cambridge, 1996).

[13] R. Rhodes, 'The Hollowing Out of the State: The Changing Nature of the Public Service in Britain' [1994] *Political Quarterly* 138.

[14] Conseil d'Etat, *Rapport Public* (La Documentation Française, Paris, 1994), 15 (author's translation).

an inevitable reaction set in. It is important to bear in mind that this antedated and empowered the rise of the 'New Right' to political power. It was attributable in part to the Cold War but equally to fiscal crisis, cuts and retrenchment. With that clue, using hindsight, the period from the early 1950s to the late 1960s can be seen to have been a period of steady government growth, the problems those of organizing and managing expansion; multiplication of agencies and programmes, co-ordination, planning. The latter 1960s to mid-1970s were a period of relative standstill; and hence, perhaps, of reorganizations, mergers, consolidation, review, improvement. Since the later 1970s, an undoubted contraction—not only an 'end to growth', but a drastic reduction in real resources available to public administration has been taking place'.[15]

In combination with downsizing and hiving-off, we find a wish to replace public with private law. Contract ideology expresses a concern with individual rights and freedom of choice,[16] which is central also to the ethos of NPM. As Freedland noticed,[17] downloading service-provision to agencies, competitive tendering, contracting out, internal markets, and market testing, in different ways represent a shift towards a 'contractual mode of governing'. At the same time, however, the term 'Contract Culture' expressed a shift towards the management model of administration powerfully formulated within the British Citizens' Charter[18] and 'Next Steps' programme of reform of the public-service.[19] Within law, government by contract seemed to provide an escape route from onerous public law requirements such as the public-service employment statutes contained in continental systems.[20]

In a common law context this may (at least temporarily) be true, since arguably the common law contains no ethos other than freedom of contract; broadly, it '. . . does not impose, either in general or on the Crown in particular, any constraint in the choice of contractual partners, and is prepared to offer its aid in the enforcement of almost any contractual terms'.[21] It is this positivistic neutrality which sharply distinguishes Common Law

[15] A. Dunsire, 'Challenges to Public Administration in the 1980s' (1982) 39 *Public Administration Bulletin* 8, 9–10.

[16] See R. Epstein, *Simple Rules for a Complex World* (Harvard University Press, Cambridge, Mass., 1995). See also N. Lewis, *Choice and the Legal Order, Rising Above Politics* (Butterworths, London, 1996).

[17] M. Freedland, 'Government by Contract and Public Law' [1994] *Public Law* 86.

[18] *The Citizen's Charter. Raising the Standard*, Cm 1599 (HMSO, London, 1991).

[19] See D. Goldsworthy, *Setting up Next Steps* (HMSO, London, 1991).

[20] S. Cassese, 'Le système administratif italien ou part de l'arrangement' (1993) 67 *Revue française d'administration publique* 339; G. della Cananea, 'Reforming the State. The Policy of Administrative Reform in Italy under the Ciampi Government', Discussion Paper No 37 (Nuffield College Centre for European Studies, Oxford, 1995).

[21] T. Daintith, 'Regulation by Contract: The New Prerogative' [1979] *Current Legal Problems* 41, 42.

countries where private law governs government contracts from Continental systems of administrative contract ('the State must act as an honest man'). Perceived as a deficiency by British public lawyers, the lacuna has for long given rise to demands for a new 'public law' of contract.[22] It is in Continental systems, diffused through the organs of the European Union, that answers to problems created by contemporary downsizing and downloading of the public service will have to be and can be found. In this way, public law can renew the cycle by recolonizing private law.

Private law also seems to offer an escape route from the wider malaise of complex administrative regulation in which society has become increasingly enmeshed.[23] Hood and Scott[24] describe regulation as the 'mirror image' of 'managed' public services, and Majone[25] also sees regulatory agencies as the optimum method for state regulation of industry in a transnational economic order. I am not sure that we should swallow these assumptions but, without stopping to examine them, I shall move on to observe that here administrative law has little to offer. Deregulation and administrative law are unlikely confederates. Complex bureaucratic regulation is one of the less attractive features of administrative law regimes and, as I have already pointed out, it is private law which seemingly offers the exit.

The clash of ideology which lies behind the private/public, contract/administrative law and management/public service dichotomies makes it hard for proponents of the public side of these three debates to see any good in the new State forms. The assumption tends to be that, because NPM techniques are derived from the market, they are necessarily undemocratic. Yet Hirschman,[26] an advocate of citizen participation, uses the very same market metaphor of the three primary choices open to consumers: exit, voice, and loyalty—to present the State as a market in democratic goods, while Lewis, a radical proponent of NPM, bases his theory of public service on the market concept of choice.[27] Again, ideology and machinery are not inseparable, and machinery may be put to many uses.

[22] See J. Mitchell, 'The Causes and Effects of the Absence of a System of Public Law in the United Kingdom' [1965] *Public Law* 95 and, more recently, I. Harden, *The Contracting State* (Open University Press, Milton Keynes, 1992).

[23] See R. Cotterell, 'Law's Community: Legal Theory and the Image of Legality' (1992) 19 *J of Law and Soc.* 405.

[24] C. Hood and C. Scott, 'Bureaucratic Regulation and New Public Management in the United Kingdom: Mirror-Image Developments?' (1996) 23 *J of Law and Soc.* 321.

[25] G. Majone, 'The Rise of the Regulatory State in Europe' (1994) 17 *W. European Politics* 77 and *Regulating Europe* (Routledge, London, 1996).

[26] A. Hirschman, *Exit, Voice and Loyalty, Responses to Decline in Firms, Organizations and States* (Harvard University Press, Cambridge, Mass., 1970).

[27] N. Lewis, *Choice and the Legal Order, Rising above Politics* (Butterworths, London, 1996). For comment, see C. Scott, 'Choice and the Legal Order: A Jurisprudence for Contemporary Politics' (1995) 23 *J of Law and Soc.* 611.

The 'Next Steps' programme of downloading to agencies has, for example, been depicted by one British commentator as a piece of 'transferable technology' of equal value to a Labour government.[28] Local government 'contracting out' for goods or services, presently imprinted on the public mind as an instrument of competition, has in the past been used to promote policies of equal opportunities in employment.

On the other hand, we ought not to assume too readily that the ideology of public service is democratic, while that of the market is not. The market ethos is of course linked to an individualistic view that 'law exists and should be used to protect private property and its institutions'. Yet the planned state which evolves from the public service vision of law as 'existing to advance the public interest, if necessary against the interest of private property', can prove both bureaucratic and elitist. By the end of the 1970s, the degeneration of collectivism into centralized corporatism was producing a third ideology of 'citizen participation', whose cause was advancing across the political spectrum in Western societies. This pluralist and communitarian ideal saw the function of law as 'to advance the cause of public participation against both the orthodox public administration approach to the public interest and the Common Law approach of the overriding importance of private property'.[29] In short, the new ideology of citizen participation cut across the two more traditional ideals, the first impaired by its individualism, the second collective but flawed by bureaucracy, corporatism, and elitism.

There is a loose overlap between the competing ideologies of public/private and pluralist/modern classifications of citizenship. The traditional focus of citizenship is on civil and political rights and obligations. T. H. Marshall famously added to this limited liberal concept a new layer comprising the new social rights associated with the growth of the welfare state.[30] The Charter citizen is defined in economic terms as taxpayer and consumer, a 'thin' definition encapsulated in the irritating transformation of passengers, pupils, welfare clients, and patients into 'customers'. To its opponents, 'Citizen's Charter' is therefore a misnomer, a legitimating device designed to link 'charterism' to political citizenship, for which the derogatory term 'Public Customers' Charter' would be more appropriate.[31]

But this is to underplay the element of genuine empowerment which underlies the Citizen's Charter. The Charter is designed not only to raise

[28] P. Hennessy, *The Hidden Wiring, Unearthing the British Constitution* (Gollancz, London, 1995), 131.

[29] P. McAuslan, *The Ideologies of Planning Law* (Pergamon, Oxford, 1981), 2.

[30] T. H. Marshall, *Citizenship and Social Class and Other Essays* (Cambridge University Press, Cambridge, 1950).

[31] R. Hambledon and P. Hoggett, 'Rethinking Consumerism in the Public Service' (1993) 3 *Consumer Policy Review* 103.

the standards of delivery of public services but also to empower the citizen to take action when the service delivered is substandard. It has had the effect of rewriting the relationship between State and citizen in contractual terms, a theory of liberal individualism in which the State supplies services as a *quid pro quo* for taxes paid by the citizen. Yet the Charter has reinforced the idea that 'choice, wherever possible between service providers, is the best spur to quality improvement'; that information about government is a citizen's right and a government obligation; and that the users of services are to be consulted about the level and nature of those services—all points on which public service regimes have traditionally been weak.

The new techniques of NPM—audit, the rights of access to information conceded by the Charter programme, standard-setting—can become part of administrative law's machinery for accountability. Yet, criticism of the efficacy of market discipline as a form of accountability is justifiable, particularly as to the limited extent of the choices which citizens exercise. Policy-making involves choices which NPM sees as appropriate for management and inappropriate for citizen input. Here, neither public service nor market ideology has been delivered. In the sense that it left too little space for citizen-participation, the old conception of public service can be described as managerial. Market discipline, founded on the concept of choice, seeks to remedy this, but managerialism in practice also possesses autocratic and elitist tendencies. Only an enriched conception of citizenship can be of service here.

4

Public Service, Public Services, Public Functions, and Guarantees of the Rights of Citizens: Unchanging Needs in a Changed Context

ELISENDA MALARET GARCIA

1. Introduction

The notion of public service is one that may be approached in various ways and is used in widely differing conceptual areas. In the present chapter, however, an attempt will be made to focus on the legal approach, that is, to define the role of the notion of public service or similar notions in terms of government measures designed to provide guarantees for the exercise of their rights by citizens, or to ensure that collective needs are met. Such an approach necessarily takes account of the existence of an ideology of public service as legitimizing action by the State,[1] in that here the State is no longer confined to the activity of policing or maintaining public law and order, but is active in the provision of services to the public.

Although the notion of public service carries differing connotations in different Member States of the European Union, there is an *intuitive* idea which identifies certain activities as being among those properly belonging to the administration, as constituting public services and associated as such with the public authorities. True though it may be that no definition of the concept of public service can be given that is valid for all the countries of Europe, it is equally true that there exists in all the Member States a common, albeit nebulous, set of elements that can be grouped under the heading of 'public services'.[2] The common denominator underlying these activities is the fact that they are regarded as being in the general public interest, and as such are performed by public law or private law organizations under state control or subject to specific state intervention.[3] Hence

[1] See J. Chevallier, *Le service public* (2nd edn., P.U.F., Paris 1991).

[2] It has to be remembered that even in French public law the concept of public service is 'difficult to grasp and identify', as J. Chevallier has remarked (see n. 1 above), and this view is shared by large numbers of French, Italian, and Spanish legal experts.

[3] On the same point, see B. de Witte, 'L'encadrement communautaire des services publics: le chevauchement des notions d'Etat et d'entreprise', in: G. Marcou (ed.), *Les mutations du droit de l'administration en Europe: Pluralisme et convergences* (L'Harmattan, Paris 1995), 295.

the statement that there is a degree of 'uniformity of tone' in the laws of the various Member States.[4] The circumstances which gave rise to the French concept of public service exist in all the various member countries, and the legal techniques adopted are for the most part fairly similar.

Before proceeding any further I must mention here the dual significance, from the legal point of view, of the idea of public service: (a) the justification for administrative action; and (b) the basis of the rights of citizens. This duality is always present; what changes over time is the importance or role that is attributed to one facet or the other and, above all, the degree to which the rights of citizens are given concrete effect. Institutions that fulfil this dual function can be found in the different national legal systems in Europe. The reference concepts may change, and the manner in which they have been developed varies, as do the legal techniques serving them. In my view, the divergences essentially derive, on the one hand, from the place occupied by a particular country's constitution in the development of the key concepts of the law of administration,[5] and, on the other, from the role of special laws covering particular sectors.

Since the notion of public service is French in origin, I shall begin by describing the meaning of this concept in French administrative law. Given the subject and context of my chapter, however, the main criterion applied in this description is a material or functional conception which is based on the nature of the activity concerned: the function overrides the identity of the provider.[6] The purpose of this approach is to highlight the essential aspects, at the expense of factors which are incidental or more attributable to requirements inherent in French administrative law and France's system of dual jurisdictions. This choice is based on the belief that, at the present stage in the European debate, such an approach offers the only way of singling out a common language and, in particular, ensuring that the legal debate on those functions or tasks which properly devolve upon the public authorities and their sphere of responsibility is not rendered difficult or impossible by the diverse forms it may assume as a result of the differing institutional and legal traditions of individual Member States. I think it important to note that, although French legal theory always starts out from the organic/functional duality, in its subsequent development the distinction is frequently blurred, in my opinion, with public service and public administration becoming two coinciding or superimposed notions. The resultant overlap makes the concept a difficult

[4] See Conseil d'Etat, *Rapport Public* (La Documentation Française, Paris, 1994), 101.

[5] For a recent analysis of the different systems of the law of administration in Europe, see Marcou, n. 3 above, 295.

[6] Adopting a perception resembling what an author such as Kovar has dubbed 'laïcized thinking': see R. Kovar, Droit communautaire et service public: esprit d'orthodoxie ou pensee laïcisée [1996] *Rev. Trim. Droit Européen*.

one for foreign jurists to understand. Consequently, in the present context I have disregarded both the position of the idea of public service as a criterion of administrative law and those aspects of the legal regime which relate to the administration as a whole, irrespective of the particular task performed.

An approach of this kind makes it possible to establish a common way of thinking and, in particular, to eliminate misunderstandings and 'false equations'. An interpretation which gives precedence to material, rather than formal or organic, conceptions will enable us to succeed in arriving at a common language. The European tradition of public regulation of certain goods and activities of general interest is facing a crisis of legitimacy which, some believe, is calling into question the very foundations of what constitutes the European model of society. As recently stated by the Commission, the unique nature of that model is the fact that it was rebuilt upon 'a set of shared values which include the access of citizens to universal services or services of general interest that further the objectives of solidarity and equal treatment'.[7]

2. A Preliminary Issue—is the State/Market Division Obsolete and has the Public/Private Boundary Become Fluid?

Only a few years ago Bobbio was affirming that the major public/private dichotomy was still wholly relevant, in that it allowed a clear division into two comprehensive and entire spheres.[8] In my opinion, however, the situation calls for other paradigms, since the State/individual, State/market, public law/private law, contract/administrative act, and enterprise/solidarity relationships all demonstrate a crisis of this dichotomous approach. Alternatively, if this binary opposition is retained, we need to think in terms that allow a flexible response to something that exhibits hazy boundaries and uncertain outlines. When we look at the forms of intervention by the State, the first point to note is the fact that in many cases they do not fit into the traditional legal categories or, at the very least, the monolithic nature of their establishment—particularly when we remember that the process of European integration is evolving in parallel with the globalization of trade relations. European law, characterized as it is by a multiplicity of legal systems, is filled with concepts of variable content. The complexity paradigm appears to open up a way of providing solutions to the present situation.

[7] *Reinforcing the Political Union and Preparing for Enlargement*, Commission Opinion on the Intergovernmental Conference, COM(96) 90 final, 28 Feb. 1996.

[8] *Estado, gobierno y sociedad* (Ed. Plaza & Jánes, Barcelona, 1987) (Spanish translation).

State intervention in the economy takes place, as we all know, in essentially two ways. The State generates rules whose purpose is to correct the failures resulting from free operation of the economic system. But it also intervenes directly in the sense of performing economic activities through the creation of enterprises. It is at the point of intersection of these two forms of intervention that we find two phenomena which, where they overlap or have become interrelated, are the source of the present uncertainties. Competition law, which is undergoing radical developments, is a clear example of something that transcends the division between public law and private law, since its purpose is not to safeguard the individual rights of entrepreneurs but to protect the market as an institution against the consequences of the unfettered operation of free economic activity.

Similarly, in the case of public services which involve economic activities the principle of free enterprise (or freedom of trade and industry) has always introduced certain adjustments; individual freedom has to be reconciled with the right of the public authorities (particularly at local-government level) to create public services. The conditions under which the general interest is served must not be aimed at distorting competition.[9] The adjustments entailed therefore apply at two stages: when a public service is first created there must be a certain deficiency of private initiative (the familiar principle of subsidiarity) and, subsequently, when the activity has been established, a certain circle of competitors must be accommodated. Pursuing this line of reasoning, and given that the notion of public service is a clear example of the situation described, I shall attempt to demonstrate that what we are witnessing is not so much a crisis as a further mutation of a concept characterized by its very plasticity. As Hauriou one remarked, 'the public service is in a constant state of flux'.[10]

3. Emergence of the Concept of Public Service—a New Role for the State

'They have changed our state.' In my view, this famous exclamation by Hauriou[11] illustrates very clearly the significance of the theory of public service. It developed and attained its strongest influence during the period when the assignment of new functions to the State, as enshrined in the Weimar Constitution, began in real earnest. As Duguit had commented, 'civilization may be said to consist solely in the increase in the number of

[9] See F. Dreyfus, *La liberté de commerce et d'industrie* (Berger Lerault, Paris, 1973), 27.

[10] Note on the Gaz de Deville-les-Rouen decision, Conseil d'Etat, 10 Jan. 1902, which stated the principle of the adaptation of public services to new techniques.

[11] Note on the Conseil d'Etat decision of 7 Apr. 1916.

needs of every kind that can be fulfilled in less time. Consequently, as civilization progresses governmental intervention normally becomes more frequent because it alone can bring about what constitutes civilisation'.[12] The quotation is perhaps lengthy, but it demonstrates clearly the concerns and ideas underlying a doctrine which embodied a new conception of the State,[13] a theory adapted to the surrounding reality.

Thus, it consists in the construction of a justification for public intervention in areas that formerly lay outside its sphere. (It should be noted that the concept of public service operates on two levels: first, in an objective approach (where the focus is on the characteristics of the activity concerned) and, secondly, after the decision has been made, where the emphasis is on the legal regime and the link with the administration.) That justification applies both to the direct assumption of an activity (such as education or social welfare) without necessarily implying a monopoly,[14] and to intervention of a somewhat different content comprising the regulation and control of an activity which is performed by private persons, but falls within the responsibility of the administration because it has been rendered obligatory by a decision based on the sovereign powers of the State. That is, an activity in regard to which the administration places itself in a position other than that of policing. The idea is a vague one, but it must be borne in mind that we are dealing here with justifications for public intervention.

As I see it, although these same preoccupations are present in the current stage of the European process, what emerges from the complexity of our societies and the latest technological and economic changes is the fact that not only is it difficult to identify *a priori* those tasks which should be deemed to fall within the responsibility of the State, but that it is equally difficult to identify those activities which, 'by their very nature', must necessarily be performed by the State. Furthermore, it seems difficult to continue with one generalized justification; we need to look for something more precise and appropriate to the reality of the area of activity in question, even though the idea that the State must guarantee the provision of essential services still occupies a central position. The theory of public service subsequently underwent a process of development and more precise definition from the legal point of view, which it seems useful to recount here, since all the elements of the debate are still present in the current context.

[12] L. Duguit, *Traité du Droit constitutionnel* (Ed. Ancienne Lib. Fontemoing, Paris, 1927), ii, 63.

[13] The same concern is present, as he states explicitly, in Forsthoff's construct of 'provision of the means of existence' (*Daseinsvorsorge*): see *Tratado de Derecho Administrativo* (Ed. Instituto Estudos Politicos, Madrid, 1958) (Spanish translation), 95 and 116.

[14] See Duguit, n. 12 above, 63.

4. A Brief Review of Certain Elements of the Concept of Public Service—What is the Essence of the French Concept of Public Service?

Contrary to what might initially be expected of a system of law which is fundamentally built around the idea of public service, French jurists are in general agreed that the expression has no precise meaning.[15] The concept is 'difficult to grasp';[16] it is complex, general-purpose, and multifunctional.[17] It encompasses a variety of activities and is a fluid reality. Perhaps, as Truchet has commented, 'the absence of a precise definition of a concept is often the sign of a subject that is evolving'.[18] A relevant point to note, since it may help to clarify matters, is that legal scholars are agreed that the expression is used with at least two distinct meanings. In its first, organic, meaning it covers the structures of the administrative apparatus of central and local government. Alongside this approach there is a second, material, approach, in which the concept of public service is defined not in terms of personnel but according to a material criterion. It is perceived as a task or function (and hence an activity) of general interest which falls to a varying degree within the responsibility of a public law body. This second approach is the one that prevails in modern-day thinking. It is essential to bear in mind, however, that in many instances the two approaches do not coincide, since certain public service functions are performed by private law bodies. The decision whether a particular task is to be performed within the public sector or delegated to the private sector is made at the discretion of the administration—subject, clearly, to control by the courts.

In my opinion, these latter aspects are an essential starting-point for an understanding of the present situation. The 'task-based' approach is a very fruitful one, since it shows that not only has the regulator v. operator *distinction* been possible from the very outset, but such a situation manifestly existed in reality, even though the terminology itself was not used.[19] Thus, a public service is an activity with respect to which the public administration fulfils a fundamental role. As Duguit wrote long ago, public services include 'any activity that has to be governmentally regulated and controlled'. That fundamental role does not, however, consist in the direct assumption of the activity concerned in the sense of directly pro-

[15] For a compilation of the adjectives used, see A. S. Mescheriakoff, *Droit des services publics* (PUF, Paris, 1991), 10.

[16] *Ibid.*, 9.

[17] Chevallier, n. 1 above, 3–4.

[18] D. Truchet, *Les fonctions de la notion d'intérêt général dans la jurisprudence du Conseil d'Etat* (L.G.D.J., Paris 1977), 264.

[19] It is well-known that from the middle of the 19th century activities such as railways, gas, water, electricity, and telephone services were delegated to private law bodies, responsible for their day-to-day provision under the control of the public administration concerned.

viding its performance, but relates to establishing the framework and instruments for guaranteeing that the service in question is made available to citizens in accordance with characteristics laid down by the administration. It is the public administration that possesses the authority to stipulate the content, price, quality, and frequency of the service to be provided to citizens.[20] It not only specifies the conditions but, most important, has the necessary powers to guarantee their observance. Hence, there is a special link between the entity directly providing the service and the public administration which has entrusted it with that task and has consequently imposed certain obligations upon it.[21]

Every public service therefore falls within the responsibility of a public law body. There is necessarily a link between the public administration and the activity in question, even where the latter is performed by private law bodies. The power to organize such an activity remains with the public authorities even in cases where they then decide not to undertake its direct performance. The notion of the power to organize covers a wide range of decisions: creation of the service concerned, definition of the basic rules of its operation, and its discontinuance. If, however, as we have seen, a public service is essentially an activity characterized in terms of the aim pursued, the bases for a limitation of state intervention are easy to establish. Although such an approach may not be present to any great extent in French public law,[22] there is the fact that the Conseil d'Etat ruled against the assignment of responsibility for certain activities to the municipal authorities on the grounds of freedom of trade and industry.[23] Given the presumption that the public service/public provision equation is not always true, that case law must illustrate the presence of the idea of limitation.[24] The general interest, as the aim being pursued, is the element

[20] This function is reflected in the content of the contractual specifications that necessarily accompany certain concessions or licences.

[21] It should be noted that two conditions must be present for an enterprise to be classed as benefiting from Art. 90(2) of the EC Treaty: it must have a close link with the public administration and the activity entrusted to it must fulfil an important need of the community at large.

[22] On the contrary, assertions can even be found to the effect that there is no objective limit to the creation of a public service and that any societal activity may be classed as such. On this line of reasoning: see, e.g., n. 1 above, Chevallier, 98, This interpretation accounts for recent critical studies: see, in particular, D. Truchet, 'Nouvelles récentes d'un illustre vieillard. Label de service public et statut de service public' [1982] *AJDA* 427 ff., and P. Delvolvé, 'Service public et libertés publiques' [1985] *R. Fr. DA* 1.

[23] See Dreyfus, n. 9 above, 73 ff. A. S. Mescheriakoff remarks that neither the Conseil Constitutionnel nor the Conseil d'Etat has 'as yet' prohibited the creation of any particular public services on constitutional grounds (see n. 15 above, 109). However, in the conclusions to its *Rapport Public*, cited in n. 4 above, the Conseil d'Etat appears to be moving in the direction of setting limits on the power to classify activities 'under the heading of public services' (126). Given its capacity to judge upon the legality of administrative acts, this signifies something of a turning-point.

[24] For the same interpretation, see Mescheriakoff, n. 15 above, 109–10.

which justified giving precedence to the public service over individual freedoms. And that same end-purpose also constitutes the limit of public action, since all public powers are by definition limited to and subordinate to the general interest.

Before we can move forward in this process of clarification we need to add the identifying feature that characterizes a public service function: it is an activity whose content consists in providing public goods to users, who may be either private individuals or enterprises.[25] The public goods provided may take highly diverse forms, particularly when it is remembered that they are not always divisible.[26] In their provision the user is perceived not as an individual but as a citizen or member of a collectivity. The public goods provided take highly diverse forms because they evolve in response to the needs of society and in step with technological change. A public service is therefore a certain form of administrative action, a certain type of activity with a specified content whose purpose is to provide public goods. This precise purpose allows it to be distinguished from other forms of regulation.

Two questions now arise: (a) which public goods are provided, and who decides?; and (b) is their provision subject to a special legal regime, and, if so, what are its characteristic features? Since these two questions have a bearing on the problems at the centre of the current debate, it is useful to reflect on them briefly. To Duguit, a public service is 'any activity that has to be governmentally regulated and controlled because it is indispensable to the realization and development of social interdependence and is of a nature such that it cannot be fully assured save by governmental intervention' (1928).[27] If the expression 'social interdependence' is replaced by the more modern expression, 'social cohesion', this identifies very precisely the reasons which nowadays justify assigning the legal status of public service to certain activities.[28]

Since, hitherto, French administrative law, having abandoned the idea of 'services which are public by nature', appears to be moving towards the recognition of total governmental freedom, the question of identifying the particular public goods to be provided does not arise. Some reflection on

[25] This identification is not always accepted in French legal theory (as witness the notion of services that perform sovereign functions), but is in my view a key element in the context of the current debate.

[26] As is manifestly demonstrated by, e.g., household refuse collection, street lighting, and national-grid electricity supply.

[27] The conception is described as objective in so far as public services meet what is objectively regarded as a need, as opposed to the idea that the State is free to decide arbitrarily where needs of general interest exist which justify the creation of a public service: see P. Esplugas, *Conseil constitutionnel et service public* (Librairie Générale de Droit et de Jurisprudence, Paris, 1994), 36.

[28] The adoption of this expression is permissible, given that Duguit's thinking is widely recognized as falling within the traditional theory of solidarity.

the matter can, however, be detected in the emergence of a preoccupation with social cohesion and opposition to fragmentation, as also in the debate surrounding the centrality of the notion of the network.[29] It should be noted that the network concept is the subject of widespread reflection, as the constant references to regional planning demonstrate; there is also a spatial aspect to solidarity. The dominant notion is that of the general interest; this is the common denominator and the constant element.[30] It denotes, in particular, the collective needs of the population at large. Any such need necessarily incorporates the individual interest of each user,[31] but goes beyond it. It is this public need,[32] this social need or quality of being in the general public interest,[33] that is, the importance of the activity for the collectivity concerned, which explains the special link or particular relationship with the public administration which created the body that performs the task in question, or entrusted it to private law persons.

According to this line of reasoning the answer to the question of who decides is axiomatic: governments, that is, political authorities possessing democratic legitimacy. The existence of general interest in a given case is determined either by Parliament or by the public administration. The creation and organization of public services therefore lie with the political authorities which possess the power to define and give concrete effect to the general interest. Even where the administration is not to provide the service itself, it retains all the powers necessary to guarantee that the delegated task properly fulfils the general interest (powers of direction, control, and sanction).

5. A Special Legal Regime—A Regime that Must Satisfy the Principles of Equality, Continuity, and Adaptability

As noted above, the activities which constitute public service functions have a specific character. This specificity of the activity or purpose calls for special legal rules—an appropriate legal regime. The question thus arises of defining the characteristic elements of that regime and, in particular, the

[29] See various contributions in the special issue of *Revue des Affaires Européennes*, July 1994, entitled 'Les services publics en Europe. Entre monopole et concurrence'.

[30] J. F. Lachaume, *Grands services publics* (Masson, Paris, 1989), 27.

[31] *Ibid.*, 38.

[32] The definition proposed by Hauriou explicitly introduced this idea, although in his view the service rendered to the public had to be provided by a public law organization: see *Précis de droit administratif et de droit public* (Ed. Lib. L. Larose, Paris, 1903).

[33] This notion (*utilité publique*) is coming into widespread use in Europe nowadays, possibly because it seems free from any connotations too closely linked to French administrative law. Yet it was used as long ago as in the Commissary General's Opinion in the 'Société des Etablissements Vezia' case of 20 Dec. 1935. The notion of 'public utilities' which forms part of the British and American tradition is not the equivalent of the French concept of public service, since it is closely linked with the idea of monopoly.

extent or significance of its special nature. In my view, changes in private law and public law are converging towards a meeting-point in the realm of public service provision. Public services are regulated to varying degrees by an exceptional regime, i.e. one creating an exception to the general law. The public service/administrative law equation is not always complete. It is merely a starting assumption. This is the case where a public service is provided directly by a public law body, but the nature of the service (industrial or commercial) means that private law is involved to a greater or lesser extent. It is in these sectors that the boundaries are in process of being redrawn. Where a service is entrusted to a private law body, the latter must possess real autonomy in the day-to-day provision of the public service concerned, which entails extensive recourse to private law and the jurisdiction of the ordinary courts.

The extent of the domain of administrative law depends on the method of provision chosen for a given service. It is relevant in this connection to note that in the case of services of an economic nature there is a discernible tendency towards a change of legal status: public institutions are being converted into companies. This new status offers advantages from the point of view of flexibility, particularly as regards human resource management and financial management. In parallel with this process, a certain retreat by the administration is taking place in the social- or welfare-services sectors.[34]

Following these general reflections, some more precise details are needed of the real implications of what is customarily defined as an exceptional legal regime. Only very recently, the Conseil d'Etat affirmed that the concept of public service does not axiomatically denote a *de facto* or *de jure* monopoly.[35] However, even in cases where they do not enjoy any guarantees of exclusivity, public services are not in a genuinely competitive situation. The situations in question are very heterogeneous and depend on the nature of the public goods being provided. In general, it may be said that a monopoly situation exists only in those services where the level of investment needed for infrastructures is considerable, and where it is also assumed that their financing does not devolve exclusively upon public budgets or where the financing of public goods provided under certain conditions may be ensured by applying a pricing system governed by equalization mechanisms. The need to ensure financial equilibrium is one of the fundamental considerations justifying a monopoly.

That comment is sufficient in itself to indicate that the traditional area of monopoly has been that of industrial public services, that is, public ser-

[34] The notion of social services as a legal category with its own identity is not recognized in French administrative law; the fact of such services is present but camouflaged under the notions of administrative services and/or constitutional services.

[35] See Conseil d'Etat, n. 4 above, 53.

vices of an economic nature as opposed to those of a social nature (education, health, social security, culture, etc.), which are traditionally provided in co-existence with private-sector activity. Although the existence of a monopoly and its actual extent[36] derive from considerations of an economic nature, these are secondary to aims related to the general interest. The basic justification of a monopoly is a non-economic reason. It is the task itself which justifies exemption from the rules of the market.[37] It can readily be seen that all these considerations are matters of expediency. That is, the choice is dictated by meta-legal reasons which will therefore be subject to only limited judicial control. Such control is nowadays also exercised at European level. In sectors where Community regulations exist the discretionary scope is, of course, delimited and in certain areas has even disappeared.[38] The dichotomous monopoly/competition view of things has to be moderated to take account of numerous situations and different combinations.

Just as there is no axiomatic correspondence between public service and public enterprise, so there is not necessarily any correlation between public service and public function.[39] A wide variety of scenarios is possible. As stated above, a public service provides public goods, and the subject who has the use of those goods is called the user, a term which allows their status and rights to be identified more narrowly than the concept of citizen. The user is the subject for whom the service was created and operates. The main point here is to see how French administrative law responds to this basic rule. An analysis of the status of the particular user is therefore beside the point. The only concern is to examine the importance of the fundamental principles of a public service, in so far as they characterise the activity in question; they have legal effect, in that they operate as the basis of the rights of users, and consequently presuppose special obligations for the service providers.

Those principles are so closely linked to the very idea of public service that one of the authors of the 'public-service school' dubbed them the

[36] The question of associated and complementary activities arose very early. The Conseil d'Etat allowed them provided they were a necessary complement of the function in question; see M. Long *et al.*, *Les grands arrêts de la jurisprudence administrative* (10th edn., Sirey, Paris, 1995), 264 ff.

[37] I believe that these distinctions are important and that the main justification must be spelled out, since the reason of an economic nature will be legitimate only if it is directly linked to the purpose of fulfilling the general interest. This analysis can, in my view, be applied to Community law; consequently, some interpretations of the ECJ's *Corbeau* judgment seem to me somewhat inaccurate: see, e.g., A. Wachsmann and F. Berrod, 'Les critères de justification des monopoles: un premier bilan après l'affaire Corbeau' [1994] *Rev. Trim. Droit Européen* 42.

[38] As in the case, e.g., of enterprises that operate public utility networks (rail and air transport, postal services, telecommunications, and, shortly, gas and electricity).

[39] See Conseil d'Etat, n. 4 above, 53.

'natural laws' of public service.[40] The description is a meaningful one, because it demonstrates that the operational logic of such activities is specific and derives directly from the general interest. The rules widely accepted among legal scholars as being common to all public services consist in the trinity of continuity, equality, and constant adaptation (or adaptability and adjustment in step with technical progress). In other words, functions of general interest must be provided uninterruptedly, over the whole of the geographical area concerned, to all users at uniform prices and must comply with standards of quantity and quality that are regulated by the public administration. However, although it may be true that these rules apply to all public services, it is equally true that the degree to which they apply is not uniform. The fundamental point, as I see it, is that they are a source of legal obligations and that control of their observance lies with the administrative courts, which can penalize infringements in terms of both legality and liability.

Nowadays, however, the stronger objection is to their ambiguity or lack of precise definition.[41] The problem is accentuated by the fact that they are capable of being the source of both rights and obligations, not only for users but also for the body entrusted with the provision of the public-service in question. If we take the example of the closure of certain branch railway lines in order to effect budgetary savings, the collective body of users—the general interest—may benefit (as may all citizens as taxpayers), whereas some users, as viewed individually, may suffer an infringement of their rights. That example is, moreover, relevant, in that it is circumstances relating to social factors such as regional planning (i.e. the general interest) which justify imposing obligations (referred to as 'inherent in the concept of a public service' in Article 77 of the EC Treaty) necessary to the maintenance of certain transport services at levels adequate to preserve communication links serving local areas that the carrier would not provide if it were free to consider only its own commercial interests. The obligations resting on the administration and the service provider are the direct counterpart of the rights that users are able to assert. Here, I shall merely state that the position of users is stronger when the service has already been created. Once the service exists the administration and/or the service provider must take measures to ensure equal and regular access for users as well as normal operation.

To sum up briefly, it might be said that the concept of public service was the occasion of a reshaping of the meaning and image of the State and a modification of the nature of the State/society relationship in a context of economic liberalism, but at a time when the 'municipal socialism' move-

[40] L. Rolland: hence, even today they are referred to as 'Rolland's laws'; see J. F. Lachaume, n. 30 above, 224.

[41] See, e.g., Mescheriakoff, n. 15 above, 136.

ment was already under way.[42] The period following the Second World War witnessed the nationalization of the major economic services and the emergence of large monopolies in industrial services. The justification behind this process was to some degree (but not exclusively) the 'public service' argument, superimposed on the economic theory of natural monopoly. Invoking the general interest was all that was needed in order to bring major activities, some of which had previously been the responsibility of local authorities, within the domain of the State.

What stands out clearly from the entire process and the legal construct underlying it (the notion of public service) is the pre-eminence of a logic giving precedence to the general interest, and the administrative apparatus serving it over the interests of users, even though their needs form the very basis of the creation and development of public services. The legal construct of public service starts out from the viewpoint of the administration, i.e. what it may or must do in order to fulfil, as a matter of principle, the general interest. In my opinion, however, it does not really take satisfactory account of the precise and concrete needs of users, particularly where there are requirements involving quality and diversity. It may be that the deficiency merely reflects a phenomenon found in other legal systems, namely, the incapacity to construct instruments and techniques guaranteeing the provision of public goods to citizens. Public law was constructed to limit action by the public authorities in the sphere of private citizens and has difficulty in responding to demands for provision, especially when what is involved is not the production of legal acts but a material activity requiring substantial human and financial resources.[43]

6. Provision of Services to the Public in Spanish Administrative Law

An attempt was made above to present an essential or substantive notion of public service, that is, one stripped of what might be termed the incidental or accessory. In my view, this same notion is present in both Spanish[44] and Italian administrative law; what differs is the emphasis placed on particular aspects. Hence, these two systems share a certain approach and an 'incorporation' of the theory of public service which has many elements in common. In the Spanish legal system the notion of public service developed through the spread of a certain Italian doctrine,

[42] See Dreyfus, n. 9 above, 18.

[43] Hence the paradox, criticized by J. Chevallier, whereby a public service created in order to eliminate or at least reduce social inequalities can sometimes aggravate them: see *Science administrative* (PUF, Paris, 1986), 530.

[44] See E. Malaret, 'Les services publics dans le droit administratif espagnol' [1977] *AJDA* 1997 (special issue), 136 ff.

mainly the work of Zannobini and Alessi. This operates as follows. First, it distinguishes the notion of public function from that of public service; secondly, it states that, for something to be a public service 'in the strict sense', the administration must not only undertake the service in question as an activity of its own, but also in the capacity of 'owner', an expression whose legal import is in my view obscure, since it is possible to be the owner in very different legal situations. In practice, according to this notion only activities performed on a monopoly basis, often by private-sector bodies granted a prior concession, are classed as a public service.[45] But alongside the 'public service in the strict sense' doctrine, which has a certain pre-eminence, the functional concept (based on the nature of the activity concerned) is also present. It is, however, confined to the provision of public goods directly to citizens: organizations which perform tasks to meet needs extending beyond those of users do not come under the heading of public services, except where the activity is performed on a monopoly basis.[46]

Even when we look beyond the monopoly aspect, however, the framework of the notion of public service is different. Since the starting-point is the idea that the administration does not always provide the service itself, the French system's organic concept is not present here. The problem arising at present is how to characterize private law bodies operating in fields which have not been expressly identified by the legislators and which are subject to a legal regime very similar to that of activities expressly classed as public services by the legislators. As I see it, the administration needs to have entrusted the private person in question with a certain task, and at the same time to be in a position to guarantee the performance of that task in accordance with the conditions laid down. It occupies a decisive position with respect to the resultant activity and carries a responsibility regarding the operational task or the activity[47] performed by the operator. Such delegation may be effected by unilateral act or by contract.[48] The existence of this link between the activity concerned and the role of the public administration means that the concept may be described as subjective, but this needs to be qualified further with what, in my opinion, has to

[45] On the contrast in approach between Zannobini and other authors of the time, see D. Sorace, 'Il giovane Cammeo e i servizi pubblici' (1992) 22 *Quaderni Fiorentini* 511 ff.

[46] Historically, the nature of the subject wielding the monopoly exhibits certain differences in practice in the two countries. In Italy the commonest situation in the various sectors of the economy is a strong presence or monopoly in the hands of public enterprises. In Spain, on the other hand, the grant of concessions to private enterprises occupies a significant position.

[47] On the same line of reasoning in Italian legal theory, see D. Sorace, 'Pubblico e privato nella gestione dei servizi pubblici locali mediante societa per azione', *Atti del Convegno, Le societa miste per i servizi locali*, Messina, 22–23 Nov. 1996.

[48] See E. Malaret, *Servicios publicos, funciones publicas, garantias de los derechos de los ciudadanos: perennidad de la necesidades, transformacion del contexto* (RAP, 145, 1998), 49 ff.

be the adjective *functional*. This makes it possible to demonstrate two things simultaneously: first, that the activity is not viewed in an abstract manner, other than in so far as it fulfils a social function, and, secondly, that the legal regime must also be analysed in terms of the function for which it was formulated, to guarantee the performance of the task. In this sense, it can then be said that the administration has the responsibility of guaranteeing the provision of the public goods concerned.

This subjective and functional notion is present in Spanish positive law, even if it is not shared by legal theory. The administration provides public services in a situation of co-existence with the performance of the same activity by private-sector organizations, which may even be linked to the administration when they provide public goods to users on the administration's behalf (health care, education, and social services in general). In such cases there is no monopoly, but nor is there competition between the public and private sectors, since the activity is financed by the public sector. The concept of public service thus has a fairly precise meaning in Spanish administrative law, since it identifies a certain activity on the part of the administration consisting in the provision of public goods. The public service function therefore has a characteristic purpose, enabling it to be distinguished, in principle, from other forms of action by the public authorities such as policing.

The fact that the concept of public service denotes an activity on the part of the administration whose objective is to provide public goods[49] means that it is fundamentally a material and technical activity, and it is this characteristic which results in its possibly being performed by private law organizations. Given that the creation of a public service has certain implications for the principle of free enterprise, at least as regards its operation in practice, the final question arising is that of establishing, in cases where statute law is silent on the matter of classification, when an activity performed by the administration is to be classed as a public service and when it 'simply' constitutes economic activity. This delimitation has significant consequences from the point of view of competition.[50] Observance of the rules on competition derives from the principle of free enterprise as enshrined in Article 38 of the Spanish Constitution.[51]

The diversity and complexity of the problems posed explain the differences of opinion to be found among legal scholars. What interests us here, however, is whether this concept serves to legitimize administrative action in the form of action by the public authorities directed at the

[49] See R. Parada, *Derecho Administrativo* (7th edn., Marcial Pons, Madrid, 1996), i, 474 and F. Garrido Falla (10th edn., Tecnos, Madrid, 1992), ii, 321.

[50] Art. 90 of the EC Treaty gives this question a European dimension.

[51] E. Malaret, *Regimen juridico-administrativo de la reconversion industrial* (Ed. Civitas, Madrid, 1991), 105.

provision of public goods and, in particular, whether public services are a source of rights of citizens. It must be pointed out in this connection that in the Spanish system of law the concept of public service does not occupy a central position;[52] this explains, in my view, why the legal regime for the activity of providing public goods remains full of uncertainties, even though the principles of equality and continuity have been accorded some degree of accommodation. It is in this context that we need to analyse the concept of the social State.

7. Constitutional Basis of Positive Action by the Public Authorities—the Concept of the Social State and the Objective Dimension of Fundamental Rights in Spanish Law

The basis which legitimizes action by the public authorities derives directly from the Constitution. The concept of the social State is given direct recognition in the 1978 Constitution. It is, in fact, one of the features characterizing the State, which is defined in Article 1.1 of the Constitution as social, democratic, and subject to the rule of law. This quality is accorded great value, both in legal theory and in the case law of the Constitutional Court (*Tribunal Constitucional*), since it has the force of a constitutional principle directly applicable in the interpretation of any administrative acts. This has consequences as regards defining the content and significance of individual rights, with the emergence of a less 'individualistic' interpretation that takes account of the idea of social equality. But its importance lies mainly in the fact that it implies a mandate for positive action.[53] This duty to act, which has to be given concrete effect by the legislators, is greatly reinforced by the 'guiding principles of economic and social policy' enshrined in Title I of the Constitution relating to fundamental rights and duties. Certain provisions under this heading proclaim rights that include 'the right to health protection', 'the right to decent and adequate housing', and 'the right to enjoy an environment in which the development of the personality is possible'.

The legal force of these rights is limited by the fact that they are not covered by the reinforced judicial protection inherent in the special right of appeal to the Constitutional Court (*recurso de amparo*), and their content cannot be deduced directly from the Constitution, which expressly excludes direct judicial protection. This does not, however, mean that they have no normative content; the Constitution establishes directly that they

[52] E. Malaret, n. 51 above, 105.

[53] See A. Navarro, 'El marco constitucional de los derechos sociales en el ordenamiento español' [1997] *Diritto Pubblico* (2), 136 ff.

possess a precise hermeneutic value, and these constitutional principles must be observed both in all legislative activity and in court practice. This rule must be viewed in the context of a legal system such as that in Spain, whose institutions include control of the constitutionality of laws (direct and indirect). The presence of the concept of the social State means, therefore, that the State is deemed to have a responsibility in shaping the social and economic system. This implies recognizing the inadequacy or self-regulation by the market and, consequently, accepting that in certain areas competition has a limited role.

The resultant justification for the regulation of economic activities is, however, one of a general nature which starts from the idea that there is no clear dividing line between State and society. This line of reasoning is then supplemented, depending on the circumstances, by recourse to other more specific provisions in the Constitution, in the form of the limits of the rights already envisaged directly in constitutional provisions, the 'guiding principles of economic and social policy' or the objective function of fundamental rights. Thus, the case law of the Constitutional Court frequently invokes the importance of constitutional values and uses as the legal basis for public action the obligation to safeguard certain legally protected interests—a more 'flexible' idea than that of personal rights, but one which serves as a 'cover' for legislative activity. In as important a field as television, for instance, the Constitutional Court ruled that a monopoly (initially public, but subsequently opened up to competition restricted to three private television companies) was not an infringement of freedom of expression, since it made it possible to guarantee 'the right to be given correct information'.

The concept of the social State presumes the existence of a constitutional principle which as such is applicable to all public authorities, and in particular to the legislators. This is reflected in two fundamental rules. According to the Constitution 'the content of the right of ownership shall be determined by its social function', where this task is entrusted to the legislators; and 'the public authorities shall protect and guarantee the principle of free enterprise in accordance with the needs of the national economy'. The role of the law is to establish the 'practical reconciliation' of the various rights present. In this necessary task of definition the proportionality principle operates as the parameter for setting the limits and providing a framework for the legislators. The growing importance of the control of constitutionality must not go unremarked. Its introduction changes the perspective of the legislators and entails placing a different construction on the ever-open question of the role of the State in economic and social activity.

The constitutionalization of rules that establish objectives for public action, i.e. mandates for positive action, and of rules that directly 'authorize' public intervention,[54] means that the legal effect of the concept of public service is 'relativized'. There is no need to invoke it in order to legitimize action by the public authorities. However, although the concept of public service does not fulfil that function, it is also true that the Constitution establishes 'claims on the state' (particularly of a social nature) which require the creation of public services. It is important to note, in my view, that in the areas concerned (such as education, health, social security, and social services for the elderly) the creation of public services is imposed directly by the Constitution. The existence of certain public services therefore derives directly from the Constitution, and the competence of the legislators is specified.

That said, there is nothing to prevent those services from being provided by private persons, or no reason why the administration should not entrust the supply of the public goods concerned to a private law organization. As I see it, except in the areas of education and social security, there are no limits on the possibilities of delegation. What the Constitution requires in the areas mentioned is a public network, which may co-exist or operate in parallel with private activity since the latter cannot be prohibited.[55] The 'guiding principles of economic and social policy' enshrine social rights whose content and extent have to be defined by the legislators. It is important to note that these rules establishing material criteria endow the legislators with associated powers.[56]

Similarly, in certain areas the guarantees of fundamental freedoms may require the legislators to develop social and economic rights as a means of ensuring the effectiveness of those freedoms. This is because the *de jure* social State presupposes that fundamental rights have an institutional and objective dimension. They constitute the main elements of an objective system of values that the State must ensure. This changes the role of the State as legislator. Here, its duty is not to construct the barriers necessary to defend individual positions (these are already established in the Constitution) but to provide the conditions in which the exercise of those rights can be effective. The rights of citizens have their most solid base in the Constitution; it envisages a wide range of claims on the State, even if sometimes indirectly or implicitly. The task of the legislators lies in establishing the specific procedures and guarantees to render them effective. A

[54] Malaret, n. 51 above, and E. Alberti Rovira, *Autonomia política y unidad económica* (Ed. Civitas, Madrid, 1995).

[55] This follows, in my view, from two constitutional provisions: first, the express reference to the freedom to create educational establishments (mentioned explicitly, even though implicit in freedom of education); and secondly, the duty to guarantee the right of everyone to education not only through planning but also by creating 'educational establishments'! (Art. 27, paras. 1, 5 and 6, of the Spanish Constitution).

[56] L. Parejo Alfonso, *Estado social y administracion publica. Los postulados constitucionales de la reforma administrativa* (Ed. Civitas, Madrid, 1983), 87.

last point to note is a constant element in this field: the presence, once again, of concepts that remain elusive and difficult to grasp.

8. A Brief Review of Rights to the Provision of Public Services in German Law

German public law includes the constitutionalization of rules that establish objectives for public action, and also rules that 'authorize' public intervention as mandates for positive action.[57] The theory of fundamental rights in the social State[58] means that they operate as the basis for claims upon the State regarding what is to be provided.[59] This theory seeks to resolve the traditional dichotomy between legal freedom and real freedom.

Given the complex structure of the constitutional rules that enshrine this category of rights, it has been suggested that a distinction should be made between the social interpretation of rights conferring freedom (equality), which applies in general to the rights established in the Basic Law of the Federal Republic of Germany (*Grundgesetz*), and the social rights or rights to the provision of public goods that are given explicit recognition in some State constitutions.[60] The problem here lies in the fact that providing the public goods concerned (e.g. social welfare, education, housing) requires the use of substantial financial resources. Since it is impossible to deal with such situations through judicial application of the law, the role of these fundamental rights is deemed to be that of defining constitutional tasks; they are binding on the legislators and the executive as general rules.

Lastly, I should like to draw attention to the notion of public function that is to be found in the German legal system as applied to the task fulfilled by television. Two comments arise: (a) it is a material notion (the significant element is its part in forming the collective will); and (b) although a public monopoly is therefore not required and it is merely one possibility, the characteristics of the task mean that certain limitations as regards its organization have to be complied with. What is involved is clearly a task of general interest, and hence a special regime must be observed. The task of general interest that public service television fulfils imposes a

[57] The main supportive principle from an objective point of view (as opposed to the idea of a personal legal position warranting direct protection by the courts) resides in 'the duty of the public authorities to protect human dignity' (Art. 1.1, Basic Law). See E. W. Bockenforde, *Escritos sobre Derechos fundamentales* (Nomos, Baden-Baden, 1993) (Spanish translation).

[58] The notion of the social State figures directly in various Arts. of the Basic Law.

[59] See Bockenforde, n. 57 above, 64.

[60] R. Alexy, *Teoria de los derechos fundamentales* (Centro Estudios Constitucionales, Madrid, 1993) (Spanish translation), 483 and 420.

particular legal regime. For instance, from the technical point of view it must be organized and operated in a manner such that it provides a general service to all citizens, since it has a duty to serve the population as a whole.[61] The service provided need not constitute a minimum and, more specifically, is not confined to the gaps left by private-sector television. Financing from advertising revenues is therefore permissible, i.e. a system where the market is not excluded. The rules on competition do not have to observed, since television is not an economic activity but based on other principles.

9. Public Services in the New Context of the European Union—from the European Economic Community to the European Union

At the present stage in its evolution, the prospect of European integration obliges us to reflect on the function of public services in the development of a European Union which, as one of the strategic and institutional objectives it has set itself, seeks 'to promote economic and social progress which is balanced and sustainable, in particular through the creation of an area without internal frontiers, through the strengthening of economic and social cohesion and through the establishment of economic and monetary union'. As we all know, the process of European integration has taken place via a gradual process of economic integration developed on the basis of the guiding belief that the establishment of a common market constituted the necessary foundation for political integration.[62]

In the gradualist strategy with which the European Community was conceived, the market (a 'common'[63] and then later 'internal'[64] market) plays a fundamental and central part in regulating the construction of Europe. This choice is seen as allowing the process to be 'de-politicized' as compared with a conventional model of state regulation, in which national and ideological divergences would have been all too sharp. In this dynamic, the rules to be adopted and standards to be formulated are purely 'technical requirements to guarantee freedoms and competition'. Accordingly, its preferred actors among the Community institutions are

[61] See, in accordance with the same principle, Comm. Dec. 92/403 of 11 June 1993, 'UER/Eurovision system'.

[62] A political integration 'which transcends the nation state but which does not imply the creation of a European-scale Nation State, either federal or nonfederal, but something new', in the expressive words of J. Mertens de Wilmars, former President of the European Court of Justice, in a Foreword to the thought-provoking book by A. J. Arnaud, *Pour une pensée juridique européenne* (PUF, Paris, 1991), 17.

[63] See Arts. 2 and 8 of the EEC Treaty in its initial version.

[64] See Art. 8a, added by Art. 13 of the Single European Act, and the statement of its effect in the relevant Declaration annexed to the Act. It has now become Art. 7a as a result of the amendments introduced by the Treaty on European Union.

the Commission and the Court of Justice,[65] bodies which are free from any ties with national political authorities.

However, the progression from a 'common' market to an 'internal' market also signified a renewal and reinforcement of the European Community's principal objective. That market is not conceived solely as a free trade area, incapable as such of fulfilling the purposes set out in the EC Treaty itself. The Community's task is 'by establishing a common market and an economic and monetary union and by implementing the common policies or activities', to promote 'throughout the Community a harmonious and balanced development of economic activities, the raising of the standard of living and quality of life, and *economic and social cohesion and solidarity among Member States*' (Article 2, emphasis added). The introduction of economic and social cohesion as an objective implies the incorporation of a new dimension necessitating the adoption of policies and measures to help create a European area that is cohesive and egalitarian.[66] Article B of the Treaty on European Union makes explicit reference to that dimension. Given that the concept of a European Constitution began to be used by the Court of Justice from the time of the Single European Act's coming into force,[67] it would seem that the entire architecture of the European economic constitution must be established on these new bases.

It is in this context of a change in the nature of the European Community that the introduction of the concept of European citizenship (Article 8 of the Treaty on European Union) carries special significance. This concept, a foundation stone of democratic systems, is fundamental to the self-identity and legitimacy of the Union. Formerly, as we all know, the EEC Treaty viewed individuals not as citizens but as factors of production: hence the four economic freedoms. Nowadays, the concept of citizen cannot be viewed solely in terms of the closed context of the nation-Member States. The introduction of the notion of European citizenship demonstrates the new situation, the new relationship between the European Union and the people. Given that 'citizenship is above all a state of awareness and understanding which is only partly translatable in terms of positive law',[68] it does not seem difficult to establish in terms of citizenship the relationship via which the nationals of Member States belong to this new entity, the European Union; it need not necessarily be a State itself, provided it already constitutes a cultural and political community. The logic of this

[65] On this point in relation to the role of the Court, see H. Rasmussen, Le pouvoir de décision politique du juge européen et ses limites' (1992) *R Fr. AP*, 63, 413 ff.

[66] See Alberti Rovira, n. 54 above, 44.

[67] See M. L. Fernandez Esteban, 'La noción de Constitucion Europea en la jurisprudencia del Tribunal de Justicia de las Comunidades Europeas' [1994] *REDC* (40) 241 ff.

[68] J. H. H. Weiler, 'Les droits des citoyens européens' (1996) *R Marché Unique Européen* (3) 35 at 43.

process of union has led to a broadening of the tasks and powers allocated to the Community authorities. In this new perspective and, since the definition of the public service function is essentially a political matter, the concerns and ideas which attended the origin of the notion of public service are once again evident in the changed context of a Community law which is increasingly assuming the nature of a common law.[69]

As the Commission has stated, the notion of European citizenship is seen as developing on the basis of a European model of society which incorporates respect for fundamental rights that are enjoyed by all and an agreed spirit of solidarity between its members—a model of society built on a set of shared values which include access for citizens to universal services of general benefit that contribute to the objectives of solidarity and equal treatment.[70] In line with the mission thus assigned to services of general interest, the Commission suggested that an explicit reference to such services should be inserted in the Treaty and, most interestingly of all, that it should be formulated positively so that they could become a Community area of action.[71] The option adopted by the Treaty of Amsterdam reinforces and underlines the piece of general interest services in the European scheme. As part of the declaration of principles, and immediately before the Articles on citizenship of the Union, it has been provided that ' . . . given the place occupied by services of general economic interest in the shared values of the Union as well as their role in promoting social and territorial cohesion, the Community and the Member States . . . shall take care that such services operate on the basis of principles and conditions which enable them to fulfill their missions'.[72]

The product of this has been the emergence, within EC law, of regulation directed at fulfilling the general interest and providing services that are accessible to all citizens. Although initially the attitude of the Commission and the Court of Justice appeared to be focused entirely on ensuring the prevalence of the rules on competition,[73] more recent decisions show signs of a more moderate position. It must not be forgotten in

[69] On the relations between national laws and Community law, see: the various contributions in the special issue of the journal (1991) 14 *Droits*; the already classic paper by J. Rivero, 'Vers un droit commun européen: nouvelles perspectives en droit administratif', in M. Cappelletti *et al.*, *New perspectives for a common law in Europe* (Sithoff, Florence, 1979), 389 ff.; and, from the Spanish viewpoint, Rt. Alonso Garcia, *Derecho comunitario, Derechos nacionales y Derecho comun europeo* (Civitas, Madrid, 1989).

[70] See *Reinforcing political union and preparing for enlargement—Commission opinion for the Intergovernmental Conference*, COM(96) final, 28 Feb. 1996.

[71] See *Services of General Interest in Europe*, COM(96) 443 final, 11 Sept. 1996.

[72] New Article 7d of the Treaty; see also the Declaration on Article 7d, which draws attention to the importance of the principles of equality of treatment, quality and continuity, and the Protocol on the system of public broadcasting in the Member States.

[73] See, e.g., N. Belloubet-Frier, 'Service public et droit communautaire' [1994] *AJDA* 270 ff.

this connection that a number of recent judgments by the Court of Justice[74] and the process of 'Communitization' of policies on major industrial services (transport, gas, electricity and, notably, telecommunications) have played a decisive part in bringing the subject of public services to the forefront of the debate.[75] This is evidenced by the widespread attention attracted by the *Corbeau*[76] and *Municipality of Almelo* judgments. There is a direct reference to the concept of public service in the EC Treaty's stipulations regarding one of the above sectors: the obligations inherent in the concept of a public service are given express consideration in connection with transport policy (Article 77). It is not possible here to dwell even very briefly on the discussion of the present state of Community law in this field,[77] but a few specific comments may be made.

The first point to be noted is the eminently casuistic character of the Court of Justice judgments; the organization of the various public services of an economic nature cannot be the subject of regulation on the basis of this case law. Consequently, the most solid source of law applicable to them is to be found in the Community measures which have been adopted with the aim of harmonizing the necessary rules. The starting point for such measures has been the idea that opening the services up to competition must be done in accordance with a number of specified conditions which guarantee fulfilment of the general interest and make it possible to meet the needs of users.[78]

It may be noted in this connection that Article 90(2) recognizes the prevalence of the general interest over the rules on competition, but provides for Community control (by the Commission and the Court) of national rules and decisions. That is, the law that applies is not solely national law. This does not, however, signify that Community law can ever alone establish public services of an economic nature. Such a possibility is excluded by the principle of subsidiarity. But it has to be borne in mind that just as many public services started on a local scale and subsequently became transformed into national services as a result of

[74] ECJ Case 155/73, *Sacchi* [1974] ECR 409; although distant in time, this has recently aroused renewed interest as the judgment which originated a particular line of case law; Case 30/87, *Bodson* [1988] ECR 2479; Case 66/88, *Ahmed Saeed Flugreisen* [1989] ECR 803; Case C–260/89, *ERT* [1991] ECR I–2925; Case C–41/90, *Höfner* [1991] ECR I–1979; Case C–179/90, *Porto di Genova* [1991] ECR I–5889; Case C–18/88, *RTT* v. *GB-INNO* [1991] ECR I–5941; Case C-320/91 *Corbeau* [1993] ECR I-2533; Case C–393/92, *Municipality of Almelo* [1994] ECR I-1477; and joined Cases C–159/91 and C–160/91, *Poucet* [1993] ECR I–637.

[75] See, in particular, the various papers published in the special issue (1994) 2, of *Revue des Affaires Européennes*, and more especially that by C. Martinand, 'Le service public en France et en Europe—un double effort de reconstruction indispensable', at 80 ff.

[76] See, in particular, the Opinion of Advocate-General Tesauro .

[77] See, e.g., J. Y. Cherot, 'L'article 90, paragraphe 2, du Traité de Rome et les entreprises de reseau', (1996) *AJDA* (3) (20 Mar. 1996), 171–82 and R. Kovarn, n. 6 above.

[78] See *Services of General Interest in Europe*, COM(96) 443 final, 11 Sept. 1996.

requirements to cover the entire national market, so in this case network-structured services have a natural tendency to become 'Communitized'.

In addition to functions of general interest, such as environmental protection, secure energy supplies, or the obligation to perform certain activities in parts of the territory concerned where they would not be commercially profitable (the obligations of public service), there are also cases in which the task of general interest is linked to the universal nature of the activity. In other words, a service that must be provided to all those requesting it over the whole of the territory in question, at a reasonable price and meeting a specified standard of quality.[79] The concept of universal service reinforces that of public service and expresses it in more specific terms. It denotes an essential activity regulated by a special legal regime which may be described as based on the principles of universality, equality, continuity, and quality. Its provision is therefore an obligation on the provider, who may not deny access to it.

10. Conclusions

As we have seen, the concepts of public service, social State, and provision of public goods are used as a means of characterizing the role of an active administration in the task of ensuring the free development of the personality and human dignity. Such intervention takes place over a particular territory (defined by frontiers), and within that territory there must be a certain uniformity of treatment, or equality, since there is a discernible tendency for living standards to become increasingly uniform, even when political power is geographically distributed. The construction of the European Union, the opening up of our national economies, and the globalization of trade are bringing new challenges, particularly when the territorial area of intervention is not clear and the demands of citizens or members of the collectivity are centred not exclusively on quantity but also on quality, an element that is often difficult to measure.

The increasing use of the users' charter technique expresses a growing preoccupation with the precise definition of the public goods to be provided (standards relating to quality and time) and the implementation of users' rights. The legal force of such documents varies widely, but they normally provide specific methods of settling disputes between users and providers of the service which indicate the inadequacy of traditional systems. A new context of this kind places all public services in a competitive environment, although the room available for competition varies according to the nature of the activity. Even in the case of non-economic services,

[79] See, in particular, Council Resolution of 7 Feb. 1994 on universal service principles in the telecommunications sector (OJ 1994, C48/1).

however, market-type techniques and mechanisms (price manipulation, split-up of privileged providers, limited subcontracting, introduction of partial competition, etc.) have been proposed for reasons of efficiency, capacity, and equity.

This is the atmosphere surrounding the process of giving a precise definition to the range of activities that fall within the domain of public services. Hence the relevance of the characteristics of the public goods provided (essential v. complementary) and of those for whom they are intended (special needs v. general needs). In some cases only a few specific obligations, not the whole of the activity performed by a provider, will have the nature of a public service. In such a context, there is a tendency for a separation to be introduced between the function of regulation or organization, which properly falls to the public authorities since it implies the exercise of sovereign powers, and the function of provision, which may be performed either by public organizations endowed with management autonomy or by private enterprises or non-profit-making organizations.

Public services are situated in a grey area between State and market. There is nothing new about approaching the concept from the viewpoint of the limits of the market, but for all that it may be difficult to abandon. The origin of every public service lies in an essential or collective need which is recognized by the community at large as being impossible for private initiative to fulfil adequately. In that approach, one fundamental factor must not be overlooked: the special nature of the public goods provided. An attempt has to be made to identify the shared characteristic which lends them their extra importance and makes them warrant special attention from the public authorities. Legal scholars often have difficulty in dealing with this aspect because, as we saw earlier in connection with the function of legitimizing intervention, the boundaries between the domain of the law and the domain of ideology or the conception of relations between State and society are quickly crossed. The explanation for this difficulty may perhaps be the fact that over a lengthy period (since the Second World War, at least) the ideas that have been widely shared did not involve examining this type of problem.

Be that as it may, the public goods concerned are ones satisfying individual and collective needs which are not satisfied via the market in an acceptable manner, particularly as measured by certain parameters connected with the notion of the quality of life necessary to the development of the personality. They are needs which are perceived not only as essential from the individual point of view but also as elements of the structure that welds society together: needs of the collectivity. The notion of the person, primarily as a citizen, makes it possible to override the notion of the individual (in the atomistic sense of the word) to express integration into the social fabric; to use a concept dominant in the thinking of John Rawls, the freedom of the individual depends on the existence and continuity of the 'well-ordered society'. This brings us back to the ideas of social cohesion, social consensus,[80] and solidarity, and concerns about fragmentation. Since the market is not an adequate channel for their provision, the public authorities ensure, by employing various procedures, the performance of the activities concerned. The fact that the general interest evolves over time means that public services are born, live, and die, although some services continue to exist and have a tendency to outlive the needs that engendered them.

[80] See J. Delors, 'Le service public europeen', foreword to the special issue of (1994) 2, *Revue des Affaires Européennes* 3–4.

5

Citizenship, Fundamental Rights, and Public Services

ETIENNE PICARD

Although at first sight they might seem unconnected, citizenship, fundamental rights, and public services are actually three closely interdependent concepts which are nowadays merging increasingly into each other. In fact the notion of public service, as it may be interpreted in Europe today and as it has long existed in France, flows fairly directly from a certain conception of fundamental rights. It also derives from a renewed conception of citizenship, which has evolved considerably over the years, albeit more in mental attitudes than in positive law itself. Similarly, the notion of fundamental rights is still a fairly recent one in France: only now is it beginning to receive recognition in legal texts, as also in case law and legal theory. But the ground it is gaining in conceptual and positive terms, coupled with the new interpretation being placed upon the purely political notion of citizenship, is prompting a renewal of the concept of public service. That concept could well be lifted out of the identity crisis which it is undergoing at present (but which has actually attended it throughout its entire existence) and be established on different bases, which, although still confused, are certainly more in tune with current developments in ideas and values. Reciprocally, the deliberations regarding the notion of public service that have recently arisen at European level are lending new dimensions to the concepts of fundamental rights and citizenship.

The interdependence of the three concepts concerned is, in any event, a very close one. This is because the traditional notion of public service owes its origin (as well as its subsequent development) to a certain manner of perceiving the social and political bond, the relationship whereby ordinary subjects of rights and citizens are members of civil society and the State, with their fundamental rights and their guarantees as one combined whole. And it is a changed approach to that bond which is leading to a recasting of all these concepts. Historically, and very fundamentally, the notion of public service must be viewed as the product of a certain perception of the social and political bond (see sections 1 and 2) which liberalism itself subsequently amended (see section 3). Today, however, the changes that have already taken place and those currently in process call for a re-examination of these three concepts and their interrelationships (see sections 4 and 5).

1. Society, the State, and the Social Bond

Liberalism is based, essentially, on a dual principle (the two aspects of which we consider in this and the next section) of strict separation between society and State, accompanied by a certain subordination of the latter to the former. For liberal doctrine holds that society, or the societal bond, is the outcome of a voluntary agreement between its members themselves, i.e. the social contract, whereas the State is instituted by society for the purpose of serving its members. Thus, the societal bond is first the outcome of freedom, and in particular the freedom of contract, which itself postulates the freedom of will of the individual. It therefore rests on the will of the members of society, whose first fundamental right is freedom, a right of autonomy with respect to any position of dependence and any power, especially political power; and that right is presumed to be anterior to society, since according to social contract theory (at least in the doctrines expounded by Hobbes, Locke, and Rousseau) it is by the common assent of its holders that society is then created.

It is also certainly anterior to the State itself since, again according to these doctrines, it is the originating convention reached by voluntary agreement between men to create society which erects a State and a constitution as the means of guaranteeing the fundamental right to freedom. The law of society is primarily that of its parties, in the contractual sense of the term: a law of private and subjective rights which nevertheless has need of the State and its objective law in order to render it effective. But the establishing of institutions did not immediately or entirely replace the practice of social contract, nor did it simply absorb it. For according to the most liberal of these doctrines, which the Revolution and the Declaration of 1789 largely enshrined in positive law, the State is not instituted for the purpose of creating society (as is generally believed nowadays) nor for the purpose of managing it or taking overall responsibility for it (as subsequently happened).

Moreover, it is not the State that creates citizens, any more than it is society that creates men. On the contrary, it is men themselves who, solemnly, unconditionally, and unilaterally, proclaim their fundamental rights and, asserting their status as citizens, erect appropriate institutions to guarantee those rights. The State is instituted and constituted by society and its members (the authors of the originating and founding Declaration) purely for the purpose of fulfilling those collective functions which freedom itself could not perform directly—legislation, jurisdiction, and enforcement—in order to attain the ends of general interest that lie beyond the scope of simply recognizing freedom. That is, externally, defence through diplomacy and the armed forces; and internally, formal enshrinement and definition of rights and maintenance of public order through the drafting and enactment of laws, through the promulgation of the law and its sanction, and then through its application by the duly constituted authorities.

In these doctrines, however, the essential purpose of such public functions and ends was to guarantee the declared rights on the basis of which society was itself freely constituted and continues to be constituted day by day, functioning freely under the process of a State governed by the Rule of Law. In other words, *true* social life—that on which, at least in France from 1789 onwards, the original formation of the social bond rested—is, like the freedom underlying its creation, private in nature. It consists in a web of subjective relationships between individuals, overlapping legal exchanges, and transactions in which each individual is deemed to have an interest of his own and, what is more, to be able to assert his freedom. The true fundamental right of such a society (fundamental in the dual sense of serving as its foundation as well as its very essence) is freedom, but freedom accompanied by equality (albeit only equality of rights), since the contract, if it is not to become a diktat, presumes that the parties are equal before the law, at least in formal terms. True, those fundamental rights have to call upon the State in order to be effective; but the State stands apart from freedom and equality, as being the means of sanctioning them in law—wherein lies the ultimate source of its legitimacy.

In this interpretation of the social bond, public functions remain subsidiary, secondary, and peripheral. Essential though they may be to the guarantee of fundamental rights, they are also eminently dangerous to those rights, in that they presuppose privileges conferred by special private or particular laws: more precisely, they imply prerogatives exercised by state powers of sovereignty. Since by virtue of their very purpose they pose a threat to freedom and equality, they must be made subject to checks and controls and be confined within a clearly delimited category defined as state or public functions as distinct from societal or private functions. As the specifically liberal slogan very meaningfully put it: '[L]et the State maintain public order, and society will do the rest'.

2. Society, the State, and Fundamental Rights

The above outline reveals, therefore, the gap that separates society and State; but even in their interdependence they represent the two opposite poles of the political and legal world. Society and the State perform two kinds of activity or function which are quite different in their nature, their ends, and their regime. Society, on a basis of freedom in equality, performs management activities which may also be termed 'societal', in so far as they constitute society and make it function (production of goods and services, commerce, transport, education, medicine, and even, to a large extent, welfare assistance or charity); they are essentially material, even if expressed in legal forms. The State, for its part, fulfils functions that are essentially normative and only secondarily material, such as the recognition, guarantee, and enforcement of rights by way of the law, the courts, or the police.

Society and the State respectively accommodate rights that are almost unconnected. Within society, its members exercise rights of a subjective nature; although they implement them within the framework of objective rules of private law, this is done in their personal interest as freely (if not arbitrarily) defined from the point of view of the ends and means concerned. Within the State, the public authorities merely exercise allotted competences, i.e. objective powers arising from obligations to serve the above rights solely by virtue of and in accordance with procedures laid down by rules of public law authorizing departures from them. Their acts are acts of authority or sovereign power, and they are certainly neither unconditional nor arbitrary, even if sometimes discretionary. As defined by the Declaration and the Constitution, even in the absence of any control of the constitutionality of laws they remain intrinsically subordinate, at least politically if not legally, to their primary ends.

Thus, the fundamental rights of the individual and/or the citizen were exercised in two separate spheres and were of two different kinds. In the context of society, fundamental rights essentially were, and remain, the right to freedom in equality. The right to freedom was seen as preserving the autonomy of individuals within the private sphere with respect to activities and forms of interference, by the authorities, from the public sphere. It was therefore necessary, in accordance with the principle of restricting public action, to pay careful heed to restricting the latter. In the context of the State, by contrast, fundamental rights were, and remain, civic rights or rights of participation in power. They are the rights of the citizen to take part either as an elector or as an elected representative, i.e. as the holder of a public mandate or public office. These rights, too, are exercised on a basis of equality; here, however, that equality implies functional inequalities as compared with the powers of ordinary persons who do not have these particular tasks or competences vested in them.

Admittedly, the holders of these two categories of rights may have the same identity: persons who possess the first kind of fundamental rights in their capacity as private individuals may simultaneously enjoy and exercise the second kind, albeit in a different capacity as citizens. First, however, not all legal persons possess the capacity of citizen (minors, aliens, and juristic persons, for example); secondly (and in particular), the two categories of rights do not have the same composition. Personal or subjective rights presume the right to subjectivity, and hence full freedom of choice, albeit within the framework of the law and in accordance with the responsibilities thereby established. These rights are not directed towards any end external to themselves—on the contrary, their exercise constitutes an end in itself. Civic rights, by contrast, cannot be interpreted as subjective rights. Even if their exercise necessarily implies a free choice, they are wholly directed towards the collectivity, since their purpose lies in identifying those persons best able to assume public responsibilities. From the point of view of their holders, civic rights are much less an end in themselves than a means serving to establish the public guarantee of private rights. They are, rather, functions, and ones with a largely public relevance. Thus, the citizen is the public face of the private individual, standing in his place to effect his full emergence, on a democratic basis, as a free man in society, that is, as a true man. His 'regeneration' lay through this dichotomy: in striving to elevate himself, as a citizen, towards Universal Reasoning, he would reap the reward of increased personal freedom and accomplishment.

In the history of liberalism, however, these principles of political and legal organization, viewed though they were as ultimately serving the interest of every individual, proved incapable of ensuring complete social and political harmony. Not every individual could enjoy his freedom equally, because of existing initial inequalities of birth or circumstance which freedom, in fact, aggravated still further. Hence, democratic and liberal citizenship was not sufficient alone to serve the ends of the private individual: at all events, it operated to bring about, slowly but peaceably, the transformation of those principles. It was therefore in order to respond to this situation, fraught with risks for liberalism itself, that over the past two centuries the latter (in spite of itself, as it were) progressively instituted public services. For a long time it did so empirically; without any overall goal and, indeed, without any well-defined constitutional basis. Behind their multitude of forms, however, public services represent a more or less general questioning of the liberal view of society and the State, of their relations and of fundamental rights. To demonstrate this I shall, in the following section, consider the public service first conceptually and then in its more general context.

3. The Liberal Institution of Public Services

Essentially, public services are mainly perceived as a partial merging of two previously strictly separate spheres, one private and the other public.

From what had exclusively been its 'acts of authority' (*actes d'autorité*), the machinery of state extended its ordinary realm of influence to 'acts of management' (*actes de gestion*), which pure liberalism held to be the natural and reserved domain of society and private law. Since it set about performing these acts of management (normally private in nature) with the aid of its own customary procedures of state sovereign authority, such management became 'public'. And starting from that 'public management' (*gestion publique*), the general theory of French public law created and extensively developed the notion of 'public service'. As the body judging upon the acts of the administration, which had intuitively inspired the notion, the Conseil d'Etat (Supreme Administrative Court) strongly encouraged this; it also reaped a rich reward, because when receiving the right to deliver justice 'in the name of the French people' it was affirming and reinforcing its legitimacy with respect to the ordinary courts; that is, it was establishing firmly the scope of its own jurisdiction in domains that had previously lain outside it, while providing a doctrinal basis for the autonomy of the law it was in process of inventing.

Public services are therefore located exactly in an area of overlap of the two spheres, since they presuppose that the machinery of state will henceforth take charge, on the basis of its prerogatives, its particular procedures, and its public law, of activities which were formerly the preserve of society and its members, acting within the framework of their subjective rights for their own interests, in accordance with private law. In areas where it had issued only normative acts of authority or sovereign power in order to maintain public order, and where it had essentially performed only material acts of enforcement to ensure that its decisions were observed, the State began to adopt normative measures to make such activities its own and to organize them, and set about regularly performing material acts in order to make such services function. As a result, where there had been only an essentially rule-making State, a State of pure law, there was now a State that was a provider, a State of services.

In this way, social assistance, then education, then part of medicine, transport, energy production and distribution, etc., gradually became public services as the State took on the task of ensuring that these activities were performed satisfactorily, instead of confining itself to preventing their performance by private law bodies from prejudicing the rights of third parties or public order. In doing so the State took charge of the actual interests of society, instead of contenting itself with guaranteeing, from the outside, the necessary conditions of its existence. It began to shape, from the inside, their constituent elements, in so far as it set about providing, or at least supervising, these social or societal activities. But it altered their substance, because they formerly fulfilled only subjective rights, on the side of their suppliers as well as on that of their customers. By directing them exclusively at meeting the needs of the general public, subjecting them to public control, and entrusting them to public authorities or public law bodies exercising not rights but designated powers, it turned them into objective functions.

A public service is therefore an activity of general interest which is performed or, depending on the circumstances, merely supervised by a public authority on the basis of its special powers. Beyond this explicative but simplifying outline there is, of course, the question of the extreme diversity of types of public service (quite apart from intermediate forms such as 'private-sector activities of general interest'), which tends to make us lose sight of their fundamental unity. Here I shall mention only the main types. The machinery of state may go so far as to 'provide' these public service functions when it performs them itself. But it may also merely 'supervise' them, which is what it does when, although not performing them itself, it exercises a form of control to ensure that they are performed in accordance with the general interest as it prescribes. A public service may be national or local, characterized by the same quality distinguishing the function of provision from that of supervision. It may be state-run, in the sense of being managed by a territorial authority itself (central government, region, *département*, or *commune*), or managed by a different, non-territorial public law body (more especially a public corporation or public-interest grouping—'*groupement d'intérêt public*').

Hence, there may be a dissociation between the public authority supervising the service and its actual provider (particularly in the context of concessions and all the other forms of delegation of public services); and the latter may even be a private law natural or legal person, with all or some of the capital of the legal person belonging either to a public law body or to private individuals. Similarly, the public law body may be an entity combining public law and private law organizations (as is the case with public-interest groupings). The legal regime governing the activity concerned may be almost wholly a public law one (administrative public service) (even if it is managed by a private law organization, although in such cases not all acts of management, especially contracts, may be subject to public law) or at least partly a private law one (as is the case with industrial and commercial public services) (although then the regulation of its organization and control remains subject to public law). Public services therefore fall very much within a mixed area, mingling the sphere of state sovereign authority with that of society and private rights.

Thus, the institution of public services has entailed an essential change in the mode of existence of the State, in the ideological and axiological basis of its relations with society and the principles of their political and legal organization, and in the rights of individuals and of citizens. In liberal thinking this area of fusion still tends to be seen as one of confusion, whereas from other political viewpoints it is merely an extension of the public sphere—but one the existence of which is, basically, perfectly normal, and in any case necessary in order to fulfil all the fundamental rights whose recognition was previously subject to a kind of curtailment imposed by liberalism. What has happened is that the terms of the initial social contract (if it still has any kind of operative meaning) have evolved very considerably. Whereas the contract originally sought only to guarantee the autonomous right to freedom, it now seeks to serve other rights referred to as 'economic and social' rights.

Legally, however, this category of rights (whose name designates only their coverage) is somewhat disparate. Some economic and social rights are still rights of autonomy, which are economic or social only by virtue of their object (such as the right to strike or the right to organize), and do not in themselves signify entitlement to any provision of public goods; others, by contrast, which are those most specifically identifiable as economic or social rights, constitute claims (*'droits-créances'*) on the public authority concerned, in that their fulfilment demands the provision by that authority of the relevant public goods (such as the rights to education and health protection); and yet other economic and social rights may be classed as 'rights of participation' in the distribution of wealth and, indeed, in its production, or at least in the management of its production (such as the right of employees to participate in the management of the enterprise).

Above all, it may now be noted that public services can lay claim to having a constitutional basis in France, at least since 1946, since the Preamble to the Constitution of the Fourth Republic enshrines a large number of 'economic and social principles' which are referred to as 'principles that are particularly necessary to our times'. And for each of the principles thus identified there exist long-established corresponding public services, such as schooling or, more generally, the state education system, social assistance, family benefits, social security, hospitals, railways, etc. The right to work is perhaps the only such constitutional principle which does not have its corresponding public service.

For our purposes, however, the remarkable thing is that the present-day interpretation of these 'principles' now ranks them as 'rights', and even fundamental rights. The real question is how this evolution from principles to rights has come about, and what are its overall implications. It is no small matter to pass in this way from the objectivity of principles to the subjectivity of rights; nor is it merely anodyne to establish as 'fundamental' rights certain public goods which were formerly regarded purely as ways of remedying the liberal order of things, purely as corrections of existing inequalities whose provision is in any case dependent on economic circumstances.

4. The Changing Nature of Public Services and Fundamental Rights

Behind these analytical and descriptive considerations, we must therefore attempt to fathom the changes which have occurred or are in process of occurring, and which profoundly affect all the concepts in question. The changes attending the development of public services seem essential, even if not all of them are yet complete or established in positive law. They concern all the fundamental rights, including the most hallowed of them such as freedom and equality, but also the actual concept of citizenship. We begin by considering changes related to notions of freedom and equality in this section, and turn to consider changes related to the concept of citizenship in the next section. Freedom and equality still occupy a domain of their own where they continue to prevail in accordance with the traditional principles: a specifically private sphere, in which the public authorities may not intervene, which safeguards the autonomy of individuals equal before the law. Within that domain, therefore, the latter are still able, at least in formal terms, freely to decide their own particular ends and choose the means of achieving them, in accordance with rules of private law that are essentially identical for everyone.

But what is the extent of that sphere in regard, respectively, to the dominion of state sovereign power and to the mixed area in which private and public intermingle? In the short term and on immediate examination, the limits of the purely private sphere vary with the ebb and flow of the concurrent and recurrent waves of liberal or socialist thinking that have succeeded each other in France in recent years. In the long term, however, over the course of the past decades the private sphere has shown a clear tendency to diminish in extent—and its purity has, as it were, been adulterated. In the name of a public order which is expanding its demands to include the general interest, the choice of ends and means is becoming increasingly hemmed in by rules of all kinds, both disciplinary and statutory: authorizations, forms of approval, licences, quotas, incentives, management plans, programmes, standard contracts, checks and controls, etc.

Above all, and more profoundly, contemporary thinkers no longer regard the area where the two spheres interfere with each other as an actual area of interference. They increasingly perceive it, with spontaneous conviction, as the proper domain of the public sphere—as witness, among other signs, the French unitary conception of a public service, which encompasses under this one heading such widely diverse activities as, for example, gas and electricity distribution on the one hand and the judicial system, the police, national defence, and diplomacy on the other. It is, of course, quite true that their respective constitutional status, in particular, precludes their being perceived as exactly the same and that a clear distinction is made between 'public services fulfilling sovereign functions' and 'public services providing public goods' or 'market' public services, or between 'constitutional public services' and the others. Nevertheless, the fact remains that the enormous significance of the notion of public service in French public law has resulted in their being grouped together in this way, with very important implications. That notion, following a French tradition that dates back well before the Revolution, although it now operates by different means and in a different context, very definitely helps to reinforce the role and the legitimacy of central authority and the State as compared with those of private initiative and freedom.

What is more, this area where the public and private spheres merge has come to represent a kind of paradigm—a moral, intellectual, political, and indeed legal reference model—which exhibits a clear tendency to extend its influence and its law into the very heart of the sphere which previously remained strictly private. At the very least, that model is having the effect of insinuating its domain and its law. This is evident from the interpretation placed upon those most traditional of fundamental rights, freedom and equality. On a general level, they may perhaps be considered traditional as compared with what they have become in the area where the two spheres merge. This is more immediately obvious in the case of equality, which is changing its meaning and acquiring extra dimensions. But the evolution is far more insidious and charged with far more weighty implications in the case of freedom; the latter is losing its meaning and gradually having its inherent content removed as the state powers of sovereignty begin to a varying degree to define their ends and means for themselves, a process which implies the very negation of freedom as an unfettered right of self-determination.

First, equality is no longer merely an equality of rights, a purely legal notion of formal equality in the definition and application of legal rules—a form of equality which is in any case now much discredited, not because it no longer has any value (most appeals claiming unconstitutionality or illegality invoke it, and many are won on this ground), but because it has proved inadequate to ensure what is now perceived as social harmony, namely, no longer solely the absence of injustices suffered by the most disadvantaged to the benefit of the most advantaged, but a degree of integration of every individual into the collectivity that will achieve the overall satisfaction of all its members. Although it still bears the same name, equality no longer denotes an equality of rights pure and simple but an equalization of existing conditions. More particularly, it is aimed at a relative standardization of economic and social conditions. Consequently, in the minds of those on both sides it now signifies something quite different from how it was previously interpreted by jurists, although this has not been acknowledged explicitly and although the latter, at least in France, have not systematically given it any other name as a means of avoiding relative comparison and confusion.

The implications of such an extended perception of equality are very considerable indeed. If this is how the fundamental and constitutional right to equality is to be interpreted, a rule will not conform to the constitution merely by refraining from applying forms of discrimination, as was required by the original or formal liberal meaning of equality, which in practice demanded no more than non-discrimination; it will conform to the constitution only if it effectively militates against existing inequalities, in other words, if it treats individuals differently according to their initial inequalities in order to re-establish, as far as possible, a new material equality. If that kind of equality is deemed to be legally and generally enshrined, it is no longer a possibility but an actual obligation to afford different treatment to individuals who are placed in different circumstances. The principle of equality thus changes from a ban on discriminatory forms of treatment that create inequalities to an obligation to impose discriminatory forms of treatment that have an equalizing effect, i.e. compensatory or positive discrimination.

Whatever the circumstances, such a manner of interpreting and asserting equality postulates a process whereby conditions are levelled out, or at the very least an increasingly rigorous reduction of inequalities; and it calls for a profound change in economic and social structures. The very aim of equalizing conditions contains, as an inherent feature, a principle of indefinite expansion of the public sphere, where liberalism upheld the reverse principle of its restriction. It means that any hitherto private law activity may, and even should, become a public service. Also, new public services are always instituted in the name of 'social solidarity' the new value that has replaced the now rather outdated one of 'fraternity' that still forms part of the French republican motto alongside liberty and equality. It too, very ordinarily and instinctively, is regarded as a new but also fundamental right.

But freedom also is changing its meaning. It no longer signifies a freedom consisting of autonomy with respect to the public authorities, and more especially the political authorities. It is increasingly proclaimed as a freedom granting release, or liberation from, primarily, hardship but also from poverty and from dependence of all kinds: illness, handicap, old age, ignorance, unemployment, inadequate housing, and, in general, all the indignities of certain human conditions and of exclusion of all kinds, which are actually becoming more and more numerous and being protested against to an increasing degree. Even beyond such seriously disadvantaged social categories, however, existing inequalities are tending to be perceived as unacceptable, or certainly undesirable.

It even appears in an endemic situation of high unemployment, a context of social assistance, generalized restriction, and dependence of all kinds and an intellectual and moral climate directed more towards having than towards being, that the new pre-eminent value is not so much freedom as security: a material security against losses, vicissitudes, risks, and even liabilities of every kind. Nowadays, the individual seems to assert only a freedom of opposition, rejection, and protection (and hence a negative freedom) as opposed to an innovatory freedom of initiative, which is in practice monopolized by the major industrial or financial groups, or a genuinely creative freedom of imagination, which we are told is reserved for exceptional persons. This being so, the wish for liberation is meeting and becoming merged with the wish for equalization, something which provides yet another reason for public services to become extended and reinforced to the point where they will encompass the entire social field. Once freedom is on the way to losing its initial (and true) meaning, there is no longer any principle of an intellectual, moral, or political nature left to contain the public sphere.

5. The Changing Conception of Citizenship

In so far as the public and private spheres are tending to come together in this way and to become one and the same thing for all human activities, the private individual and the citizen are gradually ceasing to see themselves as falling within what were formerly complementary but separate categories and are naturally seeking to combine their rights. Their aim in doing so is, doubtless, the reciprocal strengthening of those rights. It is, however, quite possible that by merging the two categories of rights they may ultimately be weakening them. Although it may be liberating in certain respects, the welfare state, in anticipating and providing for all needs, undoubtedly entails more constraints than the State in its purely policing capacity. The latter confines itself to maintaining public order, while the former has assumed the task of maintaining the social order. And public order in its narrowest sense basically covers no more than the safety of people and property and the absence of public disorder and breach of the peace, whereas the social order encompasses every aspect of the life of the group.

It is here that State and society are coming to merge into each other, with their distinctive characters vanishing little by little. The process is also evidenced very meaningfully by the expression 'civil society' (not new, perhaps, but certainly used increasingly widely), which, in order to refer specifically to what remains of the non-state or non-political dimension of society, incorporates an added adjective that, until not so long ago, would have been pleonastic. Consequently, not only is the separation becoming blurred, but the situation of subordination is being reversed. For the State as the provider of every benefit is also a state that makes great demands on freedom and even requires, to a varying degree, the legitimate sacrifice of freedom when this seems necessary to the ends which it has set itself and which go largely unchallenged. Depending on the circumstances, it tends to make everyone either a user or an agent of a universal enterprise managed or headed by itself, whose fundamental law is no longer the individual freedom to arrange one's own affairs, but the general interest. That general interest, however, is no longer seen as the body of public or collective interests guaranteeing, externally, the private interest of the members of society. It is the interest both of the group as a whole and of its particular elements, with no distinction between them; an interest which is simultaneously a public or state one and one which forms the social order itself, in so far as individuals and society are deemed no longer able to operate in practice other than through the channel of public services, as beneficiaries of, or participants in, all their functions.

Fundamentally, public services certainly do not represent areas of freedom, even if the latter is still able to make its voice heard there. True though it may be that a public service is a liberating institution, in being so it removes whatever degree of individual autonomy is necessary to the achievement of its ends. Unlike the liberal view of the State as possessing sovereign powers, its reference standard is no longer the individual autonomy of persons but the needs of the general public as translated into the interest of the service, a translation that is sometimes a travesty, since public services are institutions which, like all others, show a real tendency to define their own objectives. In any event, in the legal regime of public services freedom has only whatever residual and subsidiary place it can still be accorded after proper performance of the function in question. And this principle of proper performance of the function obeys a logic of improvement, progress, and expansion which restricts freedom still further. It curtails it externally, from the point of view of third parties who could also perform the same activity on a private law basis, and it lessens it internally, from the point of view of agents or users who are dependent on its law, on its objectives and its means, and on their rules and their disciplines. Nevertheless, this increase in objectivity appears to have reached its limit and to be now accommodating, by way of rectification or compensation, new forms of subjectivization even in areas where only a short time ago the latter would still have seemed barely conceivable.

Various administrative public services have been transformed into industrial and commercial public services, over which private law wields more influence. Some such services have been delegated to private law bodies. The public law organizations have sold part of their capital to private interests. On a quite different level, but following the same philosophy, the actual status of users is tending to become more subjective, in a multitude of ways but nevertheless fundamentally. Whereas originally it was essentially legal and regulatory (i.e. entirely objective), at least within the context of administrative public services, it is now founded on genuine rights—if only as evidenced in the replacement of economic and social 'principles' by economic and social 'rights'. Thus, access to a particular service, at least according to the claims nowadays asserted, is no longer dependent on the prior existence and unilateral creation of the service in question, on its operational capacity, or on the conformity of a prospective user's situation to a status decreed by the service itself. Such access is, instead, made mandatory by an initial and, indeed, fundamental right with which the legal regime of the service must ultimately comply. This has become most obvious in, for example, the case of entry to university. But it also applies in regard to social security and to access to hospital treatment or public-authority housing. etc. Also, there is growing mention of what is a curious and hybrid category of 'subjective public rights'. The legal relations between service and user, which were formerly (at least in the case of administrative services) exclusively unilateral, are now fixed more by consent, at least in formal terms, by way of a contract or charter, although this is still statutory to some extent.

The development is not, however, in one direction only; a certain process of incorporation of public status or return to public status is also taking place. In those areas where the residues or resurgences of the most wholesale (or integrationist) liberal doctrine sought to transform the agent into an employee and the user into a customer, a more social-democratic philosophy is seeking to treat both as a kind of citizen, but citizens of a new type, in that the rights attaching to such status can now be exercised not only in the area of the State as sovereign public authority but also in that of the State as manager—in other words, more or less everywhere. This explains the emergence of new rights in regard to the administration: the right to administrative transparency, the right to the communication of administrative documents, the right to be provided with justification for decisions, and the right to participation in the management of the institution concerned or in the definition of its ends and means, to its 'democratic control'. And the magic of these rights is pervading other contexts, including purely private-sector enterprises, to the benefit of employees and of consumers.

All this is expressed, confusedly but strongly, in the newly fashionable formula of 'new citizenship'. It represents far more than a political slogan heralding the keynote of an election campaign or a general policy statement and destined to be valid only for the period of a parliament or the duration of a particular government. It is the inspiration behind a whole way of thinking that survives every change of political power, breathing fresh life into the 'social republic', and perhaps a new spirit. As thus conceived, the rights of citizenship (the term 'civil rights' is no longer applicable, since it denotes something much narrower) therefore tend to extend their field beyond the one, strictly public, sphere within which civil rights were confined. They are seen as spreading their influence over the entire area where public and private merge and, on from there, over every area where fundamental rights are exercised. The more dependent individuals become on the institutions that serve them, the more urge there is, it would appear, to mask the phenomenon—or combat it—by seeking to invest them with a status that lends them greater control over their own conditions.

Consequently, the status of citizen as interpreted in this way has the purpose not of continuing to guarantee, externally, rights of autonomy but of transporting into the economic and social system, or into the whole of the life of the group and of individuals, rights of participation which were not yet truly available there: participation in production, in management, and in their decisions, and in the distribution and equal redistribution of wealth. Such rights of participation, in a new and original synthesis, are seen as overtaking and absorbing rights of autonomy, such as those conferring claims on the State, since freedom now lies in release from forms of material dependence and equality in the equalization of conditions. However, they may perhaps do more than just absorb the freedom which consists of autonomy; they may perhaps reabsorb it, that is, negate it. But do we still set any value on it?

6. Conclusion—a Universal Synthesis?

In recent times everything has, in fact, conspired to encourage this new universal synthesis, this reconciliation of all the opposites. A certain focusing of the individual upon himself, which is only too real nowadays, has given rise to not only a discussion but also an expectation or participation, with the very word 'participation' drawing meaning from the full wealth of its ambiguity: participation in everything from which the individual feels he has always been excluded and will be excluded for ever—decision-making, wealth, knowledge, and, indeed, power. European neo-liberalism, whose interest in Europe was until very recently confined to that of making it, above and beyond Member State level, a broader society regulated solely by the market, indeed a 'single market', in which the only recognized fundamental rights were the four freedoms or movement of persons, goods, services, and capital, and from which the concept of citizen was excluded, is at last rediscovering, all at once, the other fundamental rights, citizenship and public services, even if only on the narrow basis of the second paragraph of an Article in the founding treaties that had previously gone almost unnoticed.

As subjective rights have become objectivized in the public service context, so the individual subject, taking a stand based on rights, is ceasing to accept that he is actually obliged, in every aspect of life, to remain in compliant dependence on a service but also on objective rules which have neither his conscious nor his willing consent, and which turn him into a kind of generalized and passive user or a social functionary who receives payment, but for whom any initiative is subject to an immutable hierarchical principle. He is now seeking to re-assert his identity, finding legitimate justification for doing so in invoking his status as citizen, a lofty concept whose qualities have not yet been exhausted, and is engaged in developing all the values inherent in it.

The recent dramatic moral, political, economic, and social collapse of Marxist socialism, combined with the rejection of a return to the liberalism of old, has focused reflection, in those legal systems currently being re-thought, on the duality of rights of autonomy and rights conferring claims, regarded as contradictory but now reconcilable in the emergence of a renewed republic of fully-fledged citizens. Not that the citizen will henceforth replace the individual, or block him from view. It is rather that the former is able to join forces with the latter and accompany him constantly other than just at election times, that the dichotomy is overcome and the duality even united. It is that in all his other capacities (as a customer, user, subject of the administration, subject of the judicial system, employee, consumer, etc.) the individual-as-citizen simply becomes, in all respects, a person.

6

The Liberalization and Privatization of Public Utilities and the Protection of Users' Rights: The Perspective of Economic Theory

ALESSANDRO PETRETTO

1. Introduction

Entry to the European Union automatically implies acceptance of the concept lying at the roots of its 'economic constitution': the developing of competition by means of widespread liberalization processes in the industrial sectors. The aim of this process is the gaining of the advantages associated with free competition between agents—in terms of innovation, cost minimization, price containment, and a high level of quality—independently of the private or public ownership of the enterprises operating in single markets. This therefore means liberalization, with or without privatization, above all in the basic sectors producing public-utility services such as telecommunications, energy, transport, and water supply. In some EU partners, like Italy, this concept is now slowly gaining ground at the level of policy, in the sense that some important steps have been taken in this direction. A first and fundamental stage of this process can, for example, be seen in the parliamentary approval of Statute 287/1990, which instituted the Italian regulatory authority for competition (known as the Anti-trust Authority). However, this Authority has encountered—and continues to do so—problems linked to its institutional acceptance and to a general diffidence on the part of politicians, mainly due to the time it has taken for the typically Anglo-Saxon culture of symmetric and impartial competition to gain credence in Italy as a spur to economic development.

Modern economic theory relating to public intervention is very aware of this, and has therefore moved, as a natural consequence, towards the principle of pushing for—in regard to public-utility services—the construction of a regulatory regime for services (which acts as a vigilant defender of the institutional framework and environment in which the market operates and develops) rather than a producing State (which is directly involved in the running of the services). In this chapter, an economic analysis will be offered of the institutional reorganization to which this innovative process of public intervention has given rise, and the problems connected to the institution of independent authorities for the regulation and protection of users' rights will be examined, since these last are no longer guaranteed by the direct presence of the State in the processes of production and supply. Given the transitional phase through which it is passing with regard to public-utility services, Italy lends itself very well to the verification of these theoretical approaches.

In fact, we may say that Italian public-utility reform is trying to introduce an intermediate model between the British one—strictly based on liberalization, privatization, and decentralization of industrial organization of those sectors—and the 'continental' one (typically derived from French tradition), more concerned with vertical integration of industries and centralization of public-utility supply. We have, in effect, to stress that the first model, even if it had the great merit of having opened the way to reform in Europe, can be criticized on a variety of grounds and from many aspects (especially from the point of view of users' right), while the second one seems too linked to some peculiar features of French public-sector bureaucracy. In this chapter particular attention will be devoted to several aspects of the processes of reform which underlie the Italian situation (as well as those of other EU countries), such as the rejection of direct government control, the territorial decentralization of responsibility, the settlement of the tariff structure, and the control of quality. It is in fact through the indirect control of prices (and therefore of the tariff structure) and quality that the regulatory regime ensures the rights of the users of public-utility services, defined in terms of the traditional conceptual categories of public economics, namely, those of efficiency, equity, and equality of access to services.

To be more precise, we may say that by means of efficiency we pursue the often neglected right of the user as a citizen to see applied an overall allocation of scarce resources aimed at welfare maximization of the whole of society and not of some specific constituency of the dominant group of politicians. Equity pursues the right of the citizen to receive fundamental services at 'fair' prices, i.e. consistent with the prevalent social aversion to income inequality; while equality of access aims to establish a social guarantee to standard levels of service, uniformly distributed without any kind of illegitimate discrimination among citizens. The overseeing of tariff development and qualitative standards is considered in modern economic theory of regulation as the verification over time of respect for the clauses of a contract (the regulatory contract), by means of which the indirect public intervention with which we are dealing takes its form. So the concluding sections of this chapter contain an analysis of the economic interpretation of this contract.

2. A New Theoretical and Institutional Framework for Public Utilities Policy

Starting from the premise of the strategic and social nature and the distributive content of these services, together with extended and wide-ranging examples of natural monopolies, traditional theory drew the conclusion that public intervention should stop the exploitation of users, using public enterprises as a direct instrument for putting this into practice. The direct intervention of the State in the production processes of the public-utility services was therefore justified by its intention of pursuing objectives of allocative efficiency and optimal distribution of incomes (equity), and therefore, from this point of view, to protect users' rights (quantity and quality of supply) and the community as a whole (use of scarce resources).

Modern theory, instead, turns this conclusion on its head, taking four facts as basic:[1]

(1) direct public intervention does not always guarantee the pursuance of social aims, in so far as the conflicting interests and objectives of specific subjects can prevail over those of users and the whole community;
(2) sometimes the social costs of public intervention (in terms of inefficiency) are higher than those associated with the market imperfections which it is intended to correct;
(3) technical progress tends to circumscribe the cases of natural monopoly, making concrete the possibility of the deconstruction and liberalization of these;
(4) the market, if well regulated, does not necessarily sacrifice the social and strategic characteristics of the services.

Consequently modern economic theory goes on to propose three logical steps with which to define a framework for public intervention:

(1) The first is that of the search for an 'efficient industrial configuration', that is, for a framework of reference for industrial structures which is capable of minimizing overall costs. The cases of imperfect or monopolistic competition, oligopoly, and natural monopoly appear moreover to be forms of market organization which, depending on the

[1] See, e.g., the surveys in D. P. Baron, 'Design of Regulatory Mechanisms and Institutions', in R. Schmalensee and R. Willig (eds.), *Handbook of Industrial Organization* (North Holland, Amsterdam, 1989); A. Petretto, *Mercato, organizzazione industriale e intervento pubblico*, Corso di Politica Economica (Il Mulino, Bologna, 1993); J. J. Laffont, 'The New Economics of Regulation: Ten Years After' (1994) 62 *Econometrica* 507–37 and especially in the most influential work on theory of regulation: J. J. Laffont and J. Tirole, *A Theory of Incentive in Procurement and Regulation* (MIT Press, Cambridge, Mass., 1993).

circumstances (technological characteristics, costs, and structure demand), have to be stimulated or discouraged from time to time;

(2) The second is the definition of the typologies of intervention, as follows: (a) the liberalization and trust-busting of non-natural monopolies (including public ones); (b) the separation of vertically integrated sectors (with a consequent distinction between the phases of generation, transmission, and distribution); (c) the protection of competition through the prevention of strategic barriers to entry, and the removal of eventual abuses of dominant position (in particular with regard to the interconnections and accesses to the network); (d) the regulation of the tariff structure and protection of the strategic and social characteristics (universality and widespread distribution) of the service; (e) the developing, in the case of a natural monopoly, of its conditions of 'contestability' (auctions to award concessions to be regulated by so-called programme or service contracts); (f) the stimulation of research and development of new technologies;

(3) Finally, as the concluding logical step, there is the issue of 'state withdrawal' from current management and from the organization of the services. In other words, a 'division of tasks and functions' is put into practice, so that:

(a) the public sector deals with planning and policies (legal responsibility for the services);

(b) the control of management is in principle instead entrusted to independent bodies (the so-called regulatory authorities), and

(c) the running and entrepreneurial organization, finally, is entrusted to public and/or regulated private firms within the industry.

The regulatory authorities appear therefore to be the central node in this form of the institutional structure of regulation; so we think it useful to analyse how these bodies can be considered within an economic context.

3. Public-utility Regulatory Authorities: The Division between Planning, Control, and Management

According to the predominant and traditional hierarchical structure of responsibilities in the public-utility services, public administration and enterprises tend artificially to identify with each other in the ends and processes in which they are involved, in the illusion that they represent a unique and homogenous decision-making body (see Figure 1). Of course, it should be said that it is from precisely this unity that the idea of the pursuit of social ends and the guarantee of users' rights derives. Instead,

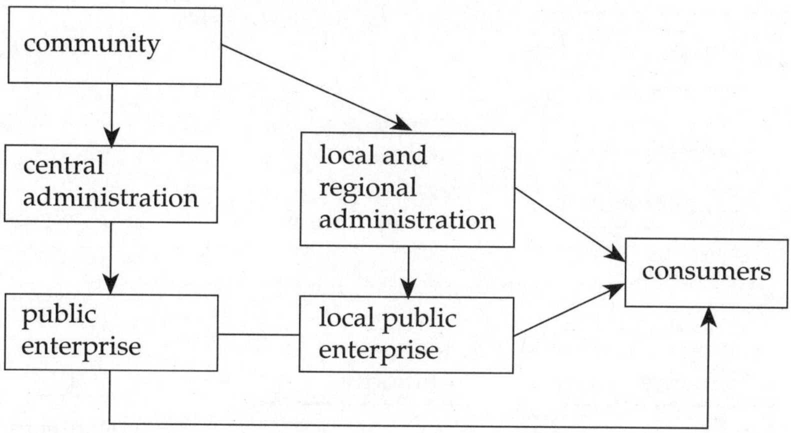

Figure 1—The traditional hierarchical structure of responsibility

according to recent economic analysis, the justifications for a wider and more highly developed hierarchy (division) of responsibilities and powers of control come from:

(1) problems of information asymmetry, according to which only enterprises comply with certain productive characteristics, and the costs depend on actions taken by enterprises but not directly observed by the public administration and bureaucracy; it is for this reason that a fundamental role can be played by an independent 'supervisor' that is flexible and equipped with the specific technical competencies (a regulatory authority, to be precise);
(2) the aim of producing a reduction in the weight of the bureaucratic apparatus of the public administration, which is too costly in terms of public spending; and
(3) some striking examples of the degeneration of political decision-making with regard to entrepreneurial matters, the result of collusion between pressure groups and private interests (not always legitimate).

A marked division between the relations which bind citizens to central and local public administrations and those which bind enterprises and users would suggest a new hierarchical structure of responsibilities. The link between the two sectors could be represented by the regulatory authorities (at both central and local level), as in the example of the British case which has now been operating for fifteen years (see Figure 2).

However, in order to 'import' these models into, for example, Italy or other European countries, we have to solve some complex problems of an

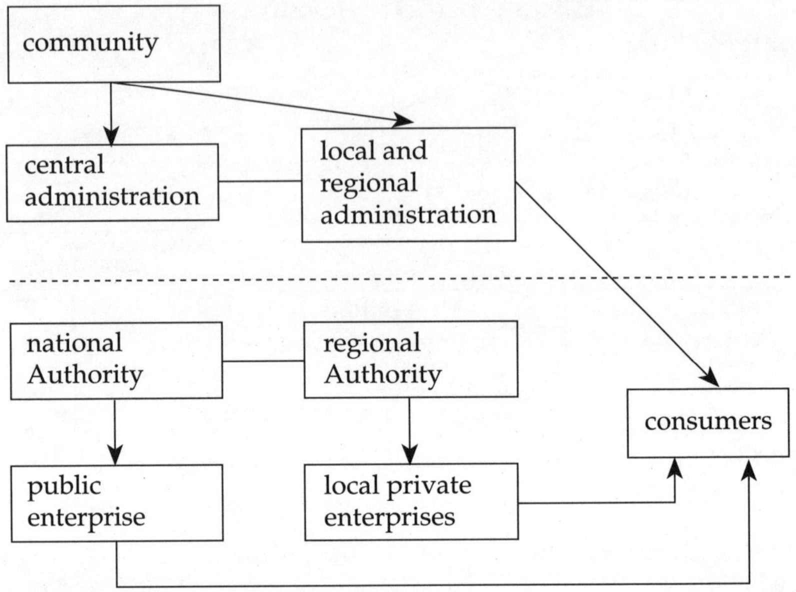

Figure 2—The new hierarchical structure of responsibility

institutional order; it is possible here to give only a general outline of these, leaving their more detailed treatment to those concerned with administrative law. In the first place it is worth pointing out that regulation through independent regulatory authorities was first implemented in presidential republics such as the USA, as a defence of the legislative powers in the face of a strong executive, while the adaptation of parliamentary republics—with what can be called 'weak' executives—necessitates numerous adjustments through the establishing of legislative and administrative guarantees (for example, in relation to appointments, lengths of tenure of office, and the legal status of staff). Moreover, in the case of Italy, it is necessary to enact several radical changes inspired by common law—which characterizes the original system—within the system of statute law which is typical of the Italian system; in other words, to move from the 'heavy' discipline of administrative law to the more flexible—although still perhaps incomplete from the point of view of market regulation—form of civil and commercial law.

Secondly, a more detailed specification is necessary for the relations between: (i) the regulatory authorities and competent ministries; (ii) the regulatory authorities and the general anti-trust authority; (iii) the regulatory authorities and the decentralized governments (the issue which is here described by the term 'service federalism'). An ideal scheme of the division of functions could assign:

(a) decisions about general industrial policy to the Ministry of Trade and Industry and/or the departments of regional governments;
(b) the 'defence' of asset value of enterprises as they are going to be privatized, to the Treasury;
(c) the planning and the legal responsibility of services mainly to the regional and local governments;
(d) the 'protection' of competition to the anti-trust authority;
(e) the 'promoting' of competition, and the regulation and control of the sector to the regulatory authorities (national and/or local).

In this regard, the recent Italian Statute No. 481 of 14 November 1995 on the competition and regulation of public-utility services constitutes a decisive and important step in the developing and modernizing of public intervention in Italy, since it pursues the general aims conforming to the general lines described above. The Statute makes provision (1) for promoting competition and efficiency in the public utility service sector; (2) for guaranteeing the levels of quality, affordability, and profitability on the part of enterprises, the availability and homogenous spread over the national territory of the public utility services, and fixed and transparent tariff systems based on pre-defined criteria; (3) for protecting the interests of users and consumers.

It is also provided that the regulatory authorities in the process of being established (for the electricity and gas industries, telecommunications, and transport) shall operate—in the manner prescribed by the theory—in full autonomy and with independent judgment and evaluation; they are also to be in charge of regulation, control, and inspection; their members are to be appointed by the President of the Republic on the recommendation of the government, but subject to the approval of the competent parliamentary committees. The part of the law dealing with the protection of users' rights is particularly substantial.[2] The regulatory authority is in fact authorised to effect inspections and to issue directives concerning the supply of the services for the purpose of assuring an equal treatment of users, and the continuity and high quality of service. To this end the regulatory authority offers itself as a 'terminal' to which users and consumers can refer complaints, requests, and report breakdowns.

All the same, several important issues remain unresolved and have been left to subsequent legislation, in particular the nature of the relations between the newly formed regulatory authorities and the privatization processes in the sectors referred to. For example, is liberalization to

[2] Art. 2(12)(*g*), (*h*), (*i*), (*l*), (*m*), and (*n*).

precede or follow the sale of the various enterprises? Is a transitional phase envisaged? General plans for the readjustment of the sectors involved are being made, from which it should be possible to deduce whether the final objective is the integral transfer of the ownership of public enterprises, or whether instead the ownership of publicly-owned enterprises will be maintained, while developing competition in the internal markets.

It should also be remembered that regulation was instituted to limit the extra profits of enterprises able to exploit their in some sense unavoidable dominant position. How is it to work in the context of enterprises which tend to be in deficit, because they are creating beneficial external effects needing to be subsidized (as in the cases of the postal service and urban transport)? In this regard, as I think that this circumstance will continue to be encountered in every application of what we may call the continental model of regulation, the following distinction can be suggested: one type of regulatory authority similar to those in Britain—limiting the amount of extra profits—and another to control the costs of the subsidized enterprises.

Moreover, the institutional structures of regulation have to take into account the phenomenon of 'service federalism', as a result of which many of the services mentioned (electricity, gas, and transport) are distributed widely over the national territory, with specific competences being managed by the local and regional administrations. In Great Britain the problem has been dealt with by instituting regional departments of the national regulatory authorities.[3] In view of the delegation of a much wider selection of functions to regional administrations of many EU countries in regard to the public-utility services, it is likely that institutions similar to regional authorities will be set up. In this case, however, problems of coordination (and separation) are likely to occur between the departments of regional governments and these decentralized independent institutions.

4. The Separation of Vertical Integrated Sectors: Generation, Transmission, and Distribution of Electricity

In the discussion of the classic problem of vertical integration of public utility industrial sectors and the related question of protection of competition, the British case, created by the radical reforms of the 1980s, is usually considered by economists as a clear benchmark. The structure of this model can be represented (in a simple form) as in Figure 3. The network

[3] See C. M. Armstrong, S. G. B. Cowan, and J. S. Vickers, *Regulatory Reform: Economic Analysis and British Experience* (MIT Press, Cambridge, Mass., 1993) and D. Helm, 'British Utility Regulation: Theory, Practice, and Reform' (1994) 10(3) *Oxford Review of Economic Policy* 17–39.

Generation — competition — some regulated private firms

- - - - - total separation - - - - -

Transmission — natural monopoly — distinct regulated private firms

- - - - - total separation - - - - -

Distribution — competition — some regulated private local firms

Figure 3—The British electricity model

operator engaged in energy transmission is a classical natural monopoly totally separated from both the sector of energy producers, which consequently have to pay an access price for supplying power to retailers, and from the sector of enterprises engaged in distribution and sale of electricity to households and firms. The generation sector is organized with oligopolistic competition, while the distribution sector is organized with competition among local firms that can apply differentiated tariffs according to the costs level of the areas served. The ownership of all the enterprises is completely private, even if the three sectors are regulated by means of the specific regulatory authority, OFTEL. The model tends to maximize efficiency by competition but could fail to some extent to defend citizens' (and consumers' and environment users') rights. Furthermore, the model does not take account of the strategic role of the public utility involved, especially for countries which are large importers of fuel and energy.

Therefore in Italy, as well in other European countries, the idea of an intermediate model is now prevailing, like the one represented in Figure 4.[4] In this model, also, the network operator is separated from the generation sector; but in this case only partially, i.e. from a technical point of view, as it can be the owner of an enterprise operating in this sector. The access price is, in this case also, strictly regulated by the specific electricity authority. The firm engaged in transmission—whose ownership can be to some extent public (the so-called 'golden share')—can also be partially involved, by means of the ownership of some local companies, in distribution and sale of electricity. Also these operations are regulated as far as quality and prices are concerned by the regulatory authority. The distribution sector here is organized by means of auctions for contracts to private

[4] See M. Polo and C. Scarpa, 'La riforma del settore elettrico in Italia: una privatizzazione al buio?', in *Le nuove frontiere della Politica Economica II* (IGIER–Il Sole 24 ore, Milano, 1996).

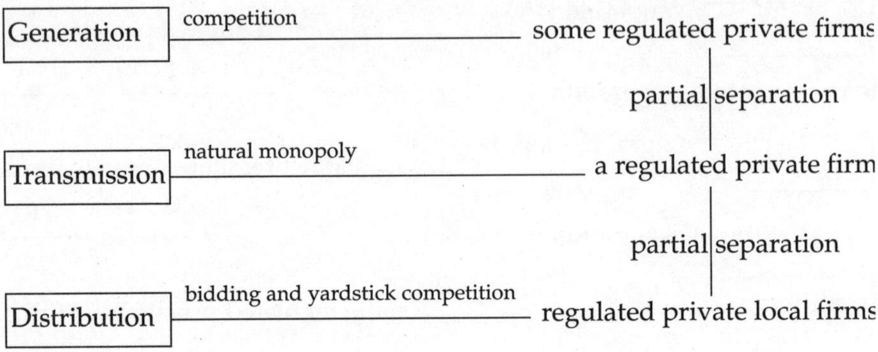

Figure 4—The 'intermediate' electricity model

local firms for which the regulatory authority manages a system of yardstick competition.[5] Those firms are required to apply a uniform structure of tariffs in the national territory.

The comparison in terms of welfare between the two models has recently been conducted by some contributions from theoretical economics, but without obtaining a definitive answer.[6] Clearly, in crude terms, the second model, in comparison with the first one, loses some of the advantages of competition but could gain in protection of users' rights and macroeconomic objectives. We may consequently say that the question is still open, and that we can choose the optimal industrial organization (which must in any case be consistent with the principle of 'separation') only by considering the specific circumstances and situations.

5. Two Examples of Decentralized Public Utilities: Financial Constraints and Consumer Protection in Water Supply and Local Transport

There are two examples of organization regarding the public-utility services which seem particularly important from the point of view of regional

[5] We recall that in such competition the regulator sets the prices (or the rate of return) not on the basis of the regulated firm's own costs, forecasts, and past performances, but rather on those of its competitors; so competition arises from the intra-firm comparison of performances: see A. Shleifer, 'A Theory of Yardstick Competition' (1985) 16 *Rand Journal of Economics* 319–27.

[6] See R. J. Gilbert and M. H. Riordan, 'Regulating Complementary Products: A Comparative Institutional Analysis' (1995) 26 *Rand Journal of Economics* 243–56 and J. S. Vickers, 'Competition and Regulation in Vertically Related Markets' (1995) 62 *Review of Economic Studies* 1–17.

decentralization: the reorganization of the water service and the reorganization of local transport according to the principles of 'inter-modal decentralization'. These are two institutional revisions which are carried out by some European countries and will have a significant effect on the fulfilment of several of the primary-demand users, linked to the use of water (in regard to its complete cycle) and to the mobility of urban areas.

In the first case, in Italy there is already a law on 'the complete cycle of water services (Statute 36/1994), which assigns:

(1) the planning of the services provided by the water supply, and the sewerage and purification systems, in particular through the constitution of optimal territorial areas, to the regional governments;
(2) the organization of and legal responsibility for the service to the local governments associated within each area;
(3) the supplying of the service to the undertaker (that is, to the enterprise winning the bidding competition and to which the franchise has been awarded).

Checks of and controls over the due performance of the contract are provided for and achieved by a number of organizational structures; for example, there is a committee in the Ministry of Public Works which has a water services inspectorate, and there are a number of monitoring bodies at the regional level which report on pre-selected territorial areas. Although these can be criticized, above all from the point of view of their actual independence—since they do not take on the clear and definite role of a regulatory authority—the new institutional structure of the water service constitutes a first and important step in the direction of a new conception of public intervention, as has been described above. Particular guarantees are, in addition, provided by the Statute for the protection of users as well as for environmental safeguarding specific to water cycles.

The Italian reform of this service is inspired by the British one based on the Water Act of 1989 that introduced the National Rivers Authority and the General Director of Water Services. This Act definitively established the previously mentioned separation between the organization of water services, assigned since 1973 to the so-called local water authorities (a somewhat misleading term), and control, regulation of tariffs, and users' defence assigned to OFWAT (the regulatory authority) and the General Director. Ten independent commissions for protecting users' rights were also constituted before proceeding to the privatization of the water authorities.

The new Italian system differs from the British one, as the liberalization process has mainly followed the idea of introducing an 'internal market' (a quasi-market) inside the public sector instead of directly and specifically pursuing a privatization design of reform. The hope of Italian reform is to gain efficiency from the principles of separation (between management and control) and competition for the market without sacrificing the aims of maximizing social and economic equity through an imposed extensive privatization of the sector.

In the case of local transport, there are only the projects which have been formulated at the level of the Ministry of Transport and the Treasury, recently partially implemented in the form of delegated legislation originally annexed to the 1996 Finance Act (Statute 549/95) and subsequently confirmed. According to these projects, a possible reform of the sector could be based on the following two criteria:

(1) the reorganization of the local markets for these services (urban and extra-urban), currently operated in the various transport modes, so as to stimulate competition between operators as much as possible and to enable them to exploit the advantages of integration of different modes of transport;

(2) a reform of the mechanisms controlling financing, moving towards the unification of all the resources—currently divided between the regional administrations, railways under licence, and the Italian State Railways (FS)—into one fund.[7] Correspondingly, an institutional separation must be made between the bodies representing the collective demand (regional and local administrations) and the supply bodies, i.e. the managing companies, by means of the instrument of concessions regulated by service contracts. The organization of the competitive processes between the managing companies should be entrusted to technical organizations on a regional basis (regulatory authorities or regional departments), which would also have the task of controlling and checking on quality standards. The national referee for these regional organizations would be the newly-formed national regulatory authority, which is to lay down the mechanisms for the distribution of funds on the basis of objective methods of standardization of costs. The distribution mechanism is to refer to an 'ordinary quota' (based on a standard increase in productivity) and a 'readjustment quota' (aimed at financing the regions which are furthest from the standard level of productivity, but with strong incentives to reduce these differences).

The Italian reform of urban transport is in some sense broadly inspired by the so-called 'London model' for organizing local transport. The underlying idea of the system applied to the English metropolis is to divide, by

[7] This is to be initiated by making a realistic estimate of the current needs, which should take into account the current levels of deficit, and establish appropriate rules for the increase in transfers by the State capable of stimulating the productivity growth of the services and of covering costs by the returns of the traffic.

a sort of fragmentation, the existing big local public enterprises in such a way as to constitute, on the one hand, a central agency of planning for the integrated service, guaranteeing the uniformity and integration of tariffs in the area, and, on the other, a set of firms for managing the service and the bus depots. The concessions to run trains on particular routes, or in particular regions, are assigned by an auction in which the firms created by the breaking up of the old public enterprise, as well some private firms, may participate. As regards railway transport, the idea is to create an 'explosion' of the FS system in order to constitute a certain number of 'service companies' for regional and local transport, operating in a network that is to remain unified and organized by the same FS. For those firms, in public as well private ownership, there is to be applied, instead of the British experience of complete privatization and deregulation, a system of yardstick competition, as regards the distribution of subsidies, managed by the central authority.

In conclusion, in the cases of both the water supply industry and local transport there seems to be a need to build a complex institutional structure for regulation inspired by, but not the same as, the radical British one. Within this structure, central, regional, and local responsibilities need to be defined, and reference needs to be made to public organizations and private enterprises, affecting the interests of a large number of citizens, not only as direct consumers but also as taxpayers and users of the environment. This process of definition depends to a significant extent on an understanding of the way in which regulatory contracts for public utilities function, and it is to that set of issues that we briefly turn our attention in the remaining sections of this chapter.

5. The Interactions Between Quality, Price, and Costs in the Standard Model of Regulation

Modern economic theory gives great importance to the information structure of the contract of regulation. In fact, the regulatory procedures of a public-utility service assume the simplified structure of a contract between the government, which has responsibility for political and economic policy, and an enterprise, which operates mainly under the terms of a monopoly. However, this kind of contract is (according to the terminology of modern theory of information) *incomplete*, that is, it is unable to account for all the contingencies and states of the world which are relevant for the parties (particularly the one representing the community and the users). The way in which this incompleteness is treated is, according to economic theory, at the heart of what can, in terms of social welfare, be achieved with regulation.

Trying to give a simple and stylized representation of the standard model of regulation we may say there are three sets of agents involved in the regulation contract (Figure 5):

(1) The *users*, subdivided according to their economic possibilities, their needs, and preferences. The structure of users' preferences and their willingness to pay for a service which displays various typologies (such as urban and trunk calls, goods and passenger transport) is usually represented by a general function depending on two crucial variables: (i) a parameter synthesising the characteristics of demand (users' preferences), which can be observed by the enterprise but not by the regulators, and (ii) an indicator of quality, the specification of which is sometimes observable but not verifiable. In economic terms a variable is said to be not verifiable when, as will be clarified below, it cannot be inserted directly into the regulation contract and submitted to a court to verify if it has been performed;

(2) The *firm*, which is usually formalized by a general cost function depending on a parameter specifying the technology that is known to the enterprise but, generally, not known to the regulator (we say that this is an 'adverse selection' variable). The cost function also depends on a variable representing the effort to reduce costs, this action being concealed from the regulator ('moral hazard' variable). The ownership of the enterprise, which in the simple model to which we refer is identified with the management, receives a reward for its productive activity consisting of the profit (or it may be the loss) plus a premium

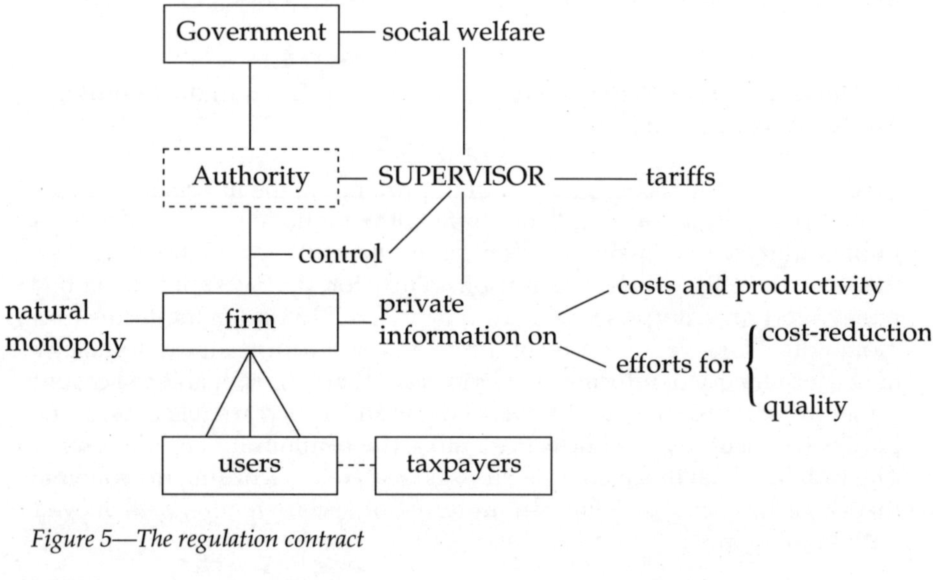

Figure 5—The regulation contract

specified in the contract. Furthermore we have to take away from this reward the costs—not necessarily monetary (disutility)—for the two efforts, respectively to reduce costs and to increase quality. For the enterprise to agree to the contract, this last should not give rise to a negative pay-off; consequently, the so-called 'participation constraint' requires that the net transfer (the payment less the financial performance) which goes to the management of the enterprise is enough to cover the costs of those two efforts;

(3) The *government* and the *regulatory authority*, jointly considered in this simplified framework as *the regulator*. As described in the preceding sections, the regulatory authority, in deference to the principle of separation between planning and the management of production, stands in a halfway position between the government and the enterprise, since, in its role of independent 'supervisor', it acquires and uses information for the government and exerts control over the keeping of the terms of the regulation contract by the enterprise. Moreover, the authority oversees the application of the agreed tariff structure and verifies, wherever this is possible, the qualitative standards of production. When these two institutions—*authority* and *government*—are not in conflict and therefore co-operate, they pursue the same objective function, which can generally be identified with an overall welfare function.[8] Included in this is the so-called *marginal cost of public funds* associated with the distortion of the taxation necessary to levy those funds from the taxpayers (who are possibly also users). This parameter aims to gather together in an analytical way the social trade-off which is set up between citizens in their role as, on the hand, users and, on the other, taxpayers.

6. Observability and Verifiability of Quality: The Problem of Regulation in General Terms

To analyse the question of the regulation of the quality of a public service produced under the conditions of a natural monopoly it is necessary to describe these goods in relation to their quality. In this regard there is a group of so-called *search goods*, about which consumers find out the quality before buying them, as well as a group of so-called *experience goods*, the quality of which is observed only after they have been bought. In the latter case, a reduction in quality tends to reduce sales, so that the monopolist will be stimulated to offer a fair level of quality; in the former, instead, an incentive will be operative only if consumers are able to repeat their

[8] For a treatment of more highly developed and complex contexts see Laffont and Tirole, n. 1 above.

consumption, thereby forcing the monopolist to defend his reputation to some extent.

In the case of a regulation contract between the public sector and an enterprise, not only is the *observability* of the quality important, but also its *verifiability*, i.e. the possibility of being able to give a prior description of the respective level and to include it in the contract so as then to be able to verify it afterwards in a court or by a special inspection body operating with the regulatory authority. A special technical committee can, for example, penalize an enterprise for inadequate quality of the water supply, for low voltage in the energy supply, or for frequent disruptions in telephonic connections. In this regard, the Italian law on the regulation of public service utilities, Statute 481/1995—following the British experience—expressly allows the regulatory authority the powers of inspection, access, and acquisition of documents to establish any eventual automatic repayments on the part of enterprises in regard to the user, where the enterprise does not respect the contractual clauses or supplies a service with levels qualitatively inferior to those established in the applicable regulations.[9]

In many cases, however, quality is not always verifiable, or else the costs of verification are too high, so that the regulator—to protect the qualitative level of supplies—has to recreate the incentives which an unregulated enterprise generally has, without losing the advantages of regulation. In particular, in the case of search goods, he has to confer a premium which is proportionate to sales, while in the case of experience goods conditions similar to a reputation effect need to be reconstructed by threatening (credibly) the non-renewal of the concession which is the foundation of the contract.

An important problem is connected to the trade-off between the incentive to contain costs and the incentive to improve quality, and therefore to the mechanism of financing the regulated enterprise. It is in fact evident that a fixed-price transfer—one, that is, at a price pre-established independently of the quantity produced and costs incurred—which produces the maximum effect in terms of an incentive to reduce costs can lead the enterprise, in the case of non-verifiability, to lower the quality of its service to recoup the margins of discretion; on the other hand, a cost-plus transfer—that is, one which repays costs plus an agreed margin—which does not give any incentive to reduce costs can lead the regulated enterprise to increase quality in order to increase its clients, off-loading the higher costs onto the regulator. The conflict is certainly clear in the case of experience goods, given that in this case it is with one instrument only—the cost-reimbursement rule—that two opposing objectives are pursued. For

[9] Art. 2(12)(*g*).

search goods the conflict can be reduced if separate instruments are used for the two objectives: the cost-reimbursement rule, and a reward linked to the volume of sales, which functions as a proxy of the level of quality.[10]

Experience of the regulatory procedures thus far applied in industrialized countries suggests that it is unusual for the regulator to be able to impose the application of prices and tariffs which follow the optimal rules of welfare maximization. More frequently, practical methods of the control of profits are applied, from which derive prices and levels of quality moving away from those practised by non-regulated monopolists to approximately optimal ones—though sometimes not even an approximation is achieved. All the mechanisms of regulation applied in practice have in common an attempt on the part of the regulator to re-establish the conditions of market pricing in respect of enterprises whose technological conditions have granted them roles as monopolists. Various methods of regulation are canvassed by economists[11] and have been analysed by the present author.[12] They are of two main types, one in which the rate of return on capital is regulated, and the other a price-capping system linked to the retail price index. The detailed exploration of the issues involved in choosing between these methods is beyond the scope of the present symposium. Suffice it to conclude that the detailed exploration strongly suggests that arriving at the best models of regulation in the overall interests of the community is an extremely complex matter, and that the creation of new business structures for the conduct of public utilities has often gone ahead before the regulatory needs have been fully met or even fully understood.

[10] For a fuller discussion of these problems, see, in particular, Laffont and Tirole, n. 1 above, ch. 4 and D. Bos, *Pricing and Price Regulation: An Economic Theory for Public Enterprises and Public Utilities* (North Holland, Amsterdam, 1994), ch. 16.

[11] There is a vast amount of economic literature on this subject; in particular we may quote: E. E. Bailey, *Economic Theory of Regulatory Constraint* (Lexington Books, Lexington, Mass., 1973); Laffont and Tirole, n. 10 above; C. Liston, 'Price-CAP versus Rate-of-Return Regulation' (1993) 5 *Journal of Regulatory Economics* 25–48; and K. E. Train, *Optimal Regulation. The Economic Theory of Natural Monopoly* (MIT Press, Cambridge, Mass., 1991). For a concrete application of these topics on regulation to the English case, see M. E. Beesley and S. C. Littlechild, 'The Regulation of Private Monopolies in U.K.' (1989) 20 *Rand Journal of Economics* 45–72; Armstrong, Cowan, and Vickers, n. 3 above; and Helm, n. 3 above.

[12] See A. Petretto, 'La regolamentazione dei prezzi e della qualità nei monopoli naturali: una sintesi della letteratura teorica', *Quaderni del Dipartimento di Economia, Università L. Bocconi di Milano*, Mar. 1997 and A. Boitani and A. Petretto, 'Le politiche di regolamentazione', in A. Ninni and F. Silva (eds.), *La politica Industriale* (Laterza, Milano, 1997).

7

Universal Service Obligations and the Emergence of Citizens' Rights in European Telecommunications Liberalization

WOLF SAUTER

1. Introduction

'When first approached, defining universal service seems quite simple, something along the lines of ensuring access to telephone services at all times and in all places to everyone at reasonable prices. But on closer examination, universal service is revealed as the stuff of myth, a slippery and ideological concept which has been used and manipulated by different parties to support their own case for special treatment.'[1]

This contribution[2] gives an account of the role which the concept of universal service has played in the recent process of liberalization of the EU telecommunications markets. It will assert that this role has been a crucial one. Universal service obligations are likewise at the heart of the ongoing debate on the introduction of competition in a number of other sectors, notably the utilities (e.g. energy, water, transport, and postal services). However, it appears that at present telecommunications provide the best example of the debate on universal service in the European Union. The relevance of the telecommunications experiences to other sectors is beyond doubt. As is widely acknowledged, the opening of telecommunications markets has gone further and faster than that in any comparable sector. In no sector previously dominated by public monopolies has the impact of the application of the competition rules of the EC Treaty (EC) been greater, and in no sector has the EC Commission been as effective in defining a policy-formulating role for itself. At international level, telecommunications liberalization has become the first area where the General Agreement on Trade in Services (GATS) negotiations in the new World Trade Organization (WTO) framework were successfully concluded. This was in

[1] C. R. Blackman, 'Universal Service: Obligation or Opportunity?' (1995) 19 *Telecommunications Policy* 171, at 171.

[2] An earlier and shorter version of this chapter appeared in (1996) 7 *Utilities Law Review* 104. I thank Juliette Ensor for her comments.

no small measure due to the effectiveness of the negotiating strategy of the EC Commission (in spite of its operating under the constraint of 'mixed competencies').[3]

At the same time, the concept of universal service was elaborated for the telecommunications sector in greater detail, and arguably with greater success, than for any other sector. Standards of universal service for telecommunications have been developed at Community level, together with the legal instruments for implementing them. Both have been transposed (and partly anticipated) by national law. In the process, individual citizens have been given legal recourse concerning universal service standards. Further, in the case of telecommunications there was a direct connection between progress on liberalization and that on universal service. Arguably, the concept of universal telecommunications service might today still be practically meaningless if it had not been for liberalization. *Vice versa*, defining and implementing universal service has been the key to resolving an apparent stalemate on telecommunications liberalization in the Community.

I will provide evidence for this thesis in three steps. First, I will distinguish and discuss the concepts of universal service, public service, and natural monopoly in telecommunications. Secondly, I will give a brief overview of the relevant primary European law. This is followed by a more detailed account of the regime change that occured in the European telecommunications markets between 1987 and 1993, focused on the universal service issue. In conclusion, I will briefly address the future development of public-service objectives in the liberalized telecommunications markets.

2. Universal Service, Public Service, and Natural Monopoly

Although the concept of universal service originated in telecommunications, this occurred in a different context than is commonly thought. Theodore Vail, President of AT&T, is widely acknowledged to have coined the term in 1907. What has been reconstructed in historical research only more recently is that the meaning Mr Vail had in mind is very different from the one which we commonly associate with universal service today.[4] Vail is also credited with having built 'the Bell system';[5] the fully

[3] See J. Enser, 'European Telecommunications Policy and the WTO', in A. Cafruny and P. Peters (eds.), *The Union and the World: The International Political Economy of a Common European Foreign Policy* (Kluwer Law, London, 1997).

[4] See the seminal work of M. Mueller, 'Universal Service in Telephone History: A Reconstruction' (1993) 17 *Telecommunications Policy* 352.

[5] See C. Graham, 'Universal Service Obligations: A Policy Review', in *Centre for the Study of Regulated Industries Proceedings* (1995), 13; S. Katus, 'The Future of Universal Service Provision in Telecoms from a Legal-Economic Point of View: The Dynamics of

vertically integrated private monopoly which dominated telecommunications in North America until it was broken up by court order in 1982. Originally, universal service formed a part of this monopoly vision.

At the time, AT&T was locked in a struggle of access competition with organized independent telephone companies. This competition began after the original Bell patents, on which telephony was based, had expired. Up to this point, telephony had largely been restricted to business use in the large urban centres of the USA. Access competition meant that AT&T and its competitors now competed in rolling out their networks across the USA, in an attempt to connect the maximum number of users, in order to make their respective services more attractive. It was this process which first led to something approaching full coverage of the national territory in the USA.

Under access competition, AT&T and the independents mutually refused to connect their respective telephone systems. That is to say, those consumers who subscribed to one service could not call subscribers to the other, unless they took out a double subscription. What Vail proposed as universal service was what today would be described as 'universal interconnection': i.e. the principle that all subscribers to telephone systems everywhere would be able to contact each other directly. The convenience of universal interconnection is evident. The vehicle for this which Vail advocated was an integrated monopoly system: the Bell system. The Bell monopoly was ultimately created, after lengthy battles for the support of public opinion, state and federal legislatures, various courts and regulators (notably, the Federal Communications Commission (FCC) and the State Public Utility Commissions). The concept of universal service as interconnectability formed a powerful argument in this struggle. The most important step in the creation of this monopoly was the exemption of telephone companies from the US antitrust laws in 1921. The result was the highly regulated private monopoly of AT&T, which lasted until the famous divestiture in 1982.[6]

Hence, the concept of universal service originated as an instrument of regulatory capture, aimed at the creation of universal monopoly:

> 'The modern reconstruction of universal service . . . was not an accurate description of a historical policy, but a retroactive rationalisation for the institution of regulated monopoly.'[7]

Proportionality within a Common Regulatory Framework', paper presented at the IBC/ICC Conference, Brussels, 27–8 Nov. 1995.

[6] See J. Huntley and D. Pitt, 'Divestiture and Market Structure: Competition and Deregulation in US Telecommunications' (1989) 10 *ECLR* 407. For a critical survey of the effects on price and competition see R. W. Crandall, *After the Breakup: U.S. Telecommnications in a More Competitive Era* (Brookings Institution, Washington, DC, 1991).

[7] Mueller, n. 4 above, at 367.

What is commonly meant by universal service today is usually the principle of 'universal access', not interconnection. That is, the idea that at the current level of societal development, every person, regardless of his or her geographical location should have the right to be connected to the public telephone system, at a reasonable (or affordable) price. The principle of universal interconnection is now generally taken for granted, perhaps because most observers have grown up under monopoly regimes which, in spite of anything else that might be brought to bear against them, have generally managed to provide such interconnection. Leaving aside the issue whether liberalization might not come to complicate the fundamental principles of interconnection, it has become clear that the conceptualization of universal service as universal access is linked to an objective of high penetration rates among the population at large. As such, universal service is also taken to be an essential element of public policy, if not the most essential element of public policy in relation to the telecommunications field.

There are several reasons why such a public-policy priority ranking makes sense. From an economic perspective, universal access forms a combination of three public goods in one:[8] first, it can be considered to constitute a basic public *social good*. That is, access to communications, as, for example, access to health facilities, is good both for the economic and social functioning of the single individual and of society as a whole. Secondly, universal access is a *transactional good*, due to the externalities of the network economics of two-way communications. That is, due to the high fixed costs of network communications, larger numbers of subscribers lower the average costs involved, whereas each additional subscriber adds to the utility of the network as a whole (since more people can be reached by using it).[9] Thirdly, universal access is a *merit good*. This means, in the present case, that in a modern democratic society citizens' access to means of information and communication is essential for the effective functioning of this social system. For this reason, it is a good thing for all members of society to be hooked up to certain networks such as telecommunications networks (regardless of their personal preferences on the matter). From a legal perspective, which is perhaps more appropriate, given the context of this contribution, it can be said that universal service as universal access is based on an egalitarian right of access,[10] a basic right for all citizens. In any event, the economic rationale discussed earlier may be read as implicit in this citizens' right.

[8] Blackman, n. 1 above, at 172.

[9] E. Noam, 'Beyond Liberalization III: Reforming Universal Service' (1994) 18 *Telecommunications Policy* 687, at 688.

[10] T. Prosser, 'Privatization, Regulation and Public Services' [1994] *Juridical Review* 3, at 13.

The universal right to access has two dimensions. The first is related to the level of penetration of the service. Traditionally, this has been seen as a requirement of non-discriminatory geographic availability. Hence, irrespective of where the citizen is located in a certain (national) territory, he or she should be connected to the public network, and receive equal treatment in terms of levels of price and services, without regard to actual cost. This 'heroic' type of universal access, involving rolling out the network across deserts, mountain ranges, and sparsely-populated agricultural areas is now in most developed countries a thing of the past.[11] Instead of *geographical* penetration, *social* penetration has now become, or—perhaps more accurately—should by now have become, the major issue. This involves both the financially disadvantaged—such as the poor—the physically disadvantaged—people in wheelchairs, deaf people—and other perhaps less obvious categories—such as those without fixed abode—homeless people. The second dimension is that of financing universal access. Obviously, a commitment to a universal right to access carries a cost to the system, in the event that such rights may require un-economic investments in infrastructure to be made. The right to access therefore has to be accompanied by some sort of (equitable) financing mechanism.

Various ways of financing universal service as universal access are imaginable. Among these are the following: internal cross-subsidies between profitable and loss-making activities within integrated monopolies; access charges levied on connections to the public network; a universal service fund based on contributions calculated by means of a telecommunications value-added account system; and direct financing based on various taxes.[12] Although it is now generally accepted that public financing from general tax revenues would minimize the economic distortions on telephone-services provision involved, it appears that different solutions may be more appropriate (and/or politically attractive) at different stages of telecommunications penetration. Because of these factors as well as local peculiarities, a wide range of systems of funding universal service is currently in use in various countries.[13] In Europe the general model has traditionally been that of internal cross-subsidies within

[11] Where geographic penetration is still an issue, as in developing countries, solutions are often sought in terms of access to satellite technology, incidentally also increasingly controlled by commercial actors. In many instances, developing countries ought to be able to use their leverage over access to the frequency resources required for satellite coverage to negotiate universal benefits for their populations.

[12] For a description of these and various other systems, see Noam, n. 9 above, at 692–3.

[13] For a cross-country comparison between different methods of providing universal service at different stages of network penetration see M. Tyler, W. Letwin, and C. Roe, 'Universal Service and Innovation in Telecommunications Services: Fostering Linked Goals Through Regulatory Policy' (1995) 19 *Telecommunications Policy* 3.

integrated public monopolies, usually imposed by law. It is this feature which has given rise to the debate in the European Community over universal service in the context of 'public service', in the sense of a publicly owned, controlled, and operated service to the (national) public of the individual Member States.

However, until recently, for these public companies the case for monopoly provision was based more on the general argument of 'natural monopoly' than on any clear universal-service obligations *per se*. The creation and expansion of telecommunications systems required large investments in infrastructure, and, at least initially, the service provided was a basic one. Hence, the industry was characterized by economies of scale and scope, and by the positive externalities generated by the large numbers of interconnected users. Given the high ratio of fixed versus variable costs a single network was perceived as optimal, both from the perspective of the provider and the users of services involved. For this reason, the provision of telecommunications infrastructure and services was generally considered to be a natural monopoly, and the rapid geographic and social spread of network connections led to actual monopolization.[14] The natural monopoly argument in itself did not necessary entail public ownership of the network. However, for various reasons including military security and network integrity, and the ambition to provide universal coverage of the national territory, formal public monopolies soon became the accepted norm in Western Europe.[15] Moreover, in many cases this development was based not so much on explicit considerations of utility as on a simple extension of the pre-existing state monopolies on telegraphy (which was long considered more essential) and on postal services.

Generally, the universal-service obligations of the national monopolies were implicit ones. That is, they were not formulated as legal rights to telephone service on demand for individual citizens. Prevailing notions of universal service were voluntaristic (or supply-, rather than demand-driven), and indeed until relatively recently telephone service was regarded as a luxury which need not be at the disposal of ordinary citizens. When a concept of universal service as 'public service' gradually developed in the course of the 1960s and 1970s, penetration ratios were anyway rising independently, simply as the result of the overall increase in living standards during this period rather than in relation to public policy. Moreover, even at this point, universal service was usually defined

14 See G. Dang Nguyen, 'Telecommunications: A Challenge to the Old Order', in M. Sharp (ed.), *Europe and the New Technologies: Six Case Studies in Innovation and Adjustment* (Pinter, London, 1985), 89. Private, although closely regulated, monopolies however persisted in a number of European countries, including Spain and Sweden.

15 K.-H. Ladeur, 'Die Neuordnung der Telekommunikation zur Funktion eines öffentlichen Unternehmens in hochkomplexer Umwelt' (1991) 74 *Kritische Vierteljahresschrift für Gesetzgebung und Rechtswissenschaft* 176.

flatly as non-discriminatory geographic access on demand. Quality standards and the concept of affordability were practically unheard of: universal service was not targeted on the basis of need.[16] Further, where *de jure* universal service obligations did exist, they were not always honoured in practice. Until a few years ago, it was not unusual for citizens of a number of EC Member States to have to wait a year or more for a connection: for example, the OECD average for 1980 was fifteen months. In Greece, as recently as 1990, more than one million applications for telephone installation were outstanding, at an average waiting time of eighty-one months.[17] Clearly, in some Member States, universal service was no more than a legal fiction, if that.

Much of this can be understood by considering the nature of the public monopolies. Until the late 1980s the provision of telecommunications in the Member States was typically entrusted to national post, telegraph and telephone ministries (PTTs). Beyond their exclusive rights to the provision of telecommunications networks and services, these PTTs were generally entrusted with extensive rule-making powers.[18] Furthermore, the PTTs' activities often extended beyond those related to their public service task, to apparently unrelated sectors such as banking, insurance, and the distribution of state benefits such as old-age and disability pensions. Further, as a matter of course, telecommunications monopolies were usually extended to cover new types of services and technologies. Where a PTT was not directly involved in the manufacture of switching and terminal equipment, it would often cultivate privileged supplier relationships, which were used to bolster national champions in consumer electronics and information technology with guaranteed high-volume contracts at artificial prices.

Hence, this 'postal-industrial complex', under only nominal control of national parliaments (often co-opted) through ministerial responsibility, was based on national networks of mutually interested parties. In a financial sense, the postal industrial complex was based on a system of financial transfers and cross-subsidies which included, but went far beyond, those based on universal-service arguments. In many cases, general

[16] N. Garnham, 'Universal Service in European Telecommunications', in N. Garnham (ed.), *European Telecommunications Policy Research: Proceedings of the Communications Policy Research Conference, 22–24 June 1988, Windsor, UK* (Amsterdam, 1989), 127.

[17] M. Cave, C. Milne, and M. Scanlan, *Meeting Universal Service Obligations in a Competitive Telecommunications Sector* (Report for DG IV, Mar. 1994), Table 1.1, at 9.

[18] Thus: 'under national legislation, telecommunications organizations are generally given the function of regulating telecommunications services, particularly as regards licensing, control of type approval and mandatory interface specifications, frequency allocation and monitoring the conditions of use. In some cases, the legislation lays down only general principles governing the operation of the licensed services and leaves it to the telecommunications organizations to determine specific operating conditions': Commission Directive 90/388/EEC on competition in the market for telecommunications services (OJ 1990 L192/10), recital 28.

cross-subsidies between telecommunications and postal services were a structural feature of the postal-industrial complex. Within telecommunications, universal service as non-discriminatory geographic access required a system of extensive cross-subsidization between profitable (usually inner-city, long-distance, and international) and unprofitable or less profitable (usually local and rural) calls, and connection charges. In general, the pricing of telecommunications services was based on political considerations, rather than on cost or considerations of affordability and social need. Other transfers occurred between the PTTs and consumers at large, and the privileged domestic suppliers (since the latter would contract to provide equipment on uncompetitive terms).

Under these conditions, the PTTs' business strategies tended to rely on technical and political considerations rather than market demand. Beyond the economics of natural monopoly, entrenched national political interests can therefore be read into the monopoly-based organization of the industry. Rural constituencies, which are generally over-represented politically, and voters in general stood to gain from these arrangements, at least in some measure. So did the labour forces of the PTTs which were generally highly unionized and tended to enjoy special public-sector employment status (which might not include the right to strike, but usually restricted lay-offs and included other privileges). Together with privileged suppliers, these groups formed a strong domestic coalition in support of monopoly provision, even where their broader interests (such as, for example, the range of available services or career prospects) were not being served by the existing arrangements.[19] Competing interests, primarily those of business users, non-privileged equipment producers, and foreign providers of equipment and services, were shut out of the market and of the relevant decision-making processes. The consumer interest (which in principle covers not only individual residential users with originally limited requirements, but also high volume corporate users with an interest in advanced services) was undifferentiated and usually ignored, except for the standard geographical coverage guarantee discussed above.

Given the vested interests at stake, and the consensus on the validity of the natural monopoly argument for telecommunications, the PTTs were (under Community law) excluded *de jure* from the liberalization of public procurement (with water, transport, and energy), and *de facto* from the application of competition policy.[20] In a formal sense, this should be understood as an

[19] See R. Cowhey, 'The International Telecommunications Regime: The Political Roots of Regimes for High Technology' (1990) 44 *International Organization* 169; J. Hills, 'Dependency Theory and its Relevance Today: International Institutions in Teleommunications and Structural Power' (1994) 20 *Review of International Studies* 169.

[20] Although they represented approximately 6% of Community GDP, the utilities were exempted from the public procurement rules: see A. Brown, 'The Extension of the Community Public Procurement Rules to Utilities' (1993) 30 *CMLRev.* 721.

application of Article 90(2) EC, since the PTTs both were revenue-producing monopolies and provided services in the general interest. Further, since most telecommunications operators were publicly owned, Article 222 EC (on Treaty neutrality *vis-à-vis* the system of property ownership in the Member States) was generally held (indirectly) to protect their monopoly status. Finally, since they were at the time constituted as government ministries and combined rule-making and operating functions, the PTTs appeared to be covered by the general sovereign powers of the Member States.

Until the 1980s, the postal-industrial complex fended off any challenges to the existing system.[21] When technological advances first began to reduce the cost, particularly of long-distance (and international) calls, prices were not reduced commensurately. The resulting growth in profit was used for further cross-subsidization of local calls, to fund network upgrading, siphoned off by the Treasury, or in a variety of other ways (in the French case including substantial cash subsidies to the struggling national electronics industry). This widening gap between actual costs and prices led to the spread of the phenomenon of by-pass: attempts by businesses to avoid the public network and construct their own infrastructure or message-forwarding routes. Increasingly therefore, the most well-heeled consumers were defecting from the system.[22] Ultimately however, monopoly provision of telecommunications was undermined worldwide by a combination of technological change, regulatory change stimulated by a shifting balance between the economic interests involved, and spill-over of regulatory change. With the introduction of digital technology and the development of advanced services, new and powerful competitors sought entry, the 'natural monopoly' argument for the monopoly provision of telecommunications was eroded, and regulatory change became all but inevitable. The watershed is generally considered to have been the conclusion of the famously protracted AT&T de-investiture case, which resulted not merely in splitting up AT&T but also in substantial deregulation and liberalization of the US market (with the important initial exception of local networks).[23]

Henceforward, the American market was to be a competitive and comparatively lightly regulated one, with liberal conditions of entry for

[21] The privileged manufacturers were able to corner their national markets where (given the long life of equipment) initial technological choices were perpetuated. The only time when the PTTs had the opportunity to cultivate new suppliers was when a new generation of equipment was introduced (i.e. once every 20 to 30 years): Dang Nguyen, n. 15 above, 101.

[22] See C. Hüttig, 'Die Deregulierung des internationalen Telekommunikationssektors: Zum Verhätnis von technischer Entwicklung und ordnungspolitischem Wandel' (1989) *Leviathan* (Special Issue No. 10) 144. There is greater detail in E. Noam, *Telecommunications in Europe* (OUP, New York, 1992).

[23] *United States* v. *American Telephone and Telegraph Co.*, 552 F Supp. 131 (DDC, 1982), aff'd. *sub nom. Maryland* v. *United States*, 460 US 1001, 103 S Ct. 1240, 75 L Ed. 2d 472 (1983).

foreign terminal equipment, and increasing cross-penetration between telecommunications and information technology firms. A situation of unbalanced market opening and rapid technical change resulted. In particular the EC Member States and Japan, which benefited from access to the US terminal market but lagged in other areas (especially in information technology and advanced services), found themselves subjected to US pressures to match the opening of the American market. This demand for reciprocity was expressed both bilaterally and in international fora, foremost the General Agreement on Tariffs and Trade (GATT). Pressures on the European telecommunications sector thus became institutional, as well as technological.[24] At the same time, in Europe, user industries and electronics industries (especially those elements which competed internationally) demanded liberalization and market opening within the Community, in order to provide them with a home market of adequate size.

Radical reform followed in the United Kingdom, albeit arguably without much pressure from the USA.[25] The continental EC Member States chose various mixtures of retrenching and reform. For them, reform was to be largely driven and directed by the European Community, where the internal-market drive had begun. The 1992 internal programme itself required (limited) liberalization in the sector in all Member States. Moreover, information technology and telecommunications were converging into 'telematics' just as the computer and electronics industries in the Community floundered. The Commission, supported by segments of industry, began to explore avenues for a more active involvement of the EC, both in the support of research and development (R&D) policy and at a more structural level. The resulting combination of liberalization and harmonization began to take shape from 1987 onwards.

[24] See G. Majone, 'Cross-national Sources of Regulatory Policy-making in Europe and the United States' (1991) 11 *Journal of Public Policy* 79; C. Scott, 'Institutional Competition and Co-ordination in the Process of Telecommunications Liberalization', in J. McCahery, B. Bratton, S. Piciotto, and C. Scott (eds.), *International Regulatory Competition and Co-ordination* (OUP, Oxford, 1996), ch. 13, 381.

[25] In the UK, the Conservative Thatcher government was ideologically predisposed toward privatization of British Telecom (BT), to complete halting reforms which had started as early as 1969. BT was privatized in 1984, after a new operator (Mercury Plc) was licensed to construct a fibre optic city service network in 1983. Hereby monopoly was replaced with a duopoly, regulated by OFTEL. It should be noted that a variety of motives laid behind liberalization in Britain. Among these were the promotion of BT as a 'national champion', relatively free from union pressure, and subject (in theory) to light-handed regulation instead of direct political control.

3. The Treaty Framework of EC Telecommunications Policy

In the debate over liberalization of the telecommunications sector in the European Community, universal service became wrapped up in the struggle over the relative merits of public-monopoly and competitive private provision of telecommunications services and networks. In the process, the more fundamental issue of the redefinition of universal service as universal access, and how such universal access can be guaranteed, was initially obscured by political posturing. More recently, however, a fairly widespread consensus has emerged on how this fundamental public-interest objective should be defined, and on ways it can be pursued under competitive conditions.

The argument of universal service initially imposed limits on the scope of liberalization, until it was successfully addressed under harmonization legislation—it was accepted that a delay in liberalization was required to guarantee the public-service role of the national monopolists. More recently, not only has the delay involved run out for the core Member States, but the dimensions of trans-European networks (TENs), consumers' rights, and citizenship have been added to the relevant universal-service concept. Hence, two phases of EC telecommunications liberalization can be distinguished. During a first phase, between 1987 and 1992, the emphasis was on extending the internal market to the telecommunications sector. Full competition was not the agenda: liberalization was limited to terminal equipment, public procurement, and certain advanced services. During the second and present phase, from 1993 onwards, liberalization was extended to all telecommunications services and infrastructure, accompanied by further harmonization in order not only to remove market barriers, but to improve multi-level policy co-ordination in the pursuit of public interest objectives, including universal service.

The break in EC telecommunications policy in 1993 was the result of the interaction between the independent dynamics of this policy, and of a change in the fundamental legal framework effected by the entry into force of the Treaty on European Union. Since the original EEC Treaty did not include any particular reference to telecommunications. Hence the original framework for Community telecommunications law and policy was formed by the general obligation to establish an internal market (Articles 2 and 8a EEC), by the rules on free movement (Articles 30 to 37), and freedom to provide services and freedom of establishment (Article 52 to 66 EEC), and the competition rules of the Treaty (Articles 3(f), 85, 86, and 90 EEC). In particular, the competition law provisions of Article 85 (control of anti-competitive agreements), Article 86 (abuse of monopoly power), and

Article 90 EEC (application of the Treaty rules to the public sector) were applied to break up the public telecommunications monopolies.[26]

Article 90 EEC played a key role in this respect. This Article is meant to reconcile the competition rules of the Treaty, and the system of undistorted competition of Article 3f EEC (3g EC), with Article 222 EC (which states that the Treaty does not prejudice the rules in the Member States governing property ownership). The exclusive and special rights on which the public telecommunications monopolies were based clearly fell under Article 90(1) EEC, and consequently the Commission used Article 90(3) EEC to specify the application of the competition rules. Most important, the application of the public-interest exception of Article 90(2) to special and exclusive rights on voice telephony and infrastructure enabled the compromise solution of phased liberalization of the telecommunications sector.[27]

Therefore, EC policy for the sector can be seen as a process of progressively redefining the balance of rights and interests that is required by Article 90 EC. Over the course of less than ten years, this balance has come full swing from vaguely defined national public-interest obligations legitimizing full monopolies within national borders, to full competition in the internal market. This occurred once less burdensome, and arguably more effective, ways of pursuing the public interest had been formulated at the Community level.[28] In the course of this process, the practical meaning of Article 222 EC has been much reduced: although the formal economic neutrality of the Treaty has been retained, the increasing constraints on the Member States' freedom of action imposed by EC law have *de facto* promoted not only liberalization and deregulation, but privatization.[29]

Further, the entry into force of the Treaty on European Union in 1993

[26] Arts. 85 and 86 concern the conduct of undertakings and not the law or regulations of the Member States. Yet by virtue of Arts. 3g and 5(2) EC, the latter are barred from adopting or maintaining in force any measures which deprive the competition rules of their effectiveness. Further, where such state measures concern public undertakings or undertakings which have been granted special or exclusive rights, Art. 90 EC applies.

[27] See C. Esteva Mosso, 'La compatibilité des monopoles de droit du secteur des télécommunications avec les normes de concurrence du traité CEE' (1993) 29 *CDE* 445; C.-D. Ehlermann, 'Managing Monopolies: The Role of the State in Controlling Market Dominance in the European Community' (1993) 14 *ECLR* 61, at 67–8.

[28] Art. 90(1) states the rule that Member States are not allowed to enact or maintain in force concerning public undertakings or undertakings to which they have granted special or exclusive rights acts contrary to the rules contained in the Treaty, in particular the competition rules. Art. 90(2) gives a limited derogation from the application of the Treaty rules to services of general economic interest and revenue-producing monopolies, in so far as these rules would obstruct the performance of the tasks of such enterprises, and to the extent that this would not be contrary to the Community interest. Art. 90(3) charges the Commission with observing the application of Art. 90, where necessary by way of directives and decisions addressed to the Member States.

[29] Regarding liberalization and privatization of undertakings (formerly) granted special and exclusive rights, notably in telecommunications: 'the EC Treaty does not in any way

has modified the fundamental legal framework. The introduction of the principle of subsidiarity for areas of concurrent competence in Article 3b EC requires that telecommunications legislation at the level of the EU be limited to topics with a Community dimension, which could not effectively be achieved by the Member States acting independently. The introduction of the co-decision procedure of Article 189b EC means that for all legislation under Article 100a EC, the approval of the European Parliament is now required on an equal footing with that of the Council, under a complex procedure involving multiple rounds of negotiation between the two legislative bodies. Hereby the residual regulatory powers of the Member States (given the acceptance of the principle of full liberalization) and the influence of the Parliament on telecommunications legislation were reinforced.

The specific changes to the EC Treaty affecting telecommunications were the introduction of Articles 3(n) and 3(s) EC, and the corresponding Titles regarding trans-European networks (TENs), and consumer protection. Telecommunications were first explicitly mentioned in the Treaty in Title XII EC (Articles 129b–d) on TENs.[30] Article 129b(1) EC states:

> 'To help achieve the objectives referred to in Articles 7a and 130a [i.e. social and economic cohesion] and to enable citizens of the Union, economic operators and regional and local comities, to derive full economic benefit from the setting up of an area without internal frontiers, the Community shall contribute to the establishment and development of trans-European networks in the areas of transport, telecommunications and energy infrastructures.'

Although this Title presumes 'the framework of a system of open and competitive markets', it establishes objectives for telecommunications policy which go beyond liberalization *per se*, notably: (i) the *interconnection*; and (ii) *inter-operability* of national networks; as well as (iii) *access* to such networks.

prejudice the ownership of such undertakings. Nevertheless, the fact remains that the entry of new competitors on to the market, combined with the limited growth for public expenditure in the Member States, will probably result in some privatization of these sectors, particularly if private enterprise can hope to benefit from an open environment' *23rd Competition Report from the Commmission: 1993* (EC Commission Publications, Brussels, 1994) para. 41. See A. Abate, 'Droit communautaire, privatisations déréglementations' (1994) 4 *Revue du Marché Unique Européen* 11; W. Devroe, 'Privatizations and Community Law: Neutrality versus Policy' (1997) 34 *CMLRev.* 267; P. Edward and D. Hoskins, 'Article 90: Deregulation and EC Law; Reflections Arising from the XVI FIDE Conference' (1995) 32 *CMLRev.* 157; R. Kovar, 'Droit communautaire et service public: esprit d'orthodoxie ou pensée laïcisée' (1996) 32 *Revue Triniestrielle de Droit Européen* 215 (pt. 1), 493 (pt. 2).

[30] Title XII aims to promote both the internal market and economic and social cohesion. It involves both co-operation and co-decision procedures, and requires consultation of the Committee of the Regions. Title XII specifically provides for the adoption, in accordance with Art. 189b EC, of guidelines which identify projects of common interest that may be supported by the Community through feasibility studies, loan guarantees, and interest-rate subsidies. Other measures may be adopted under Art. 189c EC, in particular regarding the standardization required for the inter-operability of networks.

In the context of subsidiarity, these three objectives are to be regarded as the priorities of future harmonization efforts under EC law. In particular access to telecommunications networks is fundamental to universal service.

Finally, Title M EC (Article 129a) commits the Community to contribute to protecting the health, safety, and economic interests of consumers, and to informing them adequately. This provides further standards for the public interest in liberalized telecommunications markets, again notably regarding universal service. The new emphasis on consumers' rights should also be seen as an extension of individual economic rights, and is indeed connected with enforceable citizens' rights. Under the Treaty on European Union therefore, the framework of telecommunications law and policy has been enlarged well beyond the internal market objective of negative integration by achieving the free movement of services and goods and a system of undistorted competition: the Titles regarding TENs and consumer protection now provide specific positive objectives for telecommunications legislation. Both provide a basis for Community-wide universal service obligations.

4. EC Telecommunications Liberalization and Universal Service

Parallel to the progressive elaboration of the Treaty framework, two phases of EC telecommunications-specific law and policy can be identified. The first phase, which ran from 1987 to 1992, following the publication of the 1987 Green Paper, was that of partial liberalization.[31] The second and current phase is that following the 1992 review of the sector, during which full liberalization of telecommunications was agreed, within a new regulatory framework to be established by harmonization measures.[32]

The 1987 Green Paper was preceded by widespread consultation and accompanied by intense 'reverse lobbying' of the Member States' governments by private industry groups in favour of rapid liberalization. Added to this were the general impetus of the internal market programme, and the *malaise* of the European information technology industry which expected an economic stimulus from the opening of the market. As the

[31] COM(87)290, Towards a Dynamic European Economy: Green Paper on the Development of the Common Market for Telecommunications Services and Equipment. On the development of universal service in the liberalization process see M. Haag and L. Gosling, 'Universal Service in the European Telecommunications Sector', in H. Kubicek, W. Dutton and R. Williams (eds.), *The Social Shaping of Information Superhighways. European and American Roads to the Information Society* (Campus, Frankfurt, 1997), ch. 14, 233. On telecommunications generally, see W. Sauter, Competition Law and Industrial Policy in the EU (OUP, Oxford, 1997), ch. 5, 163.

[32] SEC(92)1048, *1992 Review of the Situation in the Telecommunications Service Sector* and the Council Resolution of 22 July 1993 on the review of the situation in the telecommunications sector (OJ 1993 C213/1).

result of these various factors, and on the basis of the 1987 Green Paper, the Council reached consensus on extending the internal market to telecommunications equipment and services through a combination of liberalization and harmonization.[33] This consensus was based on a compromise which reflected the gradual adjustment of the balance between national public interests and the competition rules of the Community under Article 90(2) EC. On the one hand, the principle of progressively establishing the internal market for telecommunications by 1 January 1998 was accepted, in line with the general 1992 objective. On the other hand, it was agreed that exclusive and special rights could be maintained where this was essential to guarantee the public-service role and the financial stability of the telecommunications operators (TOs). Although this was not spelled out explicitly, in a formal sense this arrangement could be seen as an application of the public interest exception of Article 90(2) EC.

It should be noted that the 1987 Green Paper stressed the need to safeguard the financial stability of the TOs in regard to the anticipated massive public investments in network infrastructure, rather than in relation to the provision of universal service. These prospective infrastructure investments being intended mainly for upgrading to fibre-optic cable in order to facilitate digital transmission. As a political reality, even more important than considerations of public service or future investments was the fact that, since the TOs in many cases formed the largest single national undertakings, they were vital for the economies of Member States, making their future of obvious public concern. Nevertheless, under the compromise of the 1987 Green Paper, universal service as 'public service' clearly remained under the competence of the individual Member States, and in practice, the obligation to provide universal service was hereby limited to the dominant TOs.

Since both universal service and the financial stability of the TOs depended on pervasive cross-subsidies, competition and cost-based tariffs were to be phased in over time.[34] Hence, a distinction was introduced between non-reserved services, on the one hand, and a limited number of reserved services and infrastructure, on the other.[35] The TOs' exclusive

[33] Council Resolution 88/257/EEC on the development of the common market for telecommunications services and equipment up to 1992 (OJ 1988 C257/1).

[34] Commission Directive 90/388/EEC, n. 18 above, consideration 18.

[35] The reserved services, including voice telephony, accounted for the vast bulk of the market. In practice, the non-reserved services were mainly new value-added services (although not formally defined as such). In deference to the Member States, the 1987 Green Paper equated the reserved services with universal service provision: '[h]istorically, reserved services in the Member States have been telephony and telex, which have been regarded generally as "basic services" '. Both services are offered on a universal basis. This is taken to mean: (i) provided with general geographical coverage; (ii) provided on demand to all users on reasonably the same terms regardless of the user's location within the service providers territory or franchise area and the cost of interconnection to the network.' 1987 Green Paper, n. 31 above, at 66.

and special rights in the operation of reserved services (the provision of network infrastructure and 'basic' services) were subject to certain conditions, in particular their monitoring and periodic review by independent national regulatory authorities (NRAs), supervised by the Commission. The markets for non-reserved (value-added) services and terminal equipment were to be opened to competition immediately.

The implementation of liberalization was to be guaranteed by the separation of the regulatory and operational tasks of the national TOs, strict scrutiny of both public and private undertakings under the competition rules, and the harmonization of interconnection and inter-operability under conditions of open network provision (ONP). ONP was intended to provide an interface between reserved (monopoly), and non-reserved (competitive) services. For this purpose ONP was to provide open access to public networks, with the help of rules designed to compensate for unequal bargaining power, based on the principles of transparency, proportionality, and non-discrimination.

As the programme of joint liberalization and harmonization set out in the 1987 Green Paper was implemented, the scope of the public-interest exception under Article 90(2) EEC was gradually reduced. The key to this process was a 1990 Commission Directive which required the liberalization of all telecommunications services other than voice telephony, issued under Article 90(3) EEC.[36] In this Directive, the Commission reformulated and sharpened the terms of the earlier compromise with the Council in two ways. First, it formally stated that full liberalization of telecommunications services was subject only to a limited exception under Article 90(2) EEC.[37] Secondly, the validity of this exception was to be subject to review in 1992.[38] Although this Commission Directive itself was immediately challenged before the European Court of Justice, it called both the scope and the duration of the Article 90(2) EEC exception into question.

Consequently, the direction of reform was reviewed in 1992 with a round of consultations on the fixture of telecommunications regulation.[39] During the review, the Commission emphasized the competitive disadvantage of European users due to segmented national markets and the remaining monopoly on voice services, which entailed distortions in

[36] Commission Directive 90/388/EEC, n. 18 above.

[37] 'Art. 90(2) of the Treaty allows derogation from the application of Arts. 59 and 86 of the Treaty where such application would obstruct the performance, in law or in fact, of the particular task assigned to the telecommunications organizations. This task consists in the provision and exploitation of a universal network, i.e. one having general geographical coverage, and being provided to any service provider or user upon request within a reasonable period of time': *ibid.*, consideration 18.

[38] *Ibid.*, Art. 10.

[39] SEC(92)1048, n. 32 above; and COM(93)159, Communication on the Consultation on the Review of the Situation in the Telecommunications Services Sector.

prices and tariff structures, and delayed investment and innovation.[40] It pointed out that the universal service obligations imposed on the dominant TOs were often vaguely defined, did not include quality standards, and were often barely honoured in practice. The argument was raised that more effective and efficient universal service might be provided by targeted support to poorer groups. The challenge thus became to define and guarantee common universal-service goals in the context of a general review of policy objectives. The Commission was strongly supported in its views by user groups interested in the wider economic possibilities of full telecommunications liberalization, with the leading European multinationals in high technology prominent among them. A number of potential directions for future policy were set out, among which the full liberalization of telecommunications services.[41]

Meanwhile, the position of the TOs themselves was ambivalent. On the one hand they generally used the universal-service argument to protect their national monopolies, although most TOs did not have an impressive track record in this area, and seemed simply to assume that public service was a good in itself. On the other hand the more ambitious TOs envisaged a future for themselves based on expansion into new markets both at home and abroad, and believed that, in the long term, asymmetric universal-service obligations might compromise their competitiveness. Hence, although some TOs retained the view that universal-service obligations should remain the responsibility of a single undertaking, protected by special and exclusive rights, they agreed that, to the extent that markets were to be liberalized, new entrants should bear a proportionate part of the burden.[42] Unsurprisingly, the position of the Member States was similar to that of their TOs. In general they were torn between their traditional role as public owners, operators, and employers on the one hand, and the promise of new technology and innovation bringing increased private-sector growth with significant benefits to the economy as a whole on the other. As a matter of principle they resisted the independent action of the Commission taken under Article 90 EEC.

The threatened deadlock on the review of Community telecommunications policy was broken by the resolution of the legal conflict on the interpretation of Article 90 EEC. In two landmark rulings, the Court upheld the Commission Directives on the application of Article 90 EC to public undertakings and undertakings to which the Member States granted

[40] SEC(92)1050, Towards Cost Orientation and the Adjustment in Pricing Structures—Telecommunications Tariffs in the Community.

[41] 'Universal service consists in the provision and exploitation of a universal network i.e. one having general geographic coverage, and being provided to any user or service provider upon request within a reasonable period of time at affordable prices': SEC(92)1048, n. 32 above, at 23.

[42] COM(93)159, n. 39 above, at 9.

exclusive or special rights in telecommunications.[43] By this confirmation of the Commission's right to act independently under Article 90 EEC, the way was cleared for further reform (either by consensus, or under pressure from the Commission), enabling the Council to reach agreement on the need to proceed towards full services liberalization. As the sum of these various developments, the 1992–3 telecommunications policy review concluded that a common definition of universal service formed a key factor for the development of the future regulatory environment. This definition was to be based on the principles of universality (access for all, at an affordable price), equality (access independent of geographical location), and continuity (continuous provision, of a defined quality).

As a consequence of these developments, the Council in its Resolution 93/C213/EEC accepted that liberalization of telecommunications service markets was the 'inevitable result of technological and market developments'.[44] This was the beginning of the second (and current) phase of telecommunications liberalization. A new balance was struck between liberalization, harmonization, and the need to guarantee universal service. On the one hand, the principle of full liberalization of public voice telephony was accepted. On the other hand, political agreement was found on the need to retain the protection of Article 90(2) EEC for the TOs until 1998, in order to allow time for structural adjustment, notably tariff rebalancing. This rebalancing effort was not limited to the cross-subsidies related to universal service *per se*. Rather, it was necessary to introduce transparent and cost-oriented tariffs in general. Sheltered from competition, but not from the demands of political patronage, most TOs had long ago lost all track of the relationship between price, cost, and productivity. In what could be regarded as a side-bargain to the fundamental compromise involving the core States (notably France and Germany), additional adjustment periods up to 2003 were provided for Member States with less developed or very small networks. This would allow them to complete network build-out, occasionally supported by Community investment measures.

In this context, Resolution 93/C213/EEC recognized the need to safeguard universal service and maintain the financial stability of the sector while proceeding with the adjustment of tariff structures. Further, the application of harmonized open network provision (ONP) measures was

[43] Commission Directive 88/301/EEC on competition in the markets in telecommunications terminal equipment (OJ 1988 L131/72); and Commission Directive 90/388/EC, n. 18 above. The challenges to these Directives were decided in Case 202/88, *French Republic* v. *Commission* [1991] ECR I–1223; and Joined Cases C–271/90, C–281/90, and C–289/90, *Spain, France, Belgium and Italy* v. *Commission* [1992] ECR I–5833. See P. Ravaioli and P. Sandler, 'The European Union and Telecommunications: Recent Developments in the Field of Competition' (1994) 2 *The International Computer Lawyer* (Part 1) 2; (Part 2) 20.

[44] [1993] OJ C213/1.

identified as the basis for the definition of universal service.[45] The essence of the principles of the universal obligation, stated as making available 'a defined minimum service of specified quality to all users at an affordable price' was held to be embodied in the existing ONP legislation and proposals under consideration.[46] Hereby, the main battle over universal service as a justification of (public) monopoly provision had been fought before a common definition of universal service had even been adopted. Yet divergent national definitions would create market barriers, whereas the financing problem could obstruct the rebalancing necessary to allow the TOs to face competition. Therefore, beyond the problem of finding an acceptable definition, the main issue which remained was that of the financing of universal service.

To address these issues, the Commission produced a document on universal service principles in November 1993. This identified a common definition of universal service on the basis of the elements of ONP, notably the principles of transparency, non-discrimination, and proportionality, and the provision of a defined minimum set of offerings to be made available on a Community basis.[47] Under subsidiarity, the Member States would be able to introduce complementary obligations, in so far as these did not create

[45] Also, Resolution 93/C213/01 recognized: 'the importance, to the individual consumer, and for the competitiveness of Community industry and commercial users, of a Community telecommunications system offering all users, including specific social groups, reasonable and affordable charges for access and use, high quality of service and technological innovation': ibid.

[46] These concerned in particular (i) the initial provision of service; (ii) special public-service features (including pay-phones and emergency services; users directories and information; and international access); (iii) quality of service; (iv) prices; provision of dispute resolution procedures; and (v) minimum service features: see COM(93)159, n. 38 above, at 22–3; Council Directive 90/387/EEC on the establishment of the internal market for telecommunications services through the implementation of open network provision (OJ 1990 L192/l); Council Directive *944/EEC* on the application of ONP to leased lines (OJ 1992 L165/27); Council Recommendation 92/382/EEC on the application of open network provision to public packet switched data services (OJ 1992 L200/1); Council Recommendation 92/383/EEC on the application of open network provision to 1SDN(OJ 1992 L200/10); Proposal for a European Parliament and Council Directive on the application of open network provision (ONP) to voice telephony (COM(92)247/COM(94)689 OJ 1995 C122/4); Amended Proposal for a European Parliament and Council Directive on the mutual recognition of licenses and other national authorisations to operate telecommunications services (COM(92)254/COM(94)41). Given however that universal service and voice telephony are still practically synonymous, and given the level of detail paid to the elements of universal service in the proposed directive, the proposed ONP Directive on voice telephony formed the core piece of legislation in this regards. On ONP in general, see W. Sauter, 'The Future of the ONP Regime', in C. Scott and O. Adéoud (eds.), *The Future of EC Telecommunications Law* (Publication Series of the Academy of European Law in Trier, Bundesanzeiger, Cologne, 1996), vol. 19, ch. 8, 53.

[47] COM(93)543, Developing Universal Service for Telecommunications in a Competitive Environment; Proposal for a Council Resolution on Universal Service Principles in the Telecommunications Sector. See also the most recent overview in the Mar. 1996 document COM(96)73, Universal Service for Telecommunications in the Perspective of a Fully Liberalised Environment. An Essential Element of the Information Society.

barriers to market entry. The methods for funding universal service identified by the Commission were internal transfers within the dominant TOs (as before), and a system of access charges, involving financial transfers between various operators, such as between new market entrants and the dominant TOs burdened with the actual universal service obligation.

On the basis of this document Council Resolution 94/C48/EC defined universal service as access to a defined minimum service of specified quality for all users at an affordable price, based on the principles of universality, equality, and continuity, and set out acceptable financing schemes (transparent, non-discriminatory, and proportional).[48] It was accepted that the main elements for making this definition operational (quality of service, pricing policy) were to be found in the context of the ONP legislation.[49] After approval by the national regulatory authorities, loss-making universal-service obligations could be financed through internal transfers, access fees, or other mechanisms which take due account of the principles of transparency, non-discrimination, and proportionality.

Moreover, the concept of universal service adopted in Council Resolution 94/C48/EC was dynamic: whereas universal service was originally associated with stagnant technology left under monopoly control while advanced services were developed under competitive conditions, the two were now linked as related elements of a general objective of high quality of service and technological innovation.[50] This meant that benefits of cost, quality, and choice of service must be passed on to all users, and that eventually universal service would extend beyond basic access to voice telephony and data services. This enlightened view of universal service was in accordance with the vision of the 'information society' which was promoted at the time as the promise and objective of full telecommunications liberalization.[51] (The information society project is closely linked

[48] i.e. 'to permit access to a defined minimum service of specified quality to all users everywhere and, in the light of specific national conditions, at an affordable price'. See Council Resolution of 7 February 1994 on universal service principles in the telecommunications sector (OJ 1994 C48/1); and the Commission Statement concerning Council resolution on universal service in the telecommunications sector (OJ 1994 C48/8),

[49] Telecommunications operators providing fixed public networks in other Member States, and operators providing public mobile telephony services in the same Member States excepted. The latter two categories have a right to interconnect. Proposed Directive on Voice Telephony, n. 46 above, Arts. 10 and 11.

[50] '[W]hereas the concept of *universal service must evolve* in particular to keep pace with technical and economic progress', and 'that the *maintenance and development* of a universal telecommunications service, ensured through adequate financing, are a key factor for the future development of telecommunications in the Community.'

[51] See High-Level Group on the Information Society, *European and the Global Information Society: Recommendations to the European Council* (Brussels, 1994), which warned that 'the main risk lies in the creation of a two-tier society of have and have-nots, in which only a part of the populations has access to the new technology': *ibid.*, 6; also in 'Growth, Competitiveness and Employment: White Paper Follow-Up', *Bull EU* Suppl. 2/94.

with, *inter alia*, the trans-European communications networks of Title XII EC.) In this context, it was held by an influential industrial group assembled for this purpose that 'all licensed public operators should assume their share of public service responsibilities', and that 'noncommercial political burdens and budgetary constraints imposed on telecommunications operators' should be removed'.[52]

The vision of an 'information society' has also inspired the last fundamental step to full liberalization of the telecommunications sector. This was initiated by the Green Paper on Infrastructure, which set the agenda and the timetable for full infrastructure liberalization. The Infrastructure Green Paper linked, as a general principle, infrastructure and services liberalization.[53] Hence, it proposed the immediate removal of all restrictions on the use of infrastructure for the provision of satellite, mobile, and other liberalized services. The networks over which voice telephony was delivered were to be liberalized in step with the service itself.

Concerning harmonization, the Infrastructure Green Paper identified the two key issues to be addressed under ONP as interconnection and universal service.[54] The Infrastructure Green Paper established three tiers of universal service. First, it repeated the 1993 definition of universal service as 'access to a defined minimum service of specified quality to all users at an affordable price based on the principles of universality, equality and continuity'.[55] This relates to the provision of basic telephone service, quality of service, and tariff policy. Secondary objectives are access to information about the service, dispute-resolution procedures for users, subscriber directories, operator assistance and directory inquiry services, public pay-phones, access to emergency services, and specific conditions for disabled users and persons with special needs. Thirdly, targets or recommendations were proposed for advanced features, such as itemized billing, touch-tone dialing, call-forwarding, calling line identification, green number or 'freephone' services, call transfer, and access to directory and operator services in other Member States.[56]

In the Green Paper, the dual aim of price re-balancing was stated as providing consumers and businesses with a diverse offering of quality telecommunications services at competitive prices while guaranteeing universal access to basic telecommunications services to all *citizens*. The

[52] *Ibid.*, 12.

[53] COM(94)440, Green Paper on the Liberalization of Telecommunications Infrastructure and Cable Television Networks. Part One: Principles and Timetable, and COM(94)682, the Green Paper on the Liberalization of Telecommunications Infrastructure and Cable Television Networks. Part Two: A Common Approach to the Provision of Infrastructure for Telecommunications in the European Union.

[54] The other fundamental regulatory issues identified in the Green Paper are ensuring a fair competitive environment and ensuring comparable and effective excess to global markets; and 'broader societal issues' (generated by multi-media convergence).

[55] Part II of the Infrastructure Green Paper, n. 53 above, at xv.

[56] *Ibid.*, at 81–2.

other key issues with respect to universal service discussed were: (i) the methods for costing universal service; and (ii) the means of financing uneconomic aspects of universal provision in a competitive environment.[57] On the costing point, the Green Paper recommends that the cost of universal service be based on calculations of long-run avoidable cost or incremental costs (the difference between all revenue generated by a customer and the actual cost of the service provided to that customer, over time). Secondly, all market players should in principle contribute to financing universal service according to mechanisms established nationally (but within a Union framework). Nevertheless, the principle of proportionality might require that new services with higher cost and lower volume (including, depending on the development of its overall market-share, mobile telephony) would be exempted from contributing, to avoid delaying their development.

Between the two acceptable methods of financing, the use of access charges and universal-service funds, the use of universal-service funds is preferred. The system of access charges is based on transfers added to interconnection charges to the dominant TO, which manages the system. Its disadvantages are possible conflicts of interest (where the dominant TO in effect charges its competitors directly), the absence of transparency of cost calculations, and the absence of competition for the more efficient provision of the non-economic service. Universal-service funds involve fewer distortions, in particular by avoiding reliance on the dominant TO. Under this system, competing operators may share in the provision of universal service (and the subsidies from the universal service fund), and make their contributions to this fund either in cash (as lump-sum payments) or in kind (by providing service). Universal-service funds would allow all market participants to provide service rather than pay into the fund, and thereby exert downward pressure on the cost involved. The funds would be independently administered. The system of access charges on the contrary presupposes that universal service is provided by the dominant TO, which also administers the system and has few, if any, incentives to reduce costs.

The NRAs will supervise the revision of the financing of universal service as part of a process in which the present general subsidies of local access are to be replaced by tariff rebalancing and the introduction of special tariffs aimed at needy or uneconomic customers. Over time, the benefits of reduced cost and improved quality over a widening range of services should be extended to all users: the dual aim of this process 'should be to provide consumers and business with a diverse offering of quality telecommunications at competitive prices whilst guaranteeing

[57] On these issues, in greater detail, see the Nov. 1996 document COM(96)608, Assessment Criteria for National Schemes for the Costing and Financing of Universal in Telecommunications and Guidelines for the Member States on Operation of such Schemes.

universal access to basic telecommunications services for all citizens'.[58] The NRA should normally rely on the negotiation of access and interconnection between the parties involved. However, under ONP rules they may intervene on their own initiative at any time, and must do so if requested by either party. The NRAs are obliged to ensure that the conditions in the agreements are non-discriminatory, fair, and reasonable for both parties, and offer the greatest benefit to all users.[59] Most important, accessible and in principle inexpensive procedures to resolve disputes between users and TOs are to be provided, through an independent body.

The Infrastructure Green Paper received strong industry support. Moreover, it was not resisted by the dominant TOs, which had concluded that rapid liberalization would also provide opportunities to get rid of burdensome government regulation. In any event, they hoped it might help to establish a clear regulatory environment as a precondition for the success of their various prospective share offerings and to establish themselves as European (and global) players at an early stage. The acceptance of these proposals by the Council was not only to lead to the full liberalization of telecommunications by 1998, wholesale privatization and market entry by (and strategic alliances with) numerous new competitors from within and outside the Community, but also to a new system of telecommunications regulation. The latter was to be based on common principles set at the Community level with implementation by the NRAs under ultimate Commission supervision, and directly enforceable users' rights.[60] For universal service, independent administration, targeted

[58] Infrastructure Green Paper, n. 53 above, at 43.

[59] Notably the European Parliament and Council Directive 95/62/EC on the application of open network provision (ONP) to voice telephony (OJ 1995 L321/6), which sets out a framework for access and interconnection to the public networks. Compare n. 46 above. The right to access is extended to all users and can be restricted only with prior agreement of the NRAs, based on the essential requirements. They are also to ensure that the agreements are entered into and implemented in an efficient and timely manner, and include conditions regarding compliance with relevant standards, essential requirements, and end-to-end quality. Cost-oriented, non-discriminatory, and fully justified access charges may be included in interconnection agreements, but are to be applied only after approval by the NRA. (Note that on 9 June 1997, the Council adopted a common position on a new Directive on the application of open network provision (ONP) to voice telephony and on universal service for telecommunications in a competitive environment). See also European Parliament and Council Directive 97/13/EC on a common framework for general authorizations and individual licences in the field of telecommunications services (OJ 1997 L117/5); and the European Parliament and Council Directive on Interconnection in Telecommunications with regard to ensuring universal service and inter-operability through the application of the principles of open network provision (ONP), adopted on 11 June 1997, not yet published.

[60] Council Resolution of 22 December 1994 on the timetable and principles for the liberalization of telecommunications infrastructure (OJ 1994 C379/04). Another important 1994 Council Resolution on the future regulatory framework for telecommunications recognizes as a key factor in the elaboration of this framework 'the maintenance and development of a universal service in accordance with the Council Resolution of 7 February 1994, and to that end, in compliance with the principles of transparency, proportionality and non-discrimination:

subsidies, and the dynamic development of its scope were to set new standards of public service, albeit increasingly provided by private operators.

5. Conclusion

Whereas the goals of completing the internal market for telecommunications, promoting new efficient services which may help relaunch the European economy, and stimulating private investment, are now widely accepted, the issue of universal service remains on the political agenda. Although many public telecommunications operators have paid lip-service to the idea of universal service in the past, the advocates of reform have been forced to come to terms with this public-interest defence of dominant position, and to integrate its achievement in their strategy for liberalization. Hence, the universal-service obligations of the dominant TOs justified the Article 90(2) EC exception of public voice telephony from liberalization until 1998 under Commission Directive 90/388/EEC on Competition in the Markets for Telecommunications Services. For a long while, the primary purpose behind this exception may have been that of buying time to allow the TOs to engage in tariff re-balancing. Yet in preparation for full liberalization the attention paid to the social dimension of the universal-service problem has increased, and, as has been seen, innovative approaches to its provision and financing have emerged.

It is likely that in the future the European Parliament will play an important role in keeping the universal service issue alive. When the guiding principles of universal service were first established at the Community level, the European Parliament was ignored. For example, although the Commission's proposals for a Community definition were simultaneously submitted to the Council and the European Parliament (as required by standard procedures), the relevant Council Resolution was adopted before the parliamentary debate had even occurred.[61] However, using its

the obligation placed on certain operators by Member States to provide a defined minimum range of telecommunications services of specified quality and, in the light of specific national conditions at an affordable price; the adoption at Union level of common principles for determining the financial compensation of operators which may be justified by such obligations, placing prime importance on achieving the highest level of productivity in the provision of universal service; the establishment by the Member States, where necessary, of the rules for calculating any corresponding net costs and the rnechanisms for sharing such costs between market players, under the control of the national regulatory authorities': Council Resolution of 18 September 1995 on the implementation of the future regulatory framework for telecommunications (OJ 1995 C258/1).

[61] See EP A3–0317/94, Committee on Economic and Monetary Affairs and Industrial Policy, *Report on the Communication from the Commission Accompanied by the Proposal for a Council Resolution on Universal Service Principles in the Telecommunications Sector* (COM(93) 543–OJ C3–0473/93): rapporteur: Mel Read; and the resolution therein (adopted). Debates of the European Parliament No 3–448/243–247 (5 May 1994); No 3–448/272 (6 May 1994).

co-decision powers under Article 189b in conjunction with Article 100a EC, the European Parliament has the opportunity to fill in the details of universal service under ONP legislation. The strength of the European Parliament's position was well illustrated when it decided to block the proposed ONP directive on voice telephony in its conflict with Council over comitology. This made the voice ONP directive the first legislative measure ever to be blocked under the rules of Article 198b EC, albeit on a matter of institutional principle rather than a fine-tuning point with regard to universal service.[62]

Further, the European Parliament has begun to take up the link between consumers' rights, and citizens' rights. For example, it proposed adding universal service to a list of citizens' rights to be included in the Treaty at the 1996–7 intergovernmental conference.[63] Although the Parliament was not successful and the Amsterdam Treaty makes only a general reference to 'services of general economic interest' this initiative suggests that at least in the medium term the link between democratic control and directly enforceable citizens' rights will be strengthened.[64] It should further be noted that such rights have already been elaborated under ONP legislation, and remain to be defined more fully at national level. Meanwhile, the European Parliament has encouraged the Commission to undertake regular monitoring of universal service developments at national level—which

[62] This proposal was caught by the co-decision rules of Art. 189b EC after the entry into force of the Treaty on European Union, and duly rejected by the newly elected European Parliament in protest against the 'comitology' provisions included in a vote on 19 July 1994.

[63] See EP A3–0254/94, Committee on Economic and Monetary Affairs and Industrial Policy, *Report on Public Undertakings, Privatization and Public Services in the European Community*, Rapporteur: Roberto Speciale; and the resolution attached (adopted). Debates of the European Parliament No 3–448/243–247 (5 May 1994); No 3–448/272 (6 May 1994). The European Centre for Enterprizes with Public Participation (CEEP) has proposed amending the Treaty to this effect, adding a Charter on services of general economic interest, and creating a monitoring 'assessment body', attached to the European Parliament: see CEEP, *Europe, concurrence and service public* (Masson/Armand Collin, Paris, 1995). In particular, the French government had come out publicly in favour of incorporating public service in the Treaty, and reducing the powers of the Commission in Art. 90 EC.

[64] The Treaty of Amsterdam will only introduce a new Treaty Art. 16 which states that '[w]ithout prejudice to Articles 77, 90 and 92, and given the place occupied by services of general economic interest in the shared values of the Union as well as their role in promoting social and territorial cohesion, the Community and the Member States, each within their respective powers and within the scope of application of this Treaty, shall take care that such services operate on the basis of principles and conditions which enable them to fulfil their missions'. The declaration on this Art. 16 annexed to the EC Treaty states that '[T]he provisions of Article 7d [new Art. 16] of the Treaty establishing the European Community on public services shall be implemented with full respect for the jurisprudence of the Court of Justice, inter alia as regards the principles of equality of treatment, quality and continuity of such services.' A separate protocol concerning public broadcasting specifies that the Treaty shall not prejudice national systems of funding insofar as granted for the fulfilment of the public service remit, and provided that such funding is acceptable under Community legal norms. These results are broadly in line with the Commission's approach. See COM(96)443, *Services of general interest in Europe.*

will stimulate convergance towards best practice.[65] Given these developments, the role of the NRAs under subsidiarity, and the new activism of the European Parliament in conjunction with the legislatures in the Member States will come to form the main dynamic factors with an impact on the progressive extension of the scope of universal service. The paradoxical result may well turn out to be that true universal service will for the first time be available throughout the European Union after liberalization has been completed. This may well provide an example for public service in other sectors which have so far resisted liberalization.

More important for the telecommunications sector itself may be new issues which go beyond established notions of universal service, such as the right to access to on-line services, and the nature of such a right (including the degree of public regulation of content). These issues arise as the result of technological developments as such, and due to the convergence between hitherto discrete economic sectors which are the result of this. In this context, it is worth noting that among the eight regulatory principles set out by the G–7 after their Brussels Global Information Society conference of February 1995, included: 'providing open access to networks; ensuring universal provision of, and access to, services; and promoting equality of opportunity to the citizen; as well as promoting equality of content, including cultural linguistic diversity'.[66] So far, few concrete results have emerged at international level. Nevertheless, this suggests that regulatory convergence on liberalization and on the redefinition of public-interest objectives has not only transcended the national level, but the Community level as well.[67] It also provides further evidence of developments that could lead to the emergence of public service objectives for the information age.

Universal service remains an important objective of the Community legal framework for telecommunications. However, issues of privacy and data security, guarantees of plurality of media ownership and access to information (necessary to protect the democratic process), diversity of content (necessary to protect linguistic and cultural diversity) are gaining in importance. So is the awareness of the danger that within an information society, a new social divide may emerge between those people who

[65] See COM(98) 101 final, First Monitoring Report on Universal Service in Telecommunications in the European Union.

[66] 'The Official Results of the G–7 Ministerial Conference on the Information Society—Chair's Conclusions', *Europe Documents* No 1923, 27 Feb. 1995.

[67] Note, in this context, the provision regarding universal service in the reference paper on regulatory conditions to the February 1997 GATS agreement on Basic Telecommunications (that came into force in February 1998): 'Any Member has the right to define the kind of universal service obligation it wishes to maintain. Such obligations will not be regarded as anti-competitive *per se*, provided they are administered in a transparent, non-discriminatory and competitively neutral manner and are not more burdensome than necessary for the kind of universal service defined by the Member'. See Enser, above n. 2.

do, and those who do not have access to information essential for their wellbeing. Such concerns are those of private businesses (such as represented in the High Level Group on the Information Society which first raised these issues alongside that of universal service) primarily to the extent that they may give rise to regulatory barriers to the spread of the new media. Yet, many of these new issues are linked to citizens' private and public (or political) and human rights, as well as with the quality of the democratic dimension of the European Union. It is to be hoped that they will be taken up and dealt with as such.

8

Citizenship and Public Services—Some General Reflections

GIULIANO AMATO

1. The Historical Roots of Public Services Regulation

Mediaeval legal systems laid down, in their extraordinarily rich fabric, a number of guiding threads for the future. The first that should be mentioned here is the identification of the function of government not with administration but with adjudication of complaints and disputes between private individuals. This was the embryo of the jurisdictional function, but as exercised initially by the King. And it was therefore the King who injected into it the characteristic features of the function of government and the typical manifestation of the State. A second embryo, which history was to correlate with the first but which, to start with, merely existed alongside it, was the development of the principle whereby economic activities of collective interest (the forerunners of public services) did not axiomatically fall within the public domain but remained part of the private sphere. The only difference was that a person offering them was subject to special liabilities, but these were additional to the private law rules that were still applicable to the contracts concerned.

The concept I am referring to was that of the *common carrier* (or also, by extension, *common calling*) which was to become established in Anglo-American law. A common carrier was a person who offered his services (not only as a transporter of goods and passengers but also as a barber, a farrier, and so on), not to particular, preselected customers, but to anyone who might request them. Inasmuch as this was so (the courts took to pronouncing) the liabilities were greater: '[i]f somebody has come to you and asked you to cure his horse for him and the horse dies after your treatment, you are not liable even if that treatment was ill-considered. But if you have publicly offered your services to anyone who chooses to bring their horse to you, you are automatically liable in the event of harm resulting from your intervention.' This was not, however, the only principle which became established during the mediaeval period. A very different embryo also emerged, namely that of the (future) public service provided by the public authorities, in the form of the principle whereby responsibility for the construction of works (bridges) and for associated activities, which by definition served a collective use, lay with the feudal lord.

Although I am simplifying things greatly, these few allusions lead me on to the well-known fact that, as a consequence of successive historical vicissitudes, there subsequently emerged from the mediaeval melting pot two divergent legal architectures. On the one hand, there was the *common law*, which became established in the United Kingdom and was then transferred to the United States, in which the primordial public function was adjudication, and economic activities, including those constituting a public service, were regulated by private law except for special additional liabilities (which did not, however, alter the normative stem onto which these activities remained grafted). On the other hand, there was the pervasive public law which developed in continental Europe, where the administrative function, and hence identification of the State with its bureaucratic machinery, became prevalent, and even economic activities, if they concerned the public interest, fell under public law, either by being entrusted directly to the State or by being made subject to special legal regimes differing from private law. The special nature of those legal regimes came to be based on the notion of the supremacy of the State and on the consequent premise that acts by the State fell outside the scope of the ordinary law, and that everything which the State absorbed into its domain was therefore to be regulated by a law derogating from the intrinsic parity-based nature of private law.

Although hardly a favourable system of law during the years of absolutism, it was to become a far more balanced system offering far more protective guarantees when, in the course of the nineteenth century, administrative law proper came into being. Despite the fact that administrative law was never to succeed in divesting itself of its genetic relationship with the authoritarian administration characterizing its origins, it is unfair to identify it with the latter. For it was administrative law which provided the procedural guarantees and judicial remedies in disputes with the administration that had not formerly existed. Admittedly, in doing so it was never to obliterate entirely those features embodying the superiority of public acts and the intrinsically unfettered discretionary nature of the function they express, through whose residual effect it in fact continues to operate even today.

So how did these two different systems—the common law and continental civil law—react in coming to grips with the new requirements continually confronting them both alike? What, to start with, was the response of the Anglo-American system of common law to phenomena requiring more analytical regulation and public supervision, when it did not possess the machinery to which we continentals were naturally able to entrust this?

2. In Common Law Countries

It is significant that, in his book entitled *Administrative Law* (mainly devoted, as such, to independent agencies), the prominent American scholar, Walter Gellhorn, opens his 'Introduction' by quoting one of the first laws of the state of Maryland (so taking us back to the seventeenth century), which was intended to deal with the increase in river transport, and hence to regulate such transport with due regard to the multiple interests involved. The statute in question, in the natural tradition of the common law, entrusted the detailed provisions to the courts with the following words: '[t]he aforesaid courts shall specify the tolls for passengers and horses carried on state ferries and shall likewise fix the number and type of boats to be used for a ferry service and the number of fit and strong men to be employed on each of the boats licensed by those courts.' Thus, in a single provision we find a whole range of functions and powers allocated: fixing prices, shaping the structure of the market (the number of operators in the ferries markets and the number of employees on each boat), and granting licences to carry on such activity. These are all functions and powers which continental Europeans would readily class as administrative and which, in continental Europe, when first being dealt with legislatively (not necessarily in the same words, of course), were obviously delegated to administrative bodies. Yet here they were entrusted to the courts.

This demonstrates how large a part has been played by the difference between the main stems onto which, in the two systems, inherently similar institutional developments have been grafted. In a system in which the State's primordial function was adjudication and economic activities were regulated almost exclusively by the common law, and hence private law, even the protection of overriding public interests was initially entrusted to the courts. In the continental systems of law, by contrast, the result was an expansion of the structures and functions of the machinery of the State. In Gellhorn's book the reference to the Maryland law on ferries is preceded by a few lines in which the author mentions the belief, widely held among American authors, that although the courts may make mistakes and although the legislators may make mistakes, it is the mistakes made by bureaucracies that can have the most disastrous consequences. Compare that view with a well-known passage from a prestigious Italian scholar of the early twentieth century, Oreste Ranelletti: 'the State can manage without courts and can manage without Parliaments, but it cannot exist without its administration and its administrative officials'.

The two strands have, obviously, generated profoundly different ideologies. Nevertheless, with the passage of history and the consequent links between the institutional solutions adopted in response to largely common problems, the two paths have begun to draw far closer together (although, clearly, still remaining different) than might be inferred from their ideologies. Take the case of common law systems. In so far as the problems that arise concern the protection and limits of the right of ownership and freedom of contract in relations between their respective holders, entrusting them to the courts was and remained the natural solution. This very fact, however, engendered a case law that afforded its protection only to infringements of property rights and freedom of contract, or infringements similar to these (and, as is well known, English law came to class under the heading of property, for the precise purpose of providing them with such protection, rights which in continental Europe have a very different legal basis, such as the right not to be subject to arbitrary expulsion from private associations). But when faced with the claims of *non habentes* and, later, collective interests defying such categorization, that case law either had no solutions or refuted the cases before it. Moreover, as the centuries passed the ancient concept of the common carrier, with the special liabilities it involved, became confined to a very small number of occupations and, as a result of the inflexibility of the courts, did not take in any new ones. The consequence was a quest for different institutional solutions which, although possibly inspired by the most familiar model (that of the courts), circumvented its inflexibility and, for the purposes of safeguarding those new interests, applied a law incorporating derogation. This was the original reason underlying the creation of the Star Chamber, which, although it was used to deal with political 'deviations' by means of exceptional procedures and punishments, also exercised an equitable jurisdiction in favour of *non habentes*, enabling them to avail themselves of services and make claims to which they would not have been entitled under the common law.

During the nineteenth century, still in the United Kingdom, town planning, public health, safety in factories, welfare, social assistance, and, indeed, education found institutional expression in forms following the same trend. In the absence of an administration and its associated body of functionaries, Parliament created legal persons upon which it conferred powers of investigation and decision-making founded not in common law but in statute law. These included *inspectors*, who were made responsible for monitoring and enforcing safety in factories, health conditions on ships transporting emigrants on the high seas, and the conditions in which minors were employed. They also included *administrative tribunals* to regulate some of the above areas and to rule on associated claims and disputes. This was the birth of English administrative law, thus established through bodies which, although bearing at least a partial resemblance to judicial bodies, enforced different rules to impose the special liabilities that did not exist (or no longer existed) under common law and were able to do so in accordance with the principles both of the fairness and openness of their proceedings (where there were any) and of the impartiality of their decisions, and, ultimately, by means of 'injunctions' that had direct effect in the same way as a writ issued by a court (which they therefore did not need).

It is no accident that, in the United States, in the early years of their existence the various *independent agencies* were called *administrative tribunals*, i.e. going by a name derived from English practice. They differed from that practice in the greater degree to which they had pre-eminently regulatory functions and powers, and were created to supervise economic activities rather than activities of social importance. Such differences aside, however, even here the new bodies and the law they applied did not entirely remove the activities they supervised from the domain of the common law (or, as we call it, private law). What they did was to make them subject, on a number of crucial points, to the precedence of rules incorporating derogation, thereby adopting what is perceived as a typical feature of administrative law, namely, derogation from the general legal regime in the name of interests that override individual interests.

This administrative law is not, of course, accompanied by either the form or the substance of what European administrative law has absorbed from its authoritarian ancestors, and consequently shares neither the preordained special supremacy of the authorities that administer it nor the separate and limited subjection to judicial review of their decisions (even though there are sometimes—I refer here to the United Kingdom—statutory sections expressly excluding judicial review, but which case law has however interpreted restrictively). According to Anglo-American authors, the typifying features of administrative law are, rather, the very principles of fairness, openness, and liability which its new authorities gradually began to impose on those under their supervision, and by which the latter are bound. And, according to the same authors, those principles themselves are part of the derogation that our doctrine sees as the identifying feature of administrative law,

It might be said that in Anglo-American law the capacity for incorporating derogation is in general shared by statute law, even if its application is still entrusted to the common law courts. We need think only of the Sherman Act to find an example of statute law replacing the common law in the legal regime governing a phenomenon which had long been regulated by the latter, namely, restraint of trade. An examination of the difference between the treatment of restrictive agreements in common law and their treatment under the Sherman Act reveals that the Act, at least initially, offered judicial protection in situations where a common law court would not have acted for fear of interfering with freedom of contract.

For example, unless it concerned essential goods or created a monopoly price over an entire market the common law courts did not rule against a horizontal price-fixing agreement, because it still constituted an expression of the parties' freedom of contract and a third party (consumer) was free to withdraw from the transaction and look elsewhere. Under the Sherman Act, on the other hand, such an agreement became actionable because it altered the natural balance between supply and demand, and the protection of that balance was thus given precedence over the parties' freedom of contract. There is undoubtedly a common element between this derogation approach and that of administrative law, as is clear from the above example. The fact remains, however, that a system of administrative law is perceived as one in which the actual application of legal regimes incorporating derogation has been entrusted to bodies other than the ordinary courts, invested with powers of action, regulation and/or adjudication and possessing direct legal effect.

3. In Continental Europe

The response that continental Europe gives to the same demands for public intervention is that activities are brought within the ambit of the administration to a quite different degree. Let us take the example of public services. As mentioned earlier, in the United States the fact of placing them under the control of agencies did not alter their fundamental nature of being private activities carrying special liabilities, in accordance with the original tradition of the common carrier. Although there was a phase during the nineteenth century when various states had conferred special and exclusive status on particular enterprises recognized as serving the collective interest, public hostility to monopolies, which were permitted to exist under common law, eventually brought this to an end. Continental Europe started from a different tradition, according to which economic activities are not necessarily private and the State is an economic agent on a par with private persons—and, indeed, taking their place when public interests are involved. Given that premise, the emergence of the public and collective interest which led to various economic activities being categorized as public services naturally resulted in their being reserved to the state and local authorities. These then provided the activities concerned either by operating enterprises of their own or by exclusive delegation through the grant of concessions characterized by a wide measure of discretion and the supreme authority of the grantor. Hence Ripert's statement that, with the expansion of public services, 'everything is becoming public law'.

Specialists in administrative law tend to stress the fact that, with all its accompaniment of statism (or, rather, discretionary absorption into the public domain), this facet of our administrative law distances it from its role as the vehicle for the authority of those in power, and in practice places it at the service of the collective interests of emergent and still subordinate social groups. It turns it, in short, into an instrument not of power but against (predominantly) private power. True though that may be, the very fact that the specialists feel the need to say it shows that our administrative law has never really cast off the aura derived from its historical origin. It is no accident that Gaetano Salvemini continued to see it as the law in the hands of those in control: administration is dictated by policy, which is in the hands of the rulers, and administration is the instrument used by the rulers in order to prevail over others.

Given these ambivalent premises, for decades there has been a singular (and mostly contradictory) interaction between the changes that have taken place and the resilience both of previous legal principles and of convictions born of the collective culture that has consolidated itself. On the one hand, the nature of the interests being protected has effectively changed and in addition, not unlike what occurred in the United States, the guarantees of protection have been improved in terms both of procedure and of administrative jurisdiction, to the extent that in the view of many the traditional difference between 'legally protected interest' and 'personal right', where it existed, has become more one of form than of substance. On the other hand, there has been no change in the legal principle whereby, if an act is administrative, it is subject to the direction and superior prerogatives of government. Nor has there been any change in the principle that a body, if it is administrative, forms part of a machinery that is subordinate to government. This has preserved, in all quarters, the aura or collective conviction that everything administrative, everything within the administration, is open to manipulation by those who govern: at one time lords, and nowadays politicians. And, as was to become evident in more recent years during times of moral crisis and de-legitimation of politicians that conviction permanently nurtures the old mistrust, and hence lack of faith in any dealings with the administration.

Nor is that all. The principle has also persisted that, if an activity involves the public interest, it may either be regulated by private law with some interference from mandatory rules of public law or, under relatively flexible conditions, reserved to the State or public agencies, and hence fall within the orbit of the old special supremacy, albeit in a revised and adjusted form. Over the years, in fact, the legal regimes governing economic activities in the public domain have become so flexible that such activities are, it may be probably be said, widely regulated by private law. Nevertheless public control, not only through the normal means of a shareholder but also through the traditional vehicles of public law, has remained largely the same, thereby acquiring not the essence but only the guise of private law.

4. The Ongoing Convergence of the Two Models

When we turn to what has begun to happen in the past few years, we find that the belief of a century ago, namely that certain economic activities involve not only individual interests but also collective public interests, remains as strong as ever. But a series of well-known developments (the process of market integration exposing everyone to competition, the advent of new technologies eroding natural monopolies and the basis of various exclusive rights, and experience demonstrating how often state intervention intended to remedy the failings of the market is rendered a failure itself through inefficiency and the prevalence of supervening interests) have shifted the area of protection of those collective interests. What has happened, in the case of continental Europe, is a change that has moved its deepest layers of rocks and has consequently weakened the centuries-old roots on which we had grown the absorption into the public domain of economic activities of collective interest and their shelter under our traditional administrative law. And that has weakened the hold over such activities of even those principles which we had not already abandoned (as I have just said) in the general run of things. The de-legitimation of politics, where it has occurred, has also assisted the change.

Because that de-legitimation is only an additional and, at most, instigating factor, it is a mistake to think that the change rests solely upon it and therefore shares its predictably temporary nature. The shift that has occurred has, in fact, brought the strand of continental law closer to the strand from which it diverged centuries ago, i.e. the common law, while in the meantime the latter has itself drawn closer as a result of the construction of its own brand of administrative law. And that approximation is bringing with it not so much a principle as a belief that is becoming a principle: the belief that economic activities now properly fall within the private domain and that this is why they are shifting towards private law, except for limitations (which are not engulfing) imposed from public law. This is still an ongoing process, as can be seen from our written law-making, and not all of the authoritative opinions accompanying it confirm it unambiguously. It continues to be said that economic activities and enterprise ownership may equally well be either public or private. And this is found in the EC Treaty itself, which has been accepted as one of the sources used to foster the change and yet still contains unamended, in its Article 222, the principle of neutrality.

However, although the texts remain unchanged the process is under way and is taking place by way of interpretation. Take the example of Article 90 of the Treaty, which, in its unambiguous wording, is based on the assumption that Member States may grant exclusive rights and prohibits them from enacting or maintaining in force any measures that permit the undertaking possessing those exclusive rights to act in a discriminatory manner. Both the Commission and the Court of Justice have adopted the interpretation (unquestionably a bold one) whereby the very grant of exclusive rights may itself be deemed a measure which permits discriminatory conduct and which, in such cases, is unlawful. On what grounds? On the grounds of the overriding principle of competition in the integrated market, which from our point of view means, however, that economic activities formerly falling within the domain of public law are being shifted over into the domain of the law regulating relations between private persons. Even a public service is no longer a service that is axiomatically provided by a public authority or public agency but a service provided by a common carrier i.e. by a private person subject to special liabilities. Another example that illustrates the process is the development taking place in all our countries in regard to public services carrying universal-service obligations. For decades, it was accepted that the existence of such obligations presupposed exclusive rights, as a kind of equivalent (or symptom) of a natural monopoly. Nowadays, Community directives make explicit provision for the distribution of the fulfilment of universal service obligations between a number of operators offering the service in question (telecommunications, for example) in competition with each other.

5. Citizenship and Public Services

Public services are increasingly provided within the framework of competitive markets, although subject to the special regulation of public agencies. That being so, are they still a facet of administrative law or are they moving into another field of law? Secondly, competition treats the end consumer as a customer, whereas in the area of public services the essential rights of the citizen are at stake. Are we not threatening those rights by promoting competition in public services? Let me start by venturing separate answers to these two questions, which will then allow me to reach conclusions suggested jointly by both. It is a fact that the link between public services and public monopolies is being abandoned for reasons extending beyond the technological limitations that prevented competition in some areas decades ago. Today, the public authorities prohibit companies from attaining dominant positions in the name of public interests. Decades ago (as regards public services, at least) they used to grant companies monopolistic positions in the name of those public interests. There has been a fundamental change in expectations, leading to a parallel change in regulations. Companies providing public services are expected to comply with the same rules as those providing any other product or service, namely, the rules of competition, rules setting the external conditions whereby the free interaction of private interests is deemed satisfactory within the permitted limits, from the viewpoint of public interests as well. We might define them as the rules enforced by referees, not by interventionist planners.

Not entirely, however. Despite this change, public services are still subject to a further degree of regulation that is enduringly interventionist: fixing tariffs, fixing the proportion of profits that must go to investments and training, and fixing conditions and obligations as to the quality of the service to be provided. None of this looks very different from the invasive regulation that traditionally belongs to administrative law. Yet even on this old side of the new coin there is a significant innovation. We entrust these interventionist regulations to new independent authorities, together with the new type of rules. Therefore, both the rules of the planner and the rules of the referee fall under the jurisdiction of an institution that has been devised and established more as a referee than a planner. Is this a compromise between the old and the new? We shall leave the matter there, for the moment. It is, without doubt, a step in a process whose final outcome is as yet unknown.

I now turn to the second question, the dilemma between the customer and the citizen. Protection of the citizen was the precise reason why, originally, public monopolies had been either invented or, more usually, designated as such (because their creation had been due to other reasons) and, secondly, administrative law had become their legal framework. What has happened in the meantime? Something that is not explained either by administrative law or by economic theories. Let us leave aside the subject of exclusive rights granted to private companies (which is a different story, more American than European, even though we ourselves had, and still have, this type of public service) and concentrate on monopolies granted to publicly-owned companies. This typically European case brought the public services concerned under the direct or indirect governance of political rulers. Little by little, not only the customers but also the employees providing the service, the companies supplying the companies providing the service, and the employees of the companies supplying the companies providing the service all became 'citizens', in the sense that all of them were seen as voters. The ultimate responsibility for public services was in the hands not of profit maximizers but vote maximizers, who (a) wanted more people hired by their companies, not because they were needed but because they brought added votes to them; (b) wanted more investments, not in order to increase productivity but to bring jobs and infrastructures into their constituencies; and (c) despite the higher expenditure resulting from these policies, wanted lower charges for customers so as not to lose their own votes.

In the end, the paradoxical outcome was that the citizen as a customer with special needs (which competition was not expected to satisfy) was left completely forgotten. He or she became the citizen as a taxpayer doomed to pay for the huge deficits produced by the protection of all those citizen-voters. Not only that, but the 'citizen' paid this heavy bill without receiving a service of good quality at an affordable price that was the only reason for being a customer who expected to be treated as a citizen. That is why many of us were forced to admit (while others were happy to demonstrate) that the 'citizen' might be better protected as a customer in a competitive market provided certain special forms of protection are preserved under the jurisdiction not of elected officials but of independent authorities.

Why are special forms of protection still perceived as necessary, despite the common assumption that competition is more efficient as regards both the quality of the services provided and the level of their prices? It must be remembered that a public service is designated as such (and consequently different from private services) because it is considered essential to the daily life of any person, who has the (consequent) right to receive it uninterruptedly and at an affordable price. Under certain conditions, however, a competitive market tends to bring about solutions (given the conflicts of interest it has to face) that may be inconsistent with the satisfaction of that right. Let us take three examples. First, telecommunications and electricity have two groups of customers, residential and business. The residential group has two features, both relevant to public services: it includes the customers who need special protection more than others and its overall demand is much more rigid than demand in the business group. A provider who feels the need to be more competitive will raise its prices in the area where demand is rigid in order to reduce them where demand is flexible. In economic terms it makes sense, but in the philosophy of public services it does not.

Secondly, any company has the right to invest its returns wherever its board deems appropriate. If financial investments are more advantageous despite the fact that new machines might improve the existing production, financial investments are a sound choice. The company is free to abandon its existing production for the sake of other profitable business. Again, in economic terms it makes sense but in the philosophy of public services it does not, because here continuity of provision is needed no less than an affordable price. Thirdly, prices under a public monopoly are generally higher than in a competitive market. In the transitional phase, when the market is being opened up and the former monopolist is facing new entrants, it tends to reduce its prices sharply (not necessarily below its costs), with the aim of making it impossible for the new entrants to gain significant market shares. In economic terms this makes sense as long as the market remains viable. It is, however, inconsistent with the principle that the customers' 'rights' have to be protected within the framework of an (actually) competitive market.

On the second of our two questions, therefore, the conclusion is that the notion of the 'citizen' has been preserved in public services. However, the very reasons which led long ago to the special protection of his or her needs under the shelter of administrative law require the citizen to be, first and foremost, a customer who is served in a competitive market today. The special forms of protection that are nonetheless maintained are devised on the basis of this premise, not in contradiction to it. Where do these preliminary conclusions jointly lead? To the quite significant discovery that the compromise being reached between 'old' protective rules and 'new' regulations for competitive public services is not simply a mixture of the old administrative rules and the new anti-trust rules. Even those rules which are undeniably interventionist, and hence old-looking, have a new aim and therefore a new meaning. Let us return for a moment to the three examples cited above. They suggest three rules. The first is 'no cross-subsidies from residential to business customers'. The second is 'reserve a share of your returns to future investment in the service you run'. The third concerns price-capping and requires it not to be too low and to include the incentive necessary to encourage new entrants. Only the first rule protects customers directly against the natural consequences of competition. The other two (which are no less interventionist, and perhaps even more so) protect and promote the competitive structure of each sectoral market.

In other words, the special needs of public services still demand interventionist rules, but those rules are conceived in accordance with the requirements of competition and aimed at their satisfaction. This has wider implications and gives us further clarification regarding the independent authorities that enforce such rules. Those authorities have to be independent not only in order to be immune from political influence but also because of the new market-oriented nature of all the rules they are expected to enforce. The compromise they embody is not between old administrative law and new competition law. It is between two sets of new rules: the rules that promote competition through intervention and the rules that *ab externo* protect competition in the still special area of public services. This is certainly not the final stage in the process. But we must, at least, understand where we are at present.

9

Employment, Citizenship, and Services of General Public Interest

ALAIN SUPIOT

Everyone knows the tale of the baker's wife, written by Jean Giono and immortalized on the screen by Marcel Pagnol and the actor Raimu. The baker's wife is fickle and deserts home and bakehouse to follow her lover. How can a baker live without a wife? He makes the bread and she sells it, and the loss of their married love means that he loses all will to carry on at all. So the baker goes on strike, as it were, making but one simple demand: if she returns so will the bread. Deprived of its bread, the entire village intervenes to bring the baker's wife back to her husband and thus restore, along with conjugal love, an employment relationship that is indispensable to the bakery.

As always, an artistic work tells us more, at a stroke, than any academic dissertation (to name but one comparison) and, indeed, tells it better. There could be no way of encapsulating more neatly the subtle relations that link employment, citizenship, and the general public interest. Although the baker is a private-sector worker and, what is more, self-employed, his work nonetheless serves the general interest. The question therefore arises whether, and to what extent, work that provides a service to the public carries special rights and obligations for the individual who performs it. Is it not the case that citizenship (membership of the village community) implies having uninterrupted and equal access to the services that are essential to the life of that community as a whole? And, conversely, that those who provide such services are entitled to special considerations?

Stating the question in these terms without preamble presupposes the acceptance of some change in the very notion of public service. Unless the baker's wife has deceived us (!), it is relatively unimportant whether the service provided to the community is public or private in nature. What matters is that it serves the interest of society as a whole. Consequently, we need to start by examining the links between the notion of services of general interest and that of citizenship: does citizenship imply guaranteed access to certain services (section 1)? If so, the next question concerns the identification of such services (section 2). We can then return to the question of the work performed in providing those services: does it call for a special legal regime, or not (section 3)? To conclude, a number of reflections are presented on the place of the notion of 'social' citizenship in an integrated Europe (section 4).

1. Services of General Interest and Citizenship

The very conception of citizenship axiomatically implies the existence of certain values of general interest that are shared by all citizens, since it is these common values which weld society into one. Originally, the notion of citizenship carried a purely political meaning deriving from Ancient Greece. In this sense it designates an equality of participation in public affairs. Power or authority lies at the centre, with all free adult males constituting a circle around it, each of them eligible to assume in turn the role of exercising it. This circular configuration finds concrete expression in the form of the agora, where all public business is debated, and contrasts with the pyramidal configuration of monarchy. Jean-Pierre Vernant has demonstrated the essential features of this citizenship:[1] substitution of the principle of equality for that of hierarchy, participation by all in the exercise of power, substitution of the spoken word for force as the means of dispute, and, lastly, contra-distinction of the private from the public. The private sphere, by its very nature, stands apart from citizenship as so defined. This private sphere encompasses the family in the etymological sense of the word: not only wife and children but also the body of household servants or slaves (*famuli*), or, in other terms, employees in a position of legal subordination.

In the nation-state model, the State constitutes the sole representative of the general interest. Consequently, citizenship tends to become identical with nationality and, equally, serving the general interest tends to become identical with serving the State. The exclusive role conferred on the State is manifested in, for example, the monopoly wielded by a country's Department of Public Prosecutions over representation of the general interest in the administration of justice. More generally, in systems of Romano-canon law it has resulted in the contra-distinction of the public sphere, as the domain of the general interest, from the private sphere, which is left to particular interests.

The Treaty of Rome, by contrast, places the concept of *serving the general interest* in a grey area which does not fall within either public law or pri-

[1] See J.-P. Vernant, *Les origines de la pensée grecque* (3rd edn., PUF, Paris, 1988), 119 ff.; and by the same author, 'Espace et organization politique en Grèce ancienne' (1965) 20 *Annales ESC* 576–95, republished in *Mythe et pensée chez les grecs* (Maspéro, Paris, 1965), 238–60.

vate law. Its Article 90(2) provides that undertakings entrusted with the operation of services of general economic interest shall be subject to the rules contained in the Treaty, and in particular to the rules on competition, 'in so far as the application of such rules does not obstruct the performance, in law or in fact, of the particular tasks assigned to them'. An area is thus explicitly designated which is identifiable neither with the exercise of state sovereign powers nor with the pursuit of free enterprise.[2] Admittedly, its contours are not delimited by the Treaty, which appears to leave it to the national laws of Member States to define which services are to be deemed 'services of general economic interest'. Nor has the Commission found it possible to structure this area entrapped in isolation between the State and the market. Nevertheless, the perspective of such a third sector, in which competition law must be reconciled with the general interest, has been upheld in the case law of the European Court of Justice, notably in the form of its *Paul Corbeau* and *Municipality of Almelo* decisions.[3] And proposals are emerging to extend its legal base in the Treaty.[4]

The above provision is to be compared with that of Article 48(4) of the Treaty, which makes 'employment in the public service' an exception to the principle of free movement of workers. In a number of well-known judgments the Court of Justice has imposed a Community definition of the notion of such employment, confining it to 'posts involving direct or indirect participation in the exercise of state sovereign authority and in duties bearing a responsibility for safeguarding the general interests of the state or other public collectivities'.[5] This functional criterion is based on the consideration that such posts presuppose a special relationship of allegiance to the State on the part of their holders and a reciprocity of the rights and obligations on which the bond of nationality is founded.[6]

The mere fact that the employer happens to be a public law body is therefore not enough to constitute exemption from the ordinary law of the labour market. Employment serving the general interest and employment serving the sovereign authority of the State, formerly perceived as identical in line, for example, with the French theory of public service, are here treated as separate notions. The reference to the 'general interests of the State or other public collectivities' suggests the existence of general

[2] See 'Les virtualités du droit communautaire: l'avenir des métiers de service public', in *Cahiers Juridiques de l'Electricité et du Gaz*, special issue, *Actualité de l'entreprise publique*, June 1994, 379 ff.

[3] Cases C–320/91, *Corbeau* [1993] ECR 2533 and C–393/92, *Municipality of Almelo and Others* [1994] ECR 1477.

[4] See CEEP, *Europe, concurrence et service public* (Masson-A.Colin, Paris, 1995).

[5] Case 149/79, *Commission* v. *Belgium* [1980] ECR 3881.

[6] Case 307/84, *Commission* v. *France* [1986] ECR 1725; Case 225/85, *Commission* v. *Italy* [1987] ECR 2625; Case 33/88, *Allué and Coonassu* v. *Università degli studi di Venezia* [1989] ECR 1591. See L. Dubouis, 'La notion d'emploi dans l'administration, publique et l'accès des ressortissants communautaires aux emplois publics' [1987] *Rev. fr. dr. adm.* 949. 962.

interests which are distinct from those of public law bodies. Such a suggestion has significant implications in that if, like the Court of Justice, we accept that nationality is inseparable from the notion of serving the interests of a given Member State, it has to be accepted that European citizenship is, in its turn, inseparable from general interests that transcend those of the Member States.

The very wording of Article 8e of the EC Treaty presents *citizenship of the Union* as an evolutive status characterized by the gradual accretion of new rights (or obligations) extending beyond the limited provisions adopted at Maastricht.[7] Such citizenship is seen as progressively acquiring substance, although without in any way encroaching on national citizenship: it is additional to the latter, not in place of it.[8] Hence it clearly designates a general interest which transcends, without negating, that of individual Member States. What, then, will be the substance of such European citizenship? The rights enumerated in Articles 8a–8d are of two kinds; first, rights of a political nature (vote and eligibility, diplomatic protection and petition) and, secondly, the extension to all such citizens of the freedom of movement and right of residence that were initially conferred only on workers. There are, therefore, two facets to this citizenship, one political and the other 'social'. The political facet, curbed as it is by the reaffirmation of national sovereignties, is perhaps unlikely ever to develop in any significant measure. By contrast, the social facet (better termed the 'socio-economic' facet) is by definition at the core of the Community dynamic. Consequently, social citizenship is potentially the most fruitful direction for the development of citizenship of the Union.

Social citizenship, just like political citizenship, may be defined as an equality of rights and obligations. They differ only in the nature of those rights and obligations, which are political in one case and socio-economic in the other. As so defined social citizenship includes, without question, equal access to certain essential services (i.e. services of general economic interest as referred to in Article 90(2) of the Treaty) of appropriate quality (not conceived in terms of universal minima). It also includes recognition of a freedom of labour construed not merely in formal terms but as the opportunity available to every individual to earn a living by performing a type of work that best expresses his or her personal talents and aspirations. This guarantee must not be confused with a right to employment (which relates only to work as an employee) but encompasses all forms of activity (on an employee or self-employed basis, market or non-

[7] Arts. 8a (freedom of movement), 8b (right to vote and to stand as a candidate in municipal and European elections), 8c (right to diplomatic protection) and 8d (right of petition). See J. Boudant, 'La citoyenneté européenne', in G. Koubi (ed.), *De la citoyenneté* (Litec, Paris, 1995); G. Sébastien, 'La citoyenneté européenne' [1993] *Rev. dr. pub.* 1263.

[8] Commission Opinion of 21 Oct. 1990, COM(90)600, *EC Bull.* 10/90, 16.

market, public or private) performed to supply something to others. Consequently, the services of general interest referred to in Article 90(2) and the notion of social citizenship of the Union invoke the same perception, in both cases, of a general interest capable of transcending national laws and Community competition law alike. But how is that perception constructed? What definition has been given, and might be given, to services of general interest in an integrated Europe?

2. The Identification of Services of General Interest

There is a certain ambiguity attaching to the notion of a public service which makes it preferable to use the alternative *service of general economic interest* as referred to in the Treaty. This is because the term 'public service' possesses two distinct meanings. In an organic sense, it designates a service provided by or under the authority of the State (as is the case, for instance, with public enterprises charged with responsibility for providing a service to the public). In a functional sense, however, the term designates a service which is indispensable to the general public, that is, a service of general interest. Such a service may equally well be provided by a public law body or a private legal person, but it is public in the sense that the general public must have uninterrupted access to it, which precludes its wholesale abandonment to competition law. Hence, a distinction needs to be drawn between serving the sovereign authority of the State and serving the public at large.

Even within an individual country, although the two largely overlap they are not identical. In France, for example, it is recognized that a private law organization may be given the task of providing a service to the public (the Social Security Offices are a case in point) or serving a general interest (the Supplementary Pension Schemes, for example), and that, conversely, certain activities performed by public bodies are subject to the rules of private law. This dissociation, originating from the famous case of 1921 referred to as the *Bac d'Eloka* judgment,[9] gave rise to the definition of the category of industrial and commercial public services, which is undoubtedly the closest to the categorization of services of general economic interest used in the Treaty of Rome. The real point is that there is no such thing as a public service by definition, since it is impossible to conceive of any service that cannot be provided through private-sector financing. The construct of a public service is therefore always an institutional one, founded on the choice of those services to which everyone must have uninterrupted and equal access. Although such choices may be influenced

[9] T.conf. 22 Jan. 1921 (*Société commerciale de l'Ouest africain*), Rec. 91; Dalloz 1921, 3, 1; Sirey 1924, 3, 34 with conclusions by Matter.

by technical considerations (territorial responsibility for networks, for example, with the argument applying as much to motorway systems as to railways or power lines) or by economic consideration (reduction of business costs, ban on *de facto* monopolies), in the final analysis it is the choice of values (or more prosaically, the choice of a type of society) which identifies the sense of community and forms part of the definition of citizenship.

As such, however, those choices fall within the sphere of positive law and are open to challenge. There is no reason why tomorrow it should not suddenly be deemed more essential to guarantee all French citizens equal access to a bakery, to banking services, or to street urinals (which, in disregard of the needs of the homeless and of the demands of the most undeniable of natural laws, have disappeared from our streets) than to air transport or the high-speed trains which daily intensify the process of rural depopulation and relentless urbanization. It is true that such choices carry with them compensation for their costs in the form of the universality, continuity, and equality of the service provided, and hence exemption from competition law. They also have redistributive effects that must be taken into account if an accurate picture of their social significance is to be obtained.

However, since their value is not universal they are manifestly vulnerable to international redefinition. The 'made in France' theory of public service, which has undoubtedly influenced the Latin countries and Catholic Belgium,[10] has not really been echoed elsewhere in Northern Europe.[11] That is not to say that these North European countries, with their Protestant culture, have failed to appreciate the necessity of guaranteeing access for everyone to certain services. What it means is that they have not made the State the pivot of the organization of those services. The notion of services of general economic interest might have been expected to be the focus of an attempt at a Community definition of *welfare*. Yet the organic criterion has been strangely dominant in the definition of these services, and Article 90 has become the repository (and an untidy one at that) of national perceptions of the general interest rather than the site of dynamic thinking on the notion of a European general interest.

[10] Conversely, the notion of a public social system or welfare state has led to the insertion into the French legal system of social-security models which are largely inspired by examples in other countries. France has exhibited little inventiveness on the matter, and its system is a costly hotchpotch of elements originally conceived in Germany and Great Britain, combined (with varying degrees of success) with specific national features: the role of mutuality, the importance attached to protected occupations, etc.: see the studies backed by MIRE, *Comparer les systèmes de protection sociale en Europe* (Rencontres d'Oxford, Imp. Nat., Paris, 1995), i, especially N. Kerschen, 'L'influence du rapport Beveridge sur le plan français de sécurité sociale', at 127 ff); *Rencontres de Berlin* (Rencontres de Florence, 1996), iii.

[11] See the overview presented on the subject by CEEP in *Europe, concurrence et service public*, n. 4 above.

Convincing evidence of this is obtained simply from examining, for example, the manner in which the common transport policy (Articles 74 ff., EC Treaty) has been implemented, particularly in the field of surface goods transport. The circumstances surrounding road transport have been changed profoundly by the effective implementation of freedom of establishment and freedom to provide services, and by the harmonization of competition conditions. The quota arrangements designed to prevent excess supply have been dismantled;[12] contributions by hauliers from one Member State towards the financing of infrastructures of which they make use in another Member State have been ruled to be in contravention of the Treaty;[13] and road haulage charges have been deregulated,[14] resulting in lower earnings for drivers and prompting some to call for a 'safety-level mileage tariff'.[15] Safety in this sector does indeed give cause for concern, with 50,000 people killed and 1.6 million injured every year on the roads of the Europe of the Twelve.[16]

In the case of rail transport, on the other hand, European integration seems as yet to have had very little impact at all, and the Europe of the railways is a juxtaposition of national networks controlled by individual Member States. The first significant Community measures are only recent, consisting in an obligation to separate infrastructure and operating accounts (the so-called *unbundling rule*) and recognition of a right of transit for the provision of international services.[17] In other words, it has been just as if the reference to services of general economic interest was relevant only at national level, even though the field in question concerns a common policy (transport), i.e. one where Community-level thinking on the general interest should surely have been a matter of course. If it is consigned to the margins of Community policy in this way, the idea of services of general interest is clearly doomed to ossification. And as viewed by public opinion, Europe gives the impression of being the grave-digger of national public services, not the inventor of transnational public services. In this context, the Swiss were not mistaken when they identified the Europe of the Community with the liberalization, with the brakes off, of heavy goods traffic. And heavy goods lorries without brakes are certainly a cause for disquiet.

The only way in which this situation can change is if the question of the general interest in regard to the surface transport of goods is considered in

12 Regulations 1841/88 (OJ 1988 L163/1) and 881/92 (OJ 1992 L95/1).

13 Case C–195/9OR, *Commission* v. *Germany* [1990] ECR I–3351.

14 Regulation 4058/89 (OJ 1989 L390/1).

15 See *Bull. Transports* 1990, 593.

16 'La politique européenne des transports à l'horizon 1992', in EC Commission, *Le dossier de l'Europe* (EC Commission, Brussels, Aug. 1992).

17 Directives 91/440 (OJ 1991 L237/25) with additional directives for its application of 19 June 1995; 95/18 (OJ 1995 L143/70) concerning operating licences; and 95/19 (OJ 1995 L143/73) concerning the allocation of infrastructure capacities.

its full context,[18] i.e. examined in terms of road transport and rail transport together. This could have some very unwelcome implications in both cases. First, it would involve accepting that considerations of the general interest are likely to impose far tighter constraints on road transport, particularly as regards working conditions and environmental aspects. Secondly, it would involve questioning the justification for the monopolies and company regulatory systems that are characteristic of the railways sector. In both cases, thinking on the general interest in regard to transport would inevitably have an impact on the legal regime of employment in the sector.

3. The Legal Regime of Employment in the Provision of Services of General Interest

Assuming that employment serving the general interest is treated as separate from employment in the service of the State, and that it therefore does not necessarily relate to employment within the public administration, is it axiomatically governed entirely by ordinary labour law? Does employment in the provision of public services have special features and, if so, what are they?[19] In the case of French law, the answer to this question has been twofold. Certain public services are categorized purely and simply as being in the service of the State, and those employed within them are therefore covered by the special service regulations governing employment in the public administration. This applies, for example, to education, postal services, and the public health service.

By contrast, so-called industrial and commercial public services are usually provided by public enterprises whose employees are covered by regimes which, although based in general on employment within the public administration, are distinct from it.[20] Unlike the special service regimes governing employment within the public administration, these regimes incorporate a link with private law: employees are bound to the enterprise through a contract of employment and are therefore in principle covered

[18] The only real example of such an approach seems to have been in regard to future policy, through the standardization of the accounting rules applicable to road, rail, and inland waterways infrastructures: Regulation 1108/70 (OJ 1970 L130/4) as amended by Regulation 1384/79 (OJ 1979 L167/1).

[19] On this point, see the following existing discussions: 'La crise de l'esprit de service public' [1989] *Dr. soc.* 777; 'L'avenir des métiers de service public et le droit communautaire', *Cahiers Juridiques de l'Electricité et du Gaz*, n. 2 above, 379–87; 'Le travail et l'opposition public/privé', in (1996) 136 *International Labour Review.*

[20] On these regulations, see two works of reference: J. Chorin, *Le particularisme des relations de travail dans les entreprises publiques à statut* (LGDJ, Paris, 1994); Ch. Garbar, *Le droit applicable au personnel des entreprises publiques* (LGDJ, Paris, 1996).

by labour law. Because this applies only within the limits prescribed by the relevant service regulations, it is often said that, in a public enterprise, the latter fulfil the role played by collective agreements in the private sector. However, the analogy quickly finds its limits, since they represent a unilateral act of a regulatory nature which is not subject to collective bargaining and whose interrelations with labour law give rise to numerous legal difficulties.

These service regimes were the cornerstone of a set of professional ethics common to managers and those managed, in which job security and security of income were inseparable from the continuity and universal accessibility of the service being provided to the public. In this, special service regimes and the State reveal their common origin: the status that gives a community its meaning.[21] Over the years, however, this close tie between public services and special service regimes has been eroded. The stringency and rigidity of these regimes make them difficult to adapt to technical and economic change. On the management side, there have been attempts by public enterprises to circumvent the obstacles they present by resorting to subcontracting or introducing legal formulas imported from the private sector (collective bargaining,[22] merit pay). But circumventing special service regimes rather than reforming them merely served to hasten their ossification. The unions, for their part, sought to combine the advantages of public law service regimes with those of private-sector employment whenever the latter were felt to be more favourable.[23] As a result, labour law has, to varying degrees, left its stamp on special service regimes, which have accommodated the right to join a union, the right to strike, and, then, the right to collective bargaining. It has thus encroached at both ends of the hierarchical ladder: at the top with the cumulation by senior managers of the advantages of both public law employment (security of tenure, relative non-accountability) and private-sector employment (*pantouflage*[24] and its derivatives), and at the bottom with the swelling

[21] See P. Legendre *Les enfants du Texte* (Fayard, Paris, 1992), 110 ff.

[22] See N. Maggi-Germain, *Négociation collective et transformation des entreprises publiques à statut* (LGDJ, Paris, 1996).

[23] Nowadays this viewpoint is supported by the Cour de Cassation, which in such cases applies the 'fundamental principle whereby, in the event of conflicting rules, that to be applied is the one most favourable to the employee'; Soc. 17 July 1996 (SNCF and EDF) Dr. Soc, 1996, 1049, concl. G Lyon-Caen.

[24] *Pantouflage* is the popular term used in France to describe the widespread practice whereby high-ranking civil servants leave public service to take up managerial posts in large private-sector enterprises. Of the 15 leading industrial enterprises in France, 12 are headed by such former civil servants, and barely 20% of the heads of large enterprises have spent their entire career in the sector. During the past 10 years all these trends have become even more marked, despite (or because of?) the privatizations that have taken place. See the report on the latest study by M. Mauer and B. Bertin-Mourot of CNRS in *Le Monde*, 17 Feb. 1995.

numbers of quasi-civil servants under job-creation contracts[25] and quasi-public employees in subcontracting enterprises.[26]

In the light of these developments, the notion of public services no longer signifies the same thing as the state administration in the form of the high-ranking *corps* of civil servants who manage them (notably those in the technical *corps*) and the ordinary public employees who work in them. For the former, the notion of public service is tending to become identified with a demand for efficiency and minimum cost that runs up against the special service regimes, which are now perceived at best as an archaism and at worst as a poison jeopardizing the very survival of public services. In the minds of many of these managers, the divorce between special service regimes and public service is already complete. By contrast, to workers and the unions special service regimes represent the last bastion of the spirit of public service; which they see as having been betrayed by those managers and by the State. For them, the defence of special service regimes is therefore identified with the defence of public services; it is at once a way of preserving their acquired rights and of reminding the State of its duties towards the public at large. In such a context, it is easy to see why special service regimes have become a particularly explosive issue. It is because the State, and hence the heads of public enterprises, no longer embody commitment to the general interest in the eyes of public-sector employees that the latter are turning to the legal regime governing their employment in order to defend their idea of that general interest. It is these developments that explain the repeated and serious labour disputes which have marked the life of public enterprises since the end of the 1980s.[27]

At first sight, the movement towards flexibilization of the law applicable to employment in the public sector in France appears to be part of a tendency common to a number of European countries. Starting from Great Britain, this movement has progressively gained ground in continental Europe, although in widely diverse forms. The most widespread tendency has been to pluck services of general economic interest from the bosom of the public administration[28] and entrust their management to

25 Code du travail Art. L.322–4–7: this refers to employment under *contrats emploi-solidarité*, i.e. fixed-term and part-time contracts of employment confined to public institutions and non-profit-making associations.

26 On this subject, see M.-L. Morin, 'Sous-traitance et relations salariales' (1994) 60 *Travail et Emploi* 23 ff.

27 See La crise de l'esprit de service publics, n. 19 above; and 'Malaise dans le social' [1996] *Dr. soc.* 115.

28 As in the case of postal services, where a recent study reveals that, of 15 enterprises in the countries surveyed, whereas in 1990 there were still 7 that had special public administration service regulations, by 1996 none did.

independent legal entities, whether public[29] or private.[30] The aim everywhere has been to create legal structures suited to the opening up of competition and hence to internationalization, decentralization,[31] and the contractualization of relations with users, who are nowadays perceived more as customers. Nowhere, however, has the movement amounted to total privatization, which would signify a straightforward alignment of services of general interest with commercial law.[32] Even where the reforms have been pursued most vigorously, as in Great Britain, the State has certainly not retreated from the scene, and still features as the ultimate guardian of the general interest. The route adopted has been the establishment of 'regulatory' authorities responsible for ensuring that this general interest is satisfied.[33] The process is thus more accurately described as one of autonomization rather than privatization: services of general economic interest are made independent of state sovereign authority without becoming identified with the sphere of private interests. Here again, therefore, we have an instance of the area of social citizenship, defined as an area of general interest distinct from the interest of the State.

This trend of development in legal structures for the provision of services of general interest has been accompanied by fresh thinking on the terms and conditions of employment of the personnel concerned in cases where they were formerly exempt from ordinary law. It is a point that needs to be emphasized, since it suggests the existence of a link between the definition of services of general interest and the legal regime for those employed in providing the services. The redefinition of the legal regime of employment in public services has varied widely from one country to

[29] See, e.g., the conversion of the Swedish and Italian railways into public enterprises (the *Statens Järnvägar* in 1988 and the *Ferrovie dello Stato* in 1986) and that of the German postal services in 1994.

[30] Such privatization may be purely legal (a commercial company with the State as its sole shareholder: *cf.* the creation in 1994 of the *Deutsche Bundesbahn AG*, a state-controlled public limited company in Germany, and similarly, since 1992, *Statens Vattenfallsverk* in Sweden in the field of electricity supply) or also economic (with the privatization of capital: see, e.g., the case in Great Britain in respect of electricity supply since 1990 and telecommunications since 1984).

[31] A borderline case is the split-up of British railways in 1994 into 25 train operating units headed by the British Railways Board. Decentralization has existed for a long time in certain sectors, such as electricity supply in Germany, where it is linked to the country's federal structure.

[32] For an overall view, see Y. Moreau, *Entreprises de service public européennes et relations sociales. L'acteur oublié* (ASPE, Paris, 1996), 222, and the collected articles in (1996) 136 *International Labour Review*, special issue.

[33] See, e.g., the role entrusted to the *Eisenbahnbundesamt* in the recent reform of German railways or to the rail regulator in Great Britain and, in the electricity supply sector, to *Svenska Kraftnät* in Sweden or to Offer in Great Britain.

another, for reasons connected both with national cultures[34] and with the negotiations that produced the reforms in question.[35]

The organic criterion of the private or public nature of the employer is therefore less likely than ever to justify any difference of treatment in the legal regime of employees providing services of general economic interest. Consequently, the natural inclination of the Community institutions, always reluctant to take bold action in matters of social policy, will probably be to leave this question to national laws, possibly invoking the principle of subsidiarity. That solution would not really be satisfactory, however, since it presumes that the legal regime of employment makes no difference to the proper performance of functions of general interest, and such a presumption is unsound. The factor which is unimportant, at Community level, is the public or private nature of the employment relationship. Article 48, as interpreted by the Court of Justice, does not make this an obstacle to the free movement of workers. It is, on the other hand, important that the terms and conditions of employment should be reconcilable with a guarantee of equal access for all European citizens to services of equal quality throughout Union territory.

The institution of this social area cannot fail to have implications for terms and conditions of employment in the services of general interest concerned. There is known to be a direct link between precariousness of employment and the incidence of accidents at work.[36] In addition to ignorance of the risks involved, the uncertainty regarding tomorrow that is characteristic of precarious employment inevitably has an effect on observance of the law. For example, the rules on driving times in the road transport sector[37] have no chance of being obeyed when the precariousness of his employment forces the driver to achieve the output required by his employer or his principal.[38] To permit fixed-term contracts or 'self-drive' (drivers who hire their vehicle) is therefore tantamount to accepting that there will be accidents. Here, safety at work goes hand in hand with job security, the only context that instils a calm approach to time in the

[34] The attachment to special service regimes is linked in France, e.g., with an exalted conception of the State which is manifestly absent in Italy.

[35] See, e.g., the German arrangement permitting the maintenance of a civil service regime for current railway employees, or the maintenance of civil service regulations in the French postal and telecommunications sector despite the abandonment of the public administration regime.

[36] From sources which also include the recital of the aims of Directive 91/383 concerning atypical employment. Testimony by witnesses, surveys, and statistics are all in agreement on this point: see *Souffrances et précarite au travail. Paroles de médecins du travail*, collected works (Syros, Paris, 1994), 357; 'Le dossier noir du travail précaire', in *Santé et Travail*, No. 8/94.

[37] Regulation 3820/85 of 20 Dec. 1985.

[38] See M. Hautdidier and P. Ramackers, 'La durée du travail est-elle contrôllable? Reflexion sur une évolution à partir de l'exemple des transports routiers' [1995] *Dr. soc.* 333; plus the numerous sociological studies devoted to this occupation, and in particular: B. Lefebvre, *Les routiers* (Syros, Paris, 1993).

employee.[39] The use of fixed-term and temporary contracts, which has been intensified in the haulage industry by the deregulation promoted at Community level, is therefore incompatible with the requirements of the general interest. Far from excluding Community intervention, the principle of subsidiarity would appear to justify it fully in this case.

The same argument can be demonstrated in the case of the maintenance of nuclear power stations. The public enterprise Electricité de France has subcontracted this maintenance work to private enterprises, which recruit employees for the purpose on a fixed-term basis. These subcontractors practise a form of 'job management by dose', terminating the contract of employment as soon as an employee has received the maximum permissible dose of radiation. As a result this encourages the employees concerned, in order to keep their jobs, to conceal the actual doses of radiation they receive.[40] The enterprise's own permanent staff, for their part, suffer a loss of expertise and control over the conditions in which the maintenance work is carried out. The link between lack of job security and lack of nuclear safety is obvious here, and the general interest should prompt a ban on the use of precarious forms of employment for such work.[41] In French law, 'protection of the health and safety of persons and property' ranks as a constitutional principle, and this can result in certain employment relationships being made subject to special rules.[42]

What has been said here regarding transport and electricity generation could equally well apply, *mutatis mutandis*, to all services of relevance to the general economic interest, regardless of whether the suppliers of those services are public or private. Social citizenship implies, for example, the possibility of being treated with the attention due to a sick person (not a customer or user) in any country within the Union in which one happens to fall ill, something which is not without its relevance to the employment regime of hospital staff. To give another example, it implies the possibility of obtaining information freely, and hence that the employment regime of journalists should protect them both from the sovereign authority of the

[39] Community law affords this fact low-key recognition when it authorizes Member States to prohibit precarious forms of employment for certain particularly dangerous types of work: Directive 91/383, Art. 5(1). But it is difficult to see how such action can be left to the judgement of individual Member States in a highly competitive and trans-border sector such as transport, which is, furthermore, the subject of a common European policy.

[40] See G. Deniol-Shaw, D. Huez, and N. Sandret, *Les intermittents du nucléaire. Enquête sur le travail en sous-traitance dans la maintenance des centrales nucléaires* (Octares, Paris, 1995), 250. Some 80.85% of the total annual radiological doses sustained by all employees who work in monitored zones are received by employees of subcontractors (*ibid.*, 193).

[41] The Ministry of Labour is envisaging the imposition of such a ban (see *Le Monde*, 23 Jan. 1997, 8). The company Manpower has retorted by warning its employees of the risk to their employment that such a measure would present (*Le Monde*, 9/10 Feb. 1997, 8).

[42] *C. const.*: dec. 80–117 DC, 22 July 1980—Protection des matières nucléaires [1980] *Dr. soc.* 441, comm. D. Turpin [1980] *Pouvoirs* No. 15, 172, comm. P. Avril and J. Gicquel; [1980] *RDP* 1652, comm. L. Favoreu (justification of a restriction of the right to strike).

State and from private interests. More generally, it implies the guarantee of continuity, equal access, and quality, and here the consequences for employment regimes cannot be general and abstract, but must be dealt with sector by sector and be unaffected by the public or private nature of the jobs concerned. Hence, the social rights of the citizen represent an ideal area for the implementation, at sectoral level, of the collective bargaining opportunities opened up by the Maastricht Agreement.

4. Citizenship and the European Social Model

There are, however, reasons for doubting that the notion of citizenship represents an adequate basis for a social model that also observes the values of liberty, equality, and solidarity. By defining a social constituency that excludes non-citizens (i.e. barbarians in Ancient Greece and non-Community nationals in modern-day Europe) it contradicts the universal nature of the rights it protects. By definition, citizenship discriminates between citizens and non-citizens in reserving for the former the full exercise of the equality and solidarity it establishes. For example, basing freedom of movement on European citizenship and no longer on the fact of being a worker means denying freedom of movement to foreign workers who are normally resident in one of the Member States. Similarly, making access to public services or social protection an attribute of European citizenship means denying that access to non-citizens.[43]

The coverage of human rights in regard to employment is not the same as that of citizenship, and basing such rights on citizenship will necessarily exclude from them all workers who are non-Community nationals. Given the respective demographic and economic trends in the Member States and their neighbours to the south and east, the already large numbers of such workers can only increase. And the influence of the European model will depend on its capacity to be a prolific melting-pot of cultures, not a confederation of the privileged inward-turning few.

The question that therefore arises is how the development of a European citizenship can be reconciled with the universality of the social rights that are recognized in Europe. For some, the only point of reference capable of transcending nationality is the market. They reason that,

[43] See J.-J. Dupeyroux and X. Prétot, 'Le droit de l'étranger à la protection sociale' [1994] *Dr. soc.* 69, comment on C. constit., dec. 93–325 DC of 13 Aug. 1993. Whereas earlier case law had based the right of foreign nationals to social protection on the principle of equality (C. constit. dec. 89–269 DC of 22 Jan. 1990, *Rec.* 33 [1990] *Dr. soc.* 352, note Prétot [1990] *RFDA* 406, note Genevois), this judgment bases it on the fundamental freedoms and rights of constitutional ranking—'although the legislators may adopt special provisions with regard to foreign nationals, it is incumbent on them to observe the fundamental freedoms and rights which are constitutionally guaranteed to all those who reside on French territory'.

whereas 'social rights' are always ultimately dependent on membership of a particular social group, 'economic rights' are, by contrast, subject to no limits other than those of the market. Since the market concept which presided over the creation of the European Community is capable of gradual extension to all the products and services of all countries, the calculated harmony which presides over market relations can, they conclude, encompass the whole of humanity. And since it is a question of regulating access to services of an economic nature, the citizen must be treated as a consumer.

The strength of this thesis (which is in the tradition of the doctrine of utilitarianism from which economic ideology emerged[44]) lies in the fact that the market is the only institution to exclude all discrimination other than that based on money. It is alone in incorporating the concept of universal formal equality. With all institutions founded on the principle of solidarity, the collective interest prevails over that of the individual, and the interest of the group members prevails over that of outsiders.[45] The thesis therefore has the merit of reminding us that every solidarity-based legal system involves a hierarchization of the interests present.

It is unconvincing, on the other hand, in the radical separation it operates between economic rights (capable of being universal) and social rights (particular by nature). To put it bluntly, this opposition of the economic and the social makes no sense: no legal bond exists which does not have both an economic dimension and a social dimension. The employment relationship, for example, is indissolubly an economic relationship and a social relationship.[46] Markets are instituted, as regards their legal aspects, in conditions that are heavily influenced by 'social' (national) factors. To talk of a common labour market within an area where, for example, some enterprises bear the cost of employees' sickness insurance while others are free of this burden because it is borne by the State[47] would be an abuse of language.

If we acknowledge the truth of these facts we are led to distinguish rights not according to their assumed economic or social natures but

[44] On economic ideology, see the classic work by Louis Dumont, *Homo œqualis. I. Genèse et épanouissement de l'idéologie économique* (2nd edn., Gallimard, Paris, 1985), 270 and *From Mandeville to Marx. The Genesis and Triumph of Economic Ideology* (Univ. Chicago Press, Chicago, Ill., 1977).

[45] Cf. the definition of the principle of solidarity adopted by the ECJ: Joined Cases C–159/91 and 160/91, C. *Poucet and Others* v. *Assurances Générales* [1993] ECR I–637 [1993] *Dr. soc.* 488, note by Laigre and Dupeyroux; Case C–244/94 *Fédération française des sociétés d'assurance* [1995] ECR L–4022 [1996] *Dr. soc.*, note by Laigre.

[46] And yet the ECJ has followed these same tramlines, deeming that the activity of social-security bodies (whose volume in financial terms exceeds the state budget in France) was not of an economic nature; and, conversely, that the activity of a public employment service was economic in nature and did not fall within the sphere of solidarity.

[47] See A. Supiot, 'Du bon usage des lois en matière d'emploi' *Dr. Soc.* 1997, 229–42.

rather according to the degree of universality that we attribute to the values they express. At one extreme there are values which possess a universal character because they attach to the human condition. They are, in particular, the values that underlie human rights. A vocabulary expressed in terms of 'rights' is perhaps not the most appropriate means of affirming the universal character of these values, given the narrowly western nature of the notion of personal rights as opposed to the general rules of law, but it is certainly suited to their affirmation and application in the European context. At the other extreme there are values which are directly linked to a narrowly defined national membership. In the words of the Court of Justice, such membership designates 'a special relationship of allegiance to the state together with a reciprocity of the rights and obligations on which the bond of nationality is founded'.[48]

Between these universal rights and national rights, with the notion of European citizenship we are immediately in an intermediate area. It would therefore be possible to accept that access to this status exists not only by virtue of national membership (of a Member State) but also by virtue of employment. Such access to citizenship by virtue of employment obviously relates, first, to non-Community nationals who work on Union territory, and as such will be accorded the same social and economic rights as Member State nationals. It could, however, be taken a step further by accepting that those who, although working outside Union territory, are so employed on behalf of European enterprises (either as posted workers or under subcontracting arrangements) should likewise enjoy at least some of the rights attaching to this 'social' (i.e socio-economic) citizenship. With a conception of citizenship expanded in such ways the European 'social model' could truly be given universal scope.

[48] See the ECJ judgments already cited: Case 307/84, *Commission* v. *France* [1986] ECR 1725; Case 225/85, *Commission* v. *Italy* [1987] ECR 2625; and Case 33/88, *Allué and Coonassu* v. *Università degli studi di Venezia* [1989] ECR 1591.

10

Labour Law—a Bridge between Public Services and Citizenship Rights

SILVANA SCIARRA

1. A New Centrality for Labour Law

One of the aims of this book is to construct a new paradigm and adopt it as a frame of reference for the formulation of new citizenship rights. The novelty of such rights consists in the fact that they are dependent on the contract of employment, thus coinciding with a traditional, albeit not exhaustive, definition of social rights; they should also be seen as a pre-condition for the granting of public service status, which has been widely analysed earlier in the book, especially in those chapters employing the language and methodology of public law. This paradigm is at the moment mainly a descriptive one, although the ambition is that it might acquire a normative relevance and influence policy-making, at both a national and a supranational level.

Labour law adds interesting insights to this methodological challenge. In most European countries this discipline has offered a very rich background to the debate on legal pluralism, not only because of the recurring co-existence of different sources in the regulation of contracts of employment, but also because of the creative role played by employers' and employees' associations in the definition of such rules.[1]

Furthermore, as a result of flexible and often original approaches adopted by legislators, combined with the innovations brought about by collective bargaining, labour law has always represented an ideal ground for both theory and practice of legal comparison and still contributes immensely to the circulation of new legal approaches and methodologies. For the same reasons, this discipline has been at the intersection of the private and public spheres of legal regulation, because of its historical ambition to cover mandatory issues on the one hand and to nurture

[1] K. W. Wedderburn, R. Lewis, J. Clark, *Labour Law and Industrial Relations: Building on Kahn-Freund* (Clarendon, Oxford, 1983); G. Balandi and S. Sciarra (eds.), *Il pluralismo e il diritto del lavoro* (Ed. Lavoro, Rome, 1982); P. Davies and M. Freedland, *Labour Legislation and Public Policy* (Clarendon, Oxford, 1993).

freedom of contract on the other. This divide did not necessarily follow the contraposition state *v.* private employment; it rather indicated an inborn ability of this relatively modern legal discipline to seek the protection of individual and collective rights of the employee through legislation of public relevance, while at the same time fully respecting the somewhat limited—and yet recognized—autonomy of the two parties entering a contract of employment.

The tendency discernible nowadays in most legal systems to demolish all divides, and to attach no relevance to the public or private nature of the employer is taken into account in the discourse that links together different contributions in this book. Privatization of the employer may mean, as has been exemplified in some of the papers, that a public service will be provided by a private entity; this will in most cases affect the nature of the employment contract and have indirect consequences for those to whom the service is addressed. Privatization may also—as in a recent Italian legislative reform[2]—be extended to the contract of employment itself, thus abolishing almost all distinctions between public and private employees and equalizing all legal treatments.[3]

The latter choice may be inspired either by the desire to eliminate old privileges associated with public contracts of employment or by the intention to inject fresh air into the apparatus of public administration, introducing new elements of competitiveness and efficiency. In both cases labour law is used as a modernizing tool, as a channel for innovation which, especially in times of economic constraint, must be able to satisfy the needs of the administration and yet continue to guarantee rights for employees.

In this very general perspective, one of the aims of this book is to link labour law with those sections of the formerly public—sometimes still public—sectors of the economy in which services of public relevance are being provided, regardless of the private or public nature of the employer. The definition of a third sector, suggested in Chapter 1, is extremely useful for an understanding of the very specific connotations which may be attributed to contracts of employment, and in particular to the employer and the employee considered individually as holders of rights and obligations.

In using this terminology we are aware of the fact that the same terminology has also been adopted in different contexts. One is the ever-growing area of the economy occupied by non-profit organizations, interesting in comparative terms as a symptom of the differentiated and

[2] See further section 9 below.

[3] A comparative perspective on this point is in Y. Moreau, *Entreprises de service public européennes et relations sociales. L'acteur oublié* (ASPE, Paris, 1996), 167 ff.

increasing demands of citizens which States are not fully capable of satisfying.[4] Even those not-for-profit or voluntary organizations operating at an intermediate level between citizens and States are, in a broad sense, service providers, and as such not far removed from the perspective adopted in this book. Nevertheless, the emphasis we put on labour law as a channel for the interpretation of new citizenship rights makes our perception of the third sector rather different and shows that the same expression may be adopted in different disciplinary approaches. A few preliminary points will be indicated in the attempt to build a bridge between labour law and new citizenship rights.

2. Rights to be Exercised within the Enterprise

One of the tasks historically assigned to labour law has been to favour the consolidation of citizenship rights within the enterprise,[5] ranging from the right to vote and to be represented to the right to free expression, freedom of speech, and so on. Trade union rights have a tradition of their own, although it can be said that they become stronger and more significant in an environment of workplace democracy. With regard to these rights, labour law may appear as a self-determined field, with its own rules and its own legitimation, an island of industrial citizenship within a wider context of political citizenship. Indeed, an analogy is often drawn between political rights and union rights, with special emphasis on the similarities which can be found or constructed in the system of representation.[6] Such an exercise may imply a misconception of collective interests supported by both management and labour as interests of very general application, whereas the tendency seems to be that they often constitute fragmented sections of the labour market and continue to ignore those who have never had access to it.

[4] To quote only significant examples in a very extensive bibliography, see H. K. Anheier and W. Seibel (eds.), *The Third Sector: Comparative Studies of Nonprofit Organizations* (Berlin-New York, 1990); P. Donati, *La cittadinanza societaria* (Laterza, Roma-Bari, 1993).

[5] A. Supiot, 'Citoyenneté et entreprise', in G. Koubi (ed.), *De la citoyenneté* (Litec, Paris, 1995); G. Lyon-Caen, *Les libertés publiques et l'emploi, Rapport au ministre du travail, de l'emploi et de la formation professionnelle* (La documentation Française, Paris, 1992). Of particular interest in this report is the proposal, *de lege ferenda* in the French system, to introduce an elected employee representative (*délegué élu aux libertés individuelles*) with the particular function—of a primarily symbolic value—of protecting individual freedoms at the place of work (see 167–8).

[6] The French debate on union 'representativeness' held a few years ago still represents an example of strong ideological confrontation. See in particular J. M.Verdier, 'Sur la relation entre représentation et représentativité syndicales' [1991] *DS* 5 ff. and G. Borenfreund, 'La représentation des salariés et l'idée de représentation' [1991] *DS* 685 ff, and also, more recently 'Pouvoir de répresentation et negociation collective' [1997] *DS* 1006.

Whatever perspective one might have chosen—totally internal to labour law or projected towards a broader political context—the enterprise level was considered a crucial one for the exercise of constitutional rights and for the shaping of legislation in a mature phase of labour law developments.[7] Even under the pressure of redistributive measures, which might have led to the redefinition—sometimes the diminution—of individual and collective rights, the enterprise remains the place in which constitutional principles are presented as the outcome of labour law developments. Such a strong contribution from a very specific disciplinary approach may or may not rest on the foundations of strong constitutional traditions and, more specifically, constitutional rights. We shall see that this difference has certain implications in comparative terms, as well as in policy orientations, especially when we come to discuss the weakness of constitutional social rights at Community level.

The constitutional foundation of rights becomes even more significant if we remember that the centrality of the enterprise is not all that obvious, whenever radical changes in production cause the decline of organizational hierarchies and favour the spread of networks. Organizational changes of this kind, strategically oriented towards wider and dynamic markets, bring with them more flexible rules at the place of work and the need to adapt to different and continually changing market demands. Citizenship rights at the enterprise level are constantly challenged. This explains the importance of constructing them as a patrimony of the individual employee, entitled to carry them with him through the various phases of his working life and following, when necessary, organizational changes occurring within the enterprise.

Citizenship rights at the enterprise level are not taken into direct account in the present analysis, although they must be accorded an indirect relevance. Rules of democracy at the place of work are included in the definition of constitutional citizenship which was offered in chapter 1; in the third sector, when the provision of public services is at stake, constitutional rights stemming from an employment relationship and rooted in the enterprise constitute a strong guarantee for the fair definition of other rules, to which the provision of the service concerned is related or on which it depends. They must, therefore, be considered a preliminary and indispensable step towards the consolidation of other citizenship rights.

The third sector is not meant to be a land of deregulation, nor a battlefield on which old constitutional traditions will be put to flight. It must be maintained that a meaningful commitment on the part of both national legislatures and European Community institutions is necessary in order to strengthen the links of the third sector with labour law and to encourage

[7] P. Davies and M. Freedland, *Kahn-Freund's Labour and the Law* (3rd edn. Stevens, London, 1983).

the definition of constitutional citizenship, while enhancing the rules of economic profitability and managerial efficiency. The declining centrality of the enterprise in other sectors of the economy makes all efforts and experiments in the third sector particularly germane. A new dimension of labour law is that of being able to cross the boundaries of the enterprise and confront constitutional citizenship outside it, while being aware of the constraints imposed by market citizenship. It must be stressed that such a dimension requires an active role on the part of employers' and employees' organizations, asked to perform their traditional function, while becoming aware of the unique characteristics of the third sector.

3. Collective Rights and Citizenship Rights

The quasi-public role acquired in most European countries by employers' and employees' organizations often leads to the conclusion in public opinion that they can be defenders of general and public interests on the economic and political scene, while continuing to be key actors in the definition and guarantee of sectoral interests. This point is relevant for the arguments developed in this book: no mechanical substitution of the political actors is envisaged, even when labour law, in various fields, refers to collective bargaining or to other functions traditionally performed by management and labour. Consequently, the general interest is not synonymous with the collective interest, if by the latter we mean—as in labour law parlance—the interests advanced by collective organizations respectively representing management and labour. This must be understood despite the fact that employees simultaneously enjoy the status of consumers and of citizens.

It is indeed crucial for the definition of the third sector to draw a line between citizens as employees and citizens as consumers. The latter may be granted special rights of access to public services and may demand that the quality and continuity of such services reach certain standards, as well as expecting that all public services are kept under close scrutiny and tariffs are controlled. External evaluators or specialized agencies—both private and public bodies acting as market authorities—are increasingly often brought into the picture, in order to establish and enforce fair rules for the provision of the service concerned. Whether as administrative agencies or as independent bodies, they bring about a system of legal guarantees for citizens/consumers which is generically different from that of the past; better protection is achieved in the market than in a system of 'vote maximizers', indifferent as such to the goals of efficiency and productivity.[8]

[8] See Amato, ch. 8 of this vol.

All this has to do with the position of consumers in a regulated market; prior to this, the decision to give substance to consumers' rights in constitutional rights—such as the right to education and the right to health—is traditionally left to national legislatures. Even in the absence of a constitution, legislators may decide that consumers are entitled to rights as citizens of the country concerned. The extension of citizenship rights of this kind to non-nationals rests in the hands of state authorities, with the possible exception of rights linked to the free movement of persons (and of workers) within the European Union.[9]

The novelty to be shown in legal analysis is that, because of the very special role played by labour law, consumers acquire a new status: their needs with regard to public services may not be disregarded even when labour law issues are at stake. Labour disputes cannot conflict with the provision of services; obligations under the contract of employment—the required proper performance of work and observance of working hours and disciplinary codes, to name but a few examples—must coincide with the welfare of consumers, that is to say with their rights as progressively defined in the process (which varies according to legal traditions in different countries) of enlarging citizenship rights.

Furthermore, through contracts of employment two separate and yet coinciding goals can be achieved: in granting rights to the employee—ranging from the protection of dignity at work to stability in employment and seniority rights—the quality of the public service is to be expected as an outcome of contractual obligations. Public interest becomes synonymous with fair implementation of employment contracts, regardless of the private or public nature of the employer. While leaving to the State the definition of general interests, employment contracts become a means to an end: they establish rules of mutual interest between the parties and yet they contribute to the strengthening of constitutional citizenship.[10] Especially when it comes to the furthering of European integration, management and labour are more than aware of the constraints imposed by market citizenship. As bearers of consensus and promoters of so-called social pacts, they are key actors in the definition of voluntary, non-binding guidelines, which then become stringent, and essential to the implementation of national and supranational economic policies.[11]

[9] See Supiot, ch. 9 of this vol., H. Verschueren, 'Libre circulation des personnes et protection sociale minimale' [1996] *R du MUE* 83 ff.

[10] Y. Moreau, 'Transformation de la relation de travail dans les entreprises de service public', in *Le travail en perspectives* (Coll. Droit et Société, LGDS 1998), 427 ff.

[11] 'Social pacts. Alliance for employment, Discussion and working papers of ETUI, 96.01.1', S. Sciarra, 'Collective Agreements in the Hierarchy of European Community Sources', in P. Davies, A. Lyon-Caen, S. Sciarra, and S. Simitis (eds.), *European Community Labour Law: Principles and Perspectives* (Clarendon, Oxford, 1996), 208 ff.

This is not irrelevant for the legal discourse to be developed in the third sector. Consumers and citizens demand the expansion of public services, thus favouring the expansion of state functions different from those traditionally exercised as a sign of authority and sovereignty.[12] In the attempt to respond to the requests coming from very diffuse groups, state powers have become increasingly dispersed and public services increasaingly disseminated and often decentralized. The 'osmotic' State, as opposed to one capable of monopolizing all rules and expressing very generalized values, operates in order to introduce efficiency at all levels of its apparatus; it coordinates the various levels of intervention, favouring competition or privatization and regulating public services wherever there is a lack of control over tariffs or the quality of the services themselves.[13]

The peculiarities of the third sector could, in perspective, influence the overall exercise of collective rights and introduce a new dimension in labour law. Collective bargaining, the uttermost expression of voluntarism and private governance when dealing with services of general interest, may include matters of public relevance within its scope, going beyond the private associations that are parties to the agreements, and orienting itself towards consumers as an undefined—and yet visible—class of citizens.[14] This is, among other reasons, a consequence of the dissemination of public services at a decentralized level and of the fact that their delivery is partially dependent on labour rules agreed collectively.[15]

Similarly, a new shadow is cast on the right to strike: when limits to its exercise are balanced against consumers' rights to have access to public

[12] M. S. Giannini, *Il pubblico potere* (Il Mulino, Bologna, 1986); S. Cassese, 'Le trasformazioni dell'organizzazione amministrativa' [1985] *Riv. Trim. Dir. Pub.* 374 ff.; G. Amato, 'Autorità semi-indipendenti e autorità di garanzia' [1997] *Riv. Trim. Dir. Pubb.* 645 ss.

[13] This scenario is described by A. Predieri, *L'emergere delle autorità amministrative indipendenti* (Passigli, Florence, 1997), 31 ff. 'Osmosis' expresses the idea of a State constantly seeking an internal equilibrium, as opposed to being a monolith, in full control of its internal hierarchy of powers. Competition rules are central to this new institutional balance and functional to the protection of other constitutional values.

[14] O. Kahn-Freund refers to 'consumers as an amorphous mass', underlining the fact that unions only represent workers as producers. See *Labour Relations, Heritage and Adjustment* (OUP, Oxford, 1979), 82.

[15] Collective agreements, especially at plant level, may link pay increases to productivity; in the third sector clauses of this kind may have a potentially disruptive effect on the quality of the service. On the other hand, collective agreements may aim at the improvement of the service providers' performance, specifying managerial responsibilities, especially at a decentralized level. See the description of such trends, common to several European countries, in Moreau, n. 3 above, 165 ff. Another example is the inclusion in collective agreements of codes of conduct or deontological rules, as in the Italian experience following the so-called privatization of public employment contracts. See section 9 below. In the first national collective agreements signed during 1995 and 1996 clauses have been included in the health sector in order to promote decentralized bargaining dealing with the duty to inform consumers' organizations of for the number of employees to be kept at work during strikes, in order to guarantee provision of essential services. See G. Albenzio, 'I principi e gli instituti comuni nei contratti collettivi dopo la riforma del pubblico impiego' [1997] *Foro It.* V, 93.

services, we are obliged to redefine its original function. As a 'species of the right to freedom of association, not a way of furthering that right',[16] the right to strike acquires its own independence and becomes adaptable to different and variable working environments. Although more exposed to judicial—and sometimes quasi-judicial—decisions, it acquires a new dimension in the public space. Structured as a more flexible right, aimed at reaching and interpreting the general interest, it responds better to legal reformulation in systems characterized by an individual entitlement, rather than by 'organic' notions,[17] where it is for the associations to resort to collective action and thereby shape individual employees' behaviour.

Two further notions have been introduced and need to be clarified. The notion of individual rights exercised collectively is typical of some—not all—European legal systems. Whether applied to freedom of association or to the right to strike, this, purely apparent, contradiction in terms proves immensely helpful for the purposes indicated earlier in this book, namely the construction of a new legal paradigm, while defining new citizenship rights. It is useful to recall that, in a wider perspective, this approach should help to avoid what proves to be a historically recurring contraposition between expansion of public services on the one hand and consolidation of social rights on the other.[18] Earlier on, it was suggested that a 'socio-economic' notion of citizenship could be attached to the status of lawfully resident citizens and also to that of citizens employed by European enterprises, even when working outside national territory.[19] This stimulating and challenging interpretation allows us to introduce further thoughts on Community developments in the field of fundamental social rights and the construction of a theory of labour law capable of crossing national frontiers and expressing a supranational concept of individual guarantees.

The second notion to be investigated more closely is that of public space, which has been adopted in legal theory as well as in theories on democracy. In this specific context, we can assume that public space is the one occupied by the third sector, and that it is partially controlled by private associations—such as employers' and employees' associations—when it comes to dealing with those limited collective interests defined by the scope of the associations themselves. The characteristics of the third sector, as we describe it in this book, have significant effects on the attitudes

[16] Framed in a wider and more general theoretical analysis of collective rights, this is the interpretation suggested by S. Leader, *Freedom of Association* (Yale Univ. Press, New Haven, Conn., 1992), 180 ff. (the quotation is at 209).

[17] Lord Wedderburn, *Employment Rights in Britain and Europe* (Lawrence & Wishart, London, 1991), 276 ff.

[18] E. Santoro, 'Le antinomie della cittadinanza: libertà negativa, diritti sociali e autonomia individuale', in D. Zolo (ed.), *La cittadinanza* (Laterza, Roma-Bari 1994), 93 ff.

[19] Supiot, ch. 9 in this vol.

of the traditional social partners. When acting within the sphere of public services, these associations are often forced to go beyond their original mandate and look at a wider angle of interests to be taken into account. Public space is the intersection of citizenship rights with social rights; it is an area of mutual reference for consumers and employees; it is a condition according to which their identities and aspirations may be confronted but not confused, nor unified in one amorphous notion of public interest.

In the public space a dominant role has been occupied by the media, whenever there has been a decline in other democratic institutions such as trade unions.[20] Public services attract the media in a very powerful way, inasmuch as they rely on information and use it as a permanent link with consumers. Consumers, on the other hand, are dependent on the media as the most visible and immediate channel through which their aspirations and demands are expressed and included in the political agenda. An even more spectacular impact is that wielded by the media when dealing with strikes restricting consumers' rights to the delivery of public services.[21] Informing consumers through the media is often the most efficient way of reaching all those potentially interested and therefore of partially protecting consumers' rights, giving them notice of the planned collective action and informing them of detailed arrangements for the delivery of services.

Labour law is present in the public space as one of the resources to which all interested parties—consumers, employees, the media—have to refer, in order to establish legal responsibilities and to expose all the actors to fair rules. Fairness may not depend on the media alone; however, it may nevertheless be acquired through them as a value, exposed to criticism and to political evaluation, as well as to judicial responses. The public space is, as one can see, an open environment in which individuals seek a link with institutions, be they the unions, the providers of public services or the media, and reflect upon issues of democracy, such as new citizenship rights. The residuary responsibility of the State, referred to in

[20] A. Touraine, *Qu'est-ce que la démocratie?* (Fayard, Paris, 1994), 213–15. When public services are at stake *'le spectacle'* of the media is at its best, according to A. Supiot, 'Malaise dans le social' [1996] *Droit Social* 119. In the shaping of public opinion, following Habermas and his ideas of free associations communicating among themselves without the State intervention, public space is the place in which 'the State has no responsibility', as indicated by P. Ladrière, 'Espace public et démocratie', in A. Cottereau and P. Ladrière (eds.), *Pouvoir et légitimité, Ecole des Hautes Etudes en Sciences Sociales* (Paris, 1992), 42. In this theoretical environment, citizens get involved in common decisions, rather than in individual exchanges, pursuing common goals. We argue that the State may have indirect responsibilities in the public space, due to the public relevance of the interests concerned. One way to prove this is through the creation of independent bodies, whose powers lie between administrative machinery and judicial constraints. An interesting approach is that chosen by J. Lenoble and A. Berten, 'L'espace public comme procedure', in the above-quoted Cottereau and Ladrière, at 83 ff.

[21] Art. 2.6 of Italian Law 146/1990, discussed below in section 2, imposes an obligation on public radio and television services to release information about strikes as well as about available alternative services.

chapter 1, is discernable in relation to labour law as it is for the provision of services. We do not wish to describe a hierarchy of powers within the public space; rather, we want to show that concurrent sources of regulation are necessary for developing the legal discourse on constitutional citizenship. We also want to prove that the self-referential exercise put into action by the State when decentralizing public services is improved by the active role played by intermediate bodies, acting as regulators of the market.[22]

The debate on whether consumers' rights are better protected through very broad rules banning distortions of competition, or whether specific rules must be made enforceable for limited sectors of the market, illustrates the difficulty for the State of abandoning completely the politicization of its administrative machinery and accepting coexistence with private institutions, enabling the latter to compete with public bodies on equal terms. Public services are the image of a 'compromise', a difficult co-ordination between the efficiency of specific sectors of the market and efficiency for the community as a whole.[23]

We maintain that changes in the structure of the State, as well as in procedures which bring citizens into contact with new manifestations of the State itself, are influenced by groups such as consumers' associations, single-issue organizations, or trade unions, and that these phenomena are slowly transforming legal systems, allowing for constant interpretation of legal principles. The new feature to be underlined is that interpretation of the law is not left exclusively in the hands of the judiciary. From the perspective of labour law, this implies a re-formulation of its function and the introduction of more flexible rules, slowly taking the place of previous mandatory rules. The perspective of public law changes, too, since new powers are recognized for citizens in bringing claims for the recognition of agreed standards in the delivery of public services.[24]

[22] It is useful to recall once more the idea of the 'osmotic' State suggested at n. 13. Independent bodies are within the context of the conflicting interests to be regulated; procedures improve the participation of different groups, whereas judges tend to remain isolated from the differentiated realities they need to evaluate. This is the point of view of Lenoble and Berten, at n. 20 above, 103–5.

[23] Moreau, n. 3 above, 188, when drawing the conclusions of a comparative analysis dealing with several European countries and with several public services.

[24] See Ch. 3 by C. Harlow in this volume, discussing the Citizens' Charter in the British experience. As for the Italian counterpart, a Charter was adopted in 1994 as a guideline issued by the Prime Minister. See S. Cassese, *La nuova costituzione economica* (Laterza, Rome-Bari, 1995). The Charter sets six fundamental principles: equality among consumers, objectivity and impartiality, continuity and regularity in the delivery of services, consumers' right to choose between service providers, consumers' participation in the delivery of services, access to information, and efficiency. One of the purposes of this book is to co-ordinate the logic of a citizens' charter with the rights of employees, in order to build up a constitutional framework which eliminates all conflicts or inconsistencies between different and often overlapping spheres of rights, as anticipated in O. Kahn-Freund's seminal work, at n. 14 above,

4. Between Networks and Hierarchies—Agencies, Authorities, Independent Bodies, and the State of the Community Debate

In the highly differentiated Community legal system, lawyers are currently forced, even more than in previous phases of transition, to understand the reasons behind legal changes and to relate the latter to new functions of the law. The complexity of such a supranational system, combined with the pressures and intrusions of the global system, through market competitiveness and constant technological challenge, favours the emergence of new institutions as an answer to new social and economic needs. The third sector—as we have repeatedly maintained in this book—is a significant example of how to construct a new paradigm for constitutional citizenship, while facing the emergence of market citizenship. It is clear by now that we are attempting to answer the question what to do with citizenship, rather than what citizenship means;[25] the very specific angle of our analysis is, despite its specificity, a way of looking at important institutional changes affecting the legal system as a whole.

It is our intention to show that in the European Union a transition is occurring from state-based to supranational constitutional citizenship, and that social rights, though still very marginal in terms of enacted reforms as well as in the discussion of future policies, are likely to acquire a more central relevance. In the debate which has taken place in most European countries during the last twenty years, neo-liberal theories have placed the emphasis on free competition and attempted to evaluate individuals with regard to their ability to survive in the market, granting them rights with totally different goals from those envisaged in early European labour law traditions.[26] Following this line of thought, consumers are better protected when no barrier is built which could impede their access to services of general interest; if labour law appears as an obstacle, it must be shaped and adapted to broader needs and demands.

At the other end of the spectrum, theories which can be broadly described as social-democratic, which place emphasis on social cohesion within the European Union, and which display a special concern about

particularly at 78, where the metaphor is that of the double mask worn by employees in the 'ghost play' of social relations.

[25] As suggested by P. Costa, 'La cittadinanza: un tentativo di ricostruzione "archeologica",' in Zolo (ed.), n. 18 above, at 50. This author adopts the view, largely shared in this chapter, of moving the research focus from the centre to the periphery, namely from the peak of the political system to its bottom, where individuals seek to enter the system itself and to find their own allocation, while defining their affiliations and their needs.

[26] References to the British case are in S. Fredman, 'The New Rights: Labour Law and Ideology in the Thatcher Years' [1992] *Oxford Jo. of Legal Studies* 24 ff. Criticism of the neo-liberals is expressed, among others, by S. Deakin, 'Labour Law as Market Regulation: The Economic Foundation of European Social Policies', in P. Davies *et al.*, at n. 11, 63 ff.

social exclusion from the floor of rights, are slowly and often unsatisfactorily emerging at supranational level. In addition to the extension to citizens of social rights which are marginal to the creation of a new political entity and to its social sphere, these theories are also concerned with the quality of public services to be delivered and favour those labour law rules which are best aimed at the protection of individuals, seen in their entire and rich dimension of employees and consumers at the same time.[27]

When looking at public services, neo-liberals overestimate consumers in their capacity for setting new universal standards in the provision of services and consequently creating an abstract legal order in which a durable definition of public interest can be found; in so doing, they obscure all clear goals pursued by labour law, ignoring the fact that previous compromises and legislative reforms have already changed the state of the discipline considerably, bringing it closer to modern systems of production and new organizational facets of the employing enterprise. They also pay very little respect to collective bargaining, both as an institution capable of adapting itself to the market and as a machinery adjustable to different industrial strategies. Social democrats,[28] on the other hand, are split between the aspiration to reconstruct social rights from the bottom in the hierarchy of norms and the conviction that fundamental principles must guide such an important new founding phase, linked to necessary but still unfinished reforms of the Treaty on European Union.

Both theories are still lacking a 'constitutional ordering', a governance structure which, overcoming the limits of markets and hierarchies, can show a new pattern of adjustment to changes 'in its context of operation, as opposed to changes within a particular context'.[29] The metaphor of 'osmosis' occurring within the State, in the process of constructing new

[27] Early and significant samples of this literature can be found in K. W. Wedderburn and W. T. Murphy (eds.), *Labour Law and the Community* (Institute of Advanced Legal Studies, London, 1982); more recently Moreau, n. 10 above. A documented critique of neo-liberal theories is offered by Wedderburn, n. 17 above, 198 ff. A comparative perspective is offered by E. Ales, 'Tutela dei diritti del cittadino e sciopero nei servizi pubblici' [1997] *Giornale di diritto del lavoro e di relazioni industriali* 139 ff.

[28] The European Commission has recently favoured discussion along these very broad lines. See the Report by the Comité des Sages, *For a Europe of Civic and Social Rights.* (EC Commission, Brussels–Luxembourg, 1996.) With regard to the strategies of social democratic governments of Western Europe during the 1970s especially in relation to full employment, an enlightening analysis is to be found in F. Scharpf, *Crisis and Choice in European Social Democracy* (Cornell University Press, 1991).

[29] This expression is taken from C. Sabel, Constitutional Ordering in Historical Context, in F. Scharpf (ed.) *Games in Hierarchies and Networks* (Campus Verlag, Frankfurt, 1993), 65 ff., in particular 79–80. His overall analysis of how to overcome the dichotomy of markets/hierarchies, is very relevant to the idea put forward in this book, namely to reflect upon a third sector in which public services are taken as indicators of emerging citizenship rights. Changes occuring in each constitutional order 'may require a reordering of the order itself: a redefinition not just of which unit is responsible for what . . . but also and more importantly a redefinition of who is entitled to be heard on which questions' (at 80).

internal equilibria and recognizing new collective interests to be taken into account, suggests that new legal techniques are necessary in order to establish coherent patterns of change. It has been suggested that a new pluralism is emerging, not only because of the growing number of different interest groups making their voices heard, but also because of the ways in which the representation of interests is organized, ranging from political representation to union and management associations, to opinion polls and referenda, and even to judicial activism.[30]

A significant reaction of the State to all these different levels of representation and to their fragmentation is to be found in the creation of independent—or quasi-independent—agencies. These are not an alternative to constitutional ordering, but contribute to its construction, suggesting rules of compatibility between competing powers; their independence from the State makes them more objective and, where necessary, more pragmatic, when it comes to understanding the functioning of the economic system and favouring changes which can improve its transparency and competitiveness; the relatively new element, useful in the context of the present analysis, is that they maintain some form of coercive power, even when dealing with private interests.

They lie between markets and hierarchies; in such a position they are asked to provide efficient rules, valid for the solution of specific conflicts of interest, without being detached from the fulfilment of general interests. Independence from the State should then imply independence from the political system—not easy to achieve, especially when appointments occur through Parliament—thus favouring the adoption of technical decisions, taken by people who are guided solely by their expertise, rather than by loyalty to a political apparatus. It is no strange coincidence that supranational institutions, whose task is to govern the global economy while monitoring changes within regional or national economic systems, have paid attention to the decentralization of state prerogatives and to all processes 'bringing policy-making and implementation closer to the communities they serve'. In indicating that priority areas—such as health, education, and the creation of infrastructures in all relevant fields—should be chosen, it is also underlined that consultative mechanisms should be established, in order fully to understand the preferences of the affected groups and to make all reforms intelligible to citizens.[31]

Desirable as these very general orientations for state policies may appear, they cannot be separated from broader reforms, such as those occurring at supranational level. Within the Community, it proved relatively easy to co-ordinate national laws with supranational antitrust

[30] Predieri, n. 13 above, 33 ff.

[31] World Bank, *World Development Report, The State in a Changing World* (OUP, Oxford, 1997), 28 and 129–30.

legislation, the former being functional to the aims of the latter, namely banning distortions in competition and the abuse of dominant positions within an integrated market. The example of competition law is a good one: it does not take concrete form in policies which offer only broad guidelines to Member States, but translates itself into binding norms to be complied with at national level.[32] The presence of intermediate bodies between markets and consumers has hitherto favoured the linking of legal rules to communities as well as to individual citizens. Whereas competition needs to be governed in a strategic way, the functioning of public services has been viewed as 'tactical',[33] subordinate to the contingent needs of specific sectors and lacking co-ordination with a harmonised and comprehensive regulation of the market.

The suggestion put forward during the IGC prior to the Amsterdam summit, namely to introduce a European charter of public services, was associated with the creation of an evaluating body, empowered to monitor the enforcement of national and Community policies, in conjunction with all interested parties.[34] The attempt in this proposal was to introduce a new 'synthesis' in what appeared to be an unco-ordinated field of legal intervention and to specify leading principles from which public services should draw inspiration. The intention to link public services to other important areas of Community action, such as consumer protection, the environment, and research, and social policies, to name but a few, was also favoured by the unsatisfactory notion of universal service[35] which was gaining ground in proposals for the reform of the Maastricht Treaty.

It is at this point in the story that the new centrality of labour law, which was suggested earlier, should again be stressed. Principles inspiring a new Community definition of public services must include continuity of provision, equal access (regardless of national origins and linguistic or cultural diversities), efficiency, quality, adaptability to new consumers' needs, transparency, and participation. Labour law is, in many respects, instrumental to all this. Services of general interest must combine competitiveness with efficiency, quality of service with modernization of management. Labour law issues are hidden between the lines: not only must

[32] S. Cassese, n. 24 above, 41.

[33] This is one of the main criticisms levelled by CEEP at Community initiatives on public services, following an analysis of secondary legislation referred to specific sectors, such as transport, postal services, telecommunications, energy, and the media. See CEEP, *Europe, concurrence et service public* (Masson, Paris, 1995), 35. The Commission's point of view is in the Communication of 11 Sept. 1996, *Services of general interest in Europe*, COM(96)443 final. Whereas universal services in telecommunications must provide for 'affordable access', with a view to protecting disadvantaged users, other general-interest services (health, welfare, education, water, and housing) must be left to national or regional responsibilities. The paradox is that, while universal services must reach the socially excluded, nothing is provided to promote the inclusion of marginal citizens within the provision of public services.

[34] CEEP, n. 33 above, 49–50.

[35] See Ch. 7 by W. Sauter.

strikes be regulated, in order to guarantee the continuity of the service concerned, but training must also be provided and human resources must be improved.[36]

Within this very broad framework, which has not fully developed into reform of the Treaty, it proves indispensable, on the one hand, to further the process of national reforms, and, on the other, to elaborate on the impact of Community social policies and on the consolidation of fundamental social rights within the Community legal order. The aim is to balance the functioning of the market against new concepts of constitutional citizenship.[37] At national level public services represent a testing ground in which to prove that the lowering of labour standards brings about false efficiency and does not add new ideas to the creation of a supranational legal system. In the following sections an attempt will be made to prove the validity of the theories presented so far by examining them against specific examples of legislation—the Law on the right to strike in public services and the Law on the privatization of employment contracts in the former public sector—taken from the Italian legal system.

No strict link can be established between the two statutes chosen for this exercise. Since both of them rely heavily on collective bargaining as a means towards better protection of consumers' rights, the opportunity will be offered to speculate on the role of private governance in the fulfilment of public and general interests. Furthermore, since both of them rest on a solid constitutional basis, to be found in the 1948 Italian Constitution, it can be argued that the combination of labour law with public law principles—right to strike v. guarantees of the fundamental freedoms of individuals, right to collective bargaining v. fair and impartial functioning of the public administration—is a challenging one, to be taken into account when discussing constitutional citizenship at Community level.

[36] CEEP, n. 33 above, 42–3, 48. Their proposal of the European Charter of services of general economic interest is set out in full in Annex II, 67 ff. This proposal, based on the inclusion of public services in the Treaty, different from the exception envisaged in Art. 90(2) of the EC Treaty, remains on the agenda of political and academic discussion. For a brief account of the limited changes in the Amsterdam Treaty, see W. Sauter's concluding remarks, to ch. 7 and in particular n. 63, and Freedland, ch. 1 pp. 11ff.

[37] The Maastricht Social Chapter (Art. 2(6)) explicitly excluded from Community competence wages, the right to organize, the right to strike, and lockout. Its inclusion in the Amsterdam Treaty does not change the substance of such exclusions, although the debate is open on whether ratification of the Treaty should include a phase of renegotiation of the Protocol and Agreement on social policy. As for the academic debate addressed to the IGC, reference can be made to R. Blanpain, B. Hepple, S. Sciarra, and M. Weiss, *Fundamental Social Rights: Proposals for the European Union* (Peeters, Leuven, 1996), and to B. Bercusson, S. Deakin, P. Koistinen, Y. Kravaritou, U. Muckenberger, A. Supiot, and B. Veneziani, *A Manifesto for Social Europe* (European Trade Union Institute of the ETUC, Brussels, 1996).

5. The Italian Law on the Right to Strike in Public Services: Proving the Centrality of Labour Law

The first item of legislation[38] chosen as an example to test the theories developed so far is the product of social unrest at the end of the 1980s, especially in rail and air transport, but also in other public services. It marks an historical turning-point in Italian labour law, which had previously been characterized by abstentionism in the field of industrial conflict; that is why a symbolic value is attached to this statute, which, for the first time in more than forty years since the enactment of the Constitution, ventured into a highly sensitive area of collective labour law.[39] The primary function of the statute is to grant a wide range of personal fundamental rights, which must be balanced against the right to strike. The individual nature of the right to strike makes its comparison with other fundamental rights—all likewise enshrined in the Constitution—a particularly challenging legal exercise, aimed at comparing different angles of the individual's sphere of constitutional prerogatives.

There were two notable factors, underlying the widespread discontent which at the time opened the way to legal intervention: one had to do with inadequate salaries, especially in key state areas (such as schools and health services); the other concerns the attack on the main large confederations of unions by new groups, not yet organized into associations but nevertheless very militant and conflictual. Although these reasons may not be deeply explored in this chapter, they need to be borne in mind for a better understanding of the social reality the legislature had to face. Another element must be mentioned: the media played an extraordinary role in accentuating the causes and the effects of conflict. Through them, public opinion had to face a situation of national emergency, caused mainly by strikes. Unions had to confront their own divided loyalties, on the one hand feeling responsible for their members, while on the other being cautious and sympathetic towards consumers.

These conflicting social demands meant that a balance had to be struck between different rights, all of constitutional relevance. Doubts were

[38] L. 12 June 1990, n. 146, Norme sull'esercizio del diritto di sciopero nei servizi pubblici essenziali e sulla salvaguardia dei diritti della persona costituzionalmente tutelati. Istituzione della Commissione di garanzia dell'attuazione della legge, GU 14 June 1990, no. 137. The ILO English translation—which does not take account of later amendments—can be found in Labour Law Documents 1990–ITA 1.

[39] A complete account of the relevant bibliography would be disproportionate to the purposes of this chapter. Materials for both historical and legal analysis are offered by U. Romagnoli and M. V. Ballestrero in their commentary on the law in G. Branca and A. Pizzorusso, *Commentario della Costituzione, sub art. 40, Supplemento* (Zanichelli, Bologna-Rome, 1994). The sociological reasons leading to social unrest in relevant areas of Italian public service are offered by L. Bordogna, *Pluralismo senza mercato* (F. Angeli, Milan, 1994).

expressed, by theorists as well as by employers' and employees' associations, as to the tools to be adopted, namely recourse to legislation instead of case law. The latter had previously acquired an important role, particularly through key decisions of the Italian Constitutional Court, and filled the gap in existing legislation, demonstrating that conflicting interests could be regulated on a case-by-case basis, yet establishing principles of general import.

Similarly, other voluntary means, such as the unions' private codes of conduct for the regulation of strikes in key areas of the economy, proved to be of little relevance, because of lack of effective sanctions owing to the private nature of the codes, which were enforceable only among union members. The latter point is more significant than might at first appear. In public opinion and particularly among advocates of legal abstentionism, the weakness of union sanctions proved that at the origin of social unrest there was an unresolved problem of conflict within the conflict. A bitter and often hard confrontation between employees belonging to different associations was taking place, demonstrating the collision between differing industrial cultures and opposing union traditions.

In the past, the long established main confederations had been able to enforce codes of conduct and exercise control over their own members, while keeping access to conflict open, thus confirming the tradition of an individual right to strike which found expression only in concerted and collective industrial action. Spontaneous groups, by contrast, did not consider themselves bound by any code of conduct, and felt free to adopt an aggressive attitude towards the confederations. Conflict within the conflict resulted in an assault on consumers' rights and provoked uncertainty among the unions, in search of an identity as guarantors of general welfare, as well as vouching for the interests of their members.

This brief analysis of the reasons behind the Italian statute being examined here confirms the centrality of rights industrial action in the Italian constitutional tradition, found in some other European countries and yet unknown to others. It can be argued that, owing to established legal traditions stronger in some legal systems than in others and because of practices enforced by unions, the dilemma between consumers' rights and the right to strike remains—to a certain extent—unresolved. Legal rules, effective in some systems, are nothing but experiments in others, subject to unpredictable responses from social rules.

That is why a combination of different measures—both legal and voluntary—has often been envisaged in the Italian labour law tradition, in order to respond to employees' demands and at the same time respect consumers' rights. As indicated above, voluntary measures may encounter a contradiction when they try to impose general rules, while lacking general enforceability. When dealing with consumers' rights, unions tend to rely on the bargaining power they have acquired as employees' representatives; they imply that a public role is the consequence of private governance and that competence in industrial relations matters brings with it a constitutional culture, broad enough to understand and interpret consumers' demands.

Regulatory techniques combining law with collective agreements or private codes of conduct often include very powerful procedural devices; rather than endowing individuals with positive rights, they rely on collective entities to shape aspirations, passing through different phases of progressive clarification as to what the outcomes of legal enforcement might be. The right to recourse to differing sanctions, including non-binding ones, is parallel to the construction of procedures; when industrial conflict is at stake, the relevance of moral sanctions may become of some importance and be included among the available answers offered by the legal system.

In the parallel debate taking place in public law, particularly when the privatization of public services occurs, procedural elements also become very central, and open to the contribution of collective organizations. This further point of contact between two different legal approaches again shows the peculiarities of the third sector. From two different perspectives—of consumers' and of employees'—procedures are seen as a guarantee of fairness and exactitude. Procedures bring the individual closer to the public service, passing through the selective filter of large organizations, as well as smaller but powerful interest groups. The crucial question remains that of how to transform this open and dynamic process into a stable system of constitutional citizenship, not dependent on the changeable strength of private bodies, nor on the unpredictable consequences of countervailing powers.

6. Which Consumers' Rights, Which Public Services?

A key element in interpreting the Italian statute is the definition of public services as regards setting limits on the right to strike; this operation is functional to the guarantee of constitutional rights referred to in the statute itself. The catalogue of rights and the wider description of services[40] are by no means to be considered exhaustive nor mandatory; it is

[40] As in Art. 1, ss. 1 and 2. Public services, described as 'essential' in the statutes, aim at guaranteeing the enjoyment of personal constitutional rights, ranging from the right to life, health, personal freedom and safety, to freedom of movement, to social security and welfare, to education, and to freedom of access to telecommunications. In ss. 2 all these very broad personal rights are more exactly specified in relation to particular public services in which limits to the right to strike need to be established.

rather the expression of significant choices which should bind those interpreting its content and preclude excessive argument over interpretation. The notion of public service, irrespective of the private or public nature of the employment relationship, derives from this kind of preliminary choice on the part of the legislature, so that all measures aimed at limiting the right to strike have to be framed within this coherent scheme.

For this purpose concurrent sources of regulation are available. First of all, the statute delegates to collective agreements the definition of important matters, without ignoring the fact that recourse to employers' unilateral decisions is the outcome of unsuccessful bargaining. This also implies that a variety of sanctions is envisaged, as we shall see later. Furthermore, an independent administrative agency[41] is established, with rather weak mandatory powers, although potentially able to gain moral force in public opinion.

Articles 1 and 2 of the statute are structured so as to be closely interrelated: guarantees provided for personal constitutional rights must imply limits on the right to strike. Therefore, notice of at least ten days is made compulsory as well as an indication of the expected duration of strikes. Essential levels of public services, preferably to be specified in collective agreements, must still be provided, even during the strike. In the rationale of the law 'indispensable' service means, in concrete terms, requiring a certain number of employees to continue to work during the strike; it may also mean that such services must be provided in accordance with certain patterns of frequency and recurrence. In both cases, the technicalities (how to choose those employees who are not to stop to work, how to organize the periodical provision of the service) have to be agreed collectively. Since no duty to bargain is envisaged under Italian law, agreements, although favoured by the law, are by no means a compulsory outcome of negotiations.

Despite the lack of a generalized legal enforceability of collective agreements under Italian law, voluntary sources are meant to play a central role in the protection of personal constitutional rights. In one of the very first opinions delivered by the Commission, it was stressed that the obligation to provide public services 'precedes' collective agreements and is somehow 'independent' of them.[42] In an overall interpretation of the law, this

[41] Which will be referred to in the text as the 'Commission'. It is made up of 9 members, to be chosen from among experts in the field of constitutional and labour law and industrial relations, appointed by the President of the Republic, following the indications of the two branches of Parliament. Members of the Commission are independent of the political system and cannot serve in other public bodies or be members of political parties, trade unions, or employers' associations. The Commission may request specialized opinions from experts in the specific public services in which conflict is at stake, as well as from leading figures in consumers' associations.

[42] *Acotral*, decided on 9 Oct. 1990, is reported at [1991] *Rivista giuridica del lavoro*, I, 528

very general principle leads to seeking final responsibility for the guarantee of individual constitutional rights in the employer's behaviour—namely in the provision of essential or indispensable quotas of the public service concerned, even when no collective agreement has been signed. This wide discretion is counterbalanced by the fact that the right to strike remains a protected constitutional right throughout. Because of the strong bias of the Italian legislature towards unions, the employer may be exposed to sanctions for anti-union activity if he goes too far in striking a balance in favour of consumers, thereby unnecessarily limiting the right to strike.[43]

Judges occupy an important position in the whole edifice of the 1990 statute. Case law has to set the borderline between two areas of equally protected constitutional rights. In order for it to do this, very pragmatic elements must be taken into account for the evaluation of the employer's behaviour, such as the designation of which sectors of the public service are instrumental to the protection of personal constitutional rights, and the correct minimum number of employees who should be required to work during the strike.

Judicial decisions may become very detailed, seeking rational criteria among the rules governing work organization and paying attention to job descriptions, as in a fact-finding exercise; yet, since they deal with extremely delicate balances between constitutional values, they must reflect the common understanding of what is thought of as 'indispensable' for consumers. It thus happens that court cases examining a particular workplace's organization and the terms and conditions of its employment contracts are made to express a general and overall conception of public interest. Even when the notion of public and 'indispensable' service is kept very broad, in order to meet the widest possible notion of general interest, the concrete definition of consumers' rights is linked, on a case-by-case basis, to local providers of public services and dependent on the concrete ways in which they are geographically distributed, efficiently organized and properly and sufficiently funded.

When a closer look is taken at this extremely complex balancing exercise, we discover that, in order to prove effective for consumers, solutions become optimal when framed in a decentralized scheme of reference; at this level the general guidelines provided for in the law and in centralized agreements must be translated into concrete measures, so as to become

[43] The reference is to Art. 28 of the Workers' Statute (L. of 20 May 1970, no. 300). Some courts followed this interpretation, which is not unanimously accepted. The opposite tendency is to consider the employer's behaviour legitimate whenever it complies with the Commission's proposal, viewed by the courts as immediately binding and used as a parameter for judicial decisions. Early case law on the 1990 statute is analysed by P. Pascucci, 'L'esercizio del diritto di sciopero nei servizi essenziali: una prima ricognizione' [1993] *Giornale di diritto del lavoro e di relazioni industriali* 369 ff.

directly functional to consumers' rights. In this respect, a gap in the statute must be pointed out: the role of consumers' associations is kept very marginal. This choice by the legislature may evidence a cultural preference for dealing with industrial organizations and a willingness to depend on their well-established capacity to resolve all disputes within a framework of agreed standards.

A case-by-case analysis and at times a fact-finding exercise is one of the tasks assigned to the Commission, which must evaluate all agreed solutions on quotas of the public service concerned to be provided during the exercise of the right to strike and, if it disagrees, issue a proposal to be notified to the parties. It can do the same when no collectively agreed solution has been reached. The problem here is to strike yet another delicate balance, since the Commission's initiative, although provided for in the statute, must not be too invasive of the autonomy of the parties, when they bargain collectively; no obligation to accept the Commission's proposal can be envisaged, since the law explicitly favours a collectively agreed definition of 'indispensable' services.

The Constitutional Court was asked to evaluate the conformity with constitutional principles of the very peculiar typology of collective agreements introduced by the 1990 statute.[44] Article 39 of the Constitution deals with the right to organize collectively and refers to future legislation the definition of criteria for granting *erga omnes* enforceability to collective agreements. The fact that no such legislation was ever enacted—as also happened with Article 40 on the right to strike, which still lacks legal regulation outside the area of public services—creates an anomaly in the entire system of labour law, the effects of which can be seen even in the interpretation of the 1990 statute. With regard to the latter, the court ruled that collective agreements, as presented within the statute, are in no way related to the category described in Article 39, because their clauses are subject to the final evaluation of the Commission, holding a negative power of veto but, nevertheless, required to assess the conformity of collectively agreed formulas with the guarantee of personal constitutional rights.

Should the interested parties not accept the Commission's negative evaluation and its proposals, reference has to be made to Article 8 of the statute, providing for the intervention of public figures (ministers or local authorities, according to the national or local relevance of the conflict in question), having the final power to impose on service providers the duty to maintain 'essential services' and 'adequate levels' in the functioning of the services themselves, while still guaranteeing exercise of the right to strike. Non-compliance with these orders is attended by administrative

[44] Corte Constituzionale, 18 Oct. 1996, no. 344 [1997] *Foro It.*, I, 381.

sanctions; there is also a right of appeal against orders issued by public authorities in administrative courts.

The multi-level system of regulation deployed here by the Italian legislature is both original and complex, especially in the attempt it makes not to ignore any of the private and public actors hit by conflicts or those initiating conflicts. A number of ideas can be framed with reference to what has been said earlier in the way of general and more theoretical remarks. The right to bargain collectively, even when used for the protection of general and public interests, does not lose its original significance, namely that of being the most important and valuable outcome of a constitutionally guaranteed right to organize. Consequently, it does not give way to other powers, such as those stemming from independent agencies, the legal nature of which still appears indistinct, at least in the example of the 1990 Italian statute.

When independent bodies are asked to step onto the scene because collective bargaining has failed, the ambiguity of their role is even more evident. It demonstrates tension, if not an actual division, between expectations and rights and suggests that, at least in the solution found by the Italian legislature, rights are potentially better enforced when rooted in collective agreements. It is also true that collective bargaining does not, by itself, have the solidity of a 'constitutional ordering': voluntary means, particularly when confronted with issues of public relevance and oriented towards the guarantee of personal constitutional rights, give way to public law and ultimately depend on the power of administrative sanctions to complete what, in the end, appears as a virtuous circle.

We shall see in the following section that recourse to private means, such as disciplinary measures available to the employer by virtue of the contract of employment, becomes more debatable, when those means are intended to be functional to the protection of public interest. It is equally debatable whether the pendulum swinging between collective agreements and an independent agency appointed through Parliament should be so clearly oriented towards the former. Reasons behind the reluctance (very visible in the statute) to grant stronger powers to the Commission, can be found in the need felt by the legislature to win social consensus, when venturing into a highly sensitive field of industrial relations, and to do so through the best-established system of private governance.

This choice confirms a prejudice, pervasive in Italian labour law, against the third-party settlement of labour disputes, even when the primary function of the law goes beyond private interests and aims at protecting personal constitutional rights. Despite all this, the legislature succeeded in having private, public, and quasi-public actors play at different tables, while all being part of the same game. This is a point to be stressed in the present analysis, since it proves that the 1990 Italian statute represents an important illustrative case in discussing how citizenship rights can be shaped in the third sector.

If we try to summarize the main elements put forward in what is not meant to be a complete exegesis of the 1990 statute, we can see that the normative function of collective agreements, despite the uncertainties of a constitutional norm never fully enforced, has its origin in the law. It is a legal provision which identifies collective agreements as the proper source to which such matters should be referred; delegation to bargainng by private parties on subject matter dealing with the limits to be applied to industrial action is a consequence of deeply rooted constitutional rights, the right to organize and the right to strike; technical expertise as expressed by an independent agency, finds its place in the interstices of such atypical collective agreements, trying to fill the gaps left by negotiators with purely persuasive powers.

The hierarchy of powers and the role assigned to each player within it both receive an *imprimatur* from the Constitutional Court, which has been successful, as was shown earlier, in raising the Commission's negative powers to the maximum point of equilibrium in the entire structure of the law, while being aware of the need not to interfere with a constitutionally based right to bargain. Finally, the courts are visible and active in administering the law; labour law and administrative law are both reflected in case law, thus proving that the third sector needs to be analysed from a multi-disciplinary perspective.

7. Sanctions—Who is Responsible for What?

It was stated in the previous section that, where consensus on minimum services to be provided during a strike cannot be achieved, the employer, and more generally the service provider, has the power to implement all organizational measures aimed at guaranteeing personal constitutional rights. This provision in the statute is very relevant when interpreting the scope of collective agreements on the definition of 'indispensable' services and placing them in a legal category of their own, not comparable to the category of collective agreements for the definition of terms and conditions of employment.

Together with the unilateral power to provide 'indispensable' services, the 1990 Italian statute has also granted the employer new disciplinary powers.[45] These are directed at individual employees who go on strike ignoring the legal and contractual requirements provided for the guarantee of personal constitutional rights. Furthermore, it is the employer's duty

[45] Art. 4. ss. 1, 2, and 3.

to enforce sanctions against unions which call an unlawful strike, regardless of the limits set in the law and in collective agreements. This implies suspending the collection and payment over of union dues and stopping paid leave for union activities for at least one month.

A third type of sanction—in the enforcement of which the employer is less actively involved—is provided against groups other than unions which call an unlawful strike; it consists in excluding such groups from negotiations for two months. The fact that this sanction, unlike the previous one, must be used against groups calling a strike on the basis of an 'indication' from the Commission does not have a rational justification. Different treatment is accorded to spontaneous groups, which are less accustomed to negotiations than large unions, and this is meant to penalize them in their attempt to acquire bargaining power. We may recall once again what was said above about an unresolved conflict within the conflict, hidden behind certain provisions in the law; even in the definition of sanctions one senses an uneasiness on the part of the legislature, sensitive enough to understand the symptoms of the disease affecting union representativeness but certainly not able to cure the disease itself.

The employer's direct involvement in issuing sanctions against unions has been challenged before the Constitutional Court on many grounds. The Court held Article 4, section 2, to be unconstitutional as no reference is made in it, in contrast to section 3, to the Commission's power to 'indicate' sanctions.[46] Beyond the technicalities, this decision is worth mentioning for reasons which go back to the original hypothesis put forward in this chapter, namely the role of labour law in setting a new paradigm of citizenship rights in the third sector. First, the Court states that the right to strike acquires an even stronger procedural element when it is exercised in public services: a whole series of intermediate requirements must be met before a stoppage of work. That is why sanctions are constructed in such a way that they can follow procedures and be differentiated according to the various phases of the procedure. Their legal nature changes too, ranging from administrative, to disciplinary, to punitive. Whereas sanctions directed at the individual employee find their justification in contracts of employment and are one further expression of a managerial prerogative, sanctions directed at the unions lack any such origin and are in fact a threat to constitutionally guaranteed union freedoms.

[46] Corte Costituzionale 24 Feb. 1995, no. 57 [1995] *Foro It.*, I, 2407.In this decision Art. 13, related to the Commssion's powers of initiative, including the one to 'indicate' sanctions, was held unconstitutional only with respect to section (c). 'Indication' is a very unusual term in public law; what it really implies in this specific context is that the employer, unlike in other cases where no power is recognized as residing in the Commission, is bound by the Commission's indication.

The Court does not think that a comparison can be drawn between individual employees and unions; it stresses, though, the irrational diversity of sanctions provided for unions in Article 4, section 2, and for other 'subjects' in Article 4, section 3. In this latter case the Commission's 'indication' must depend on the knowledge and evaluation of facts, whereas such elements are not taken into account when unions have to be sanctioned. This implies that, only with regard to unions, a discretionary power is accorded to the employer, who is also freed from any procedural requirement before enforcing the sanction. The Court is thus implying that unions should have the same right to be heard and to present their own reasons as that granted by Italian law to employees undergoing disciplinary measures. This comparison between individuals and organizations can only be read between the lines of the Court's decision; what the reasoning of the Court is more openly aimed at is discovering whether there is a clear line distinguishing economic sanctions directed at unions from punitive sanctions consisting in the exclusion of other groups from negotiations.

In the Court's decision the employer's power to sanction employees is nothing but an 'instrumental power' to ensure that limits are placed on the right to strike; as such it is strictly linked to the guarantee of a 'public interest'. It is also functional to the guarantee of quotas of public services, aimed at the protection of consumers' rights, rather than at fulfilling private interests of the employer. This implies that, as a necessary condition for applying the sanction, the Commission must intervene and evaluate the infringement of the law. This is an example of labour law bridging the gap between public services and citizenship rights: the employers' powers, born within the contractual scheme of employment, acquire a public relevance when sanctioning an employee's unlawful behaviour. This is so because the employee's choice to act unlawfully, infringing—but sometimes simply diminishing—consumers' rights to have access to public services is relevant outside the employment contract.

The lack of alternatives for the enforcement of consumers' rights leads to an abuse of labour law instruments and provokes an expansion of what were intended as private means of self-protection within employment contracts. The employer's direct power to sanction employees does not—and should not—match the definition and purpose of an administrative sanction; nor is the Commission's 'indication' a magic tool which transforms managerial prerogatives into public powers. The escape route, which makes the employer's initiative compatible with individual guarantees, is the protection granted to the employee as part of the employment contract.[47] No similar procedural guarantee exists for unions, but the constitutional right to organize is an even stronger point of reference; that

[47] Art. 2106 of the Civil Code, as amended by Art. 7 of the 1970 Workers' Statute, n. 43 above.

is why the Court underlines that sanctions in this case are directly 'functional' to consumers' rights and must be preceded by the Commission's evaluation.

The role of an independent body, such as a Commission of wise men called upon to give an expert—not a political or administrative—judgment, is in itself full of ambiguities,[48] and yet crucial in the construction of the new paradigm of constitutional citizenship. We must remember that the primary aim of the statute establishing such a body is to protect personal constitutional rights, while maintaining the right to strike in full operation. Because of this double mandate, self-restraint becomes a golden rule when evaluating essential quotas of public services negotiated in collective agreements, as well as indicating sanctions to be directed against those initiating strikes.

Labour law dominates the scene, as a consequence of the still too timid attempt made at creating an intermediate body between consumers and public services. Service providers are asked to act using employers' prerogatives, because contracts of employment are the only mediation between personal constitutional rights and the practical and technical organization of the service itself. Labour law then becomes a bridge between public and private spheres of the law: it serves the purpose of protecting a public interest, but in order to do so it relies on a third subject.

The missing actors in this play are consumers, ignored by the Italian statute even though they would seem to be centre stage. A new culture of conflict must be confronted with the willingness of these new characters to be effectively on the scene and to find new forms of collective representation. This is an issue for comparisons between European legal systems and inventive solutions at Community level. Public authorities could be made more active at local level; measures of conflict resolution could be put into action and experimented with, extending if necessary to compulsory arbitration. In all instances, consumers should be heard in order to remind labour lawyers that they have entered the discipline and represent a new core of it. Even under these new circumstances, the right to strike should not cease to be a strong social sanction, an extraordinary collective device which makes a collective voice heard. Consumers cannot be considered a counterpart to strikers: even when protected in the exercise of their constitutional rights, they may, nevertheless, be affected by conflict and undergo some inconvenience. This implies that the concrete modalities of the right to strike, without interfering with consumers' fundamental rights, help to redefine the latter's expectations and require that their needs be temporarily reshaped.

[48] See critical comments by A.Travi, 'Corte costituzionale e legge sullo sciopero' [1995] *DLRI* 346 ff.

Another decision of the Constitutional Court will be analysed in the following section, as a useful example of expanding consumers' rights through the inclusion in the statute's scope of a specific and rather different form of conflict. This new change in the 1990 Statute will help us to draw some conclusions regarding the imitative effect that the right to strike has had among professional groups of workers in a position different from that of subordinate employees and therefore not bound by contracts of employment.

8. A Further Example of Concerted Action and the Expansion of Citizenship Rights

In 1996 the Constitutional Court entered a new controversial field, in the attempt to apply the 1990 Statute to 'abstentions' by solicitors and barristers from practising the legal profession.[49] The 'administration of justice' is listed in Article 2(a) among public services, with regard to the granting of personal fundamental freedoms, especially for citizens who have been imprisoned, but also for those subject to interlocutory injunctions. Any delay in the delivery of courts' decisions, if caused by a protest by solicitors and barristers resulting in the lack of assistance during the trial, may infringe 'the parties' or consumers' constitutional rights and give rise to claims by the consumers themselves.

The core of the decision is whether a concerted protest of this kind can be assimilated to the right to strike and consequently be balanced against other constitutional rights. Following previous leading cases, the Court specifies that, whenever the right to strike may not technically be invoked, it is freedom of association which helps to interpret the abstention from work of other professional groups. Protest is lawful, even when no socio-economic dependence can be proved, just as it is for employees who are parties to contracts of employment; since the 1990 Statute it has a constitutional relevance, because the principles in Article 1 of that Statute can be widely interpreted, so as to provide concrete protection for consumers. The Court holds Article 2, sections 1 and 5 to be unconstitutional, inasmuch as they do not impose any obligation to give notice, nor set any reasonable time limit in cases of concerted abstentions by solicitors and barristers, nor do they provide for the definition of essential quotas of the service to be delivered and sanctions to be enforced.

The Court could not go any further in its decision, other than expressing the urgent need for legislative intervention on the matter, so that the gap could be filled and consumers could be fairly treated. A statute is considered necessary, because of the lack of *erga omnes* enforceability of the codes

[49] Corte Costituzionale, 27 May 1996, no. 171 [1996] Giur. It., I, 543.

of conduct adopted by professional associations. Codes normally include ethical and deontological rules which acquire a public relevance in setting standards for the whole profession; the problem is the lack of any sanction apparatus and the consequent non-enforceability of consumers' rights. The interesting story to report is that this decision prompted reactions from several institutional actors and opened up a confrontation which demonstrates once again the centrality of labour law in the settlement of disputes in which consumers—and not necessarily employers and employees—are key actors.

The Commission had indeed made its voice heard before the Constitutional Court's decision,[50] claiming its right to intervene whenever consumers' rights were seriously threatened, should this occur as a consequence of protests other than strikes. The dialogue between the Commission and the organizations of professional lawyers involved in protests developed into an exercise in setting limits to each other's competence: the Commission went beyond its powers in interpreting the Court's decision and proceeded to give itself the role of conflict mediator, despite its unclear jurisdiction.

The effect of all this was to make both public opinion and the government aware of the urgency of intervening with appropriate legislation. The Minister for Justice reluctantly responded with the insertion of certain measures in his ongoing proposals for reform: codes of conduct should include notice of at least ten days; the Minister himself was to be entitled to notice of detailed procedures to be followed in plans for abstentions involving the legal professions; no protest should last longer than thirty days or be followed by another within ninety days; and criminal sanctions should be provided for those who do not comply with the new rules.

The Commission's activism, followed by the threat of legislative intervention, drove all associations active in the legal professions into making a united response, where divisions and contrasts had previously been shown, mainly related to the still uncertain nature of different groups within the professions. This detail is not irrelevant in our perspective: no clear function can automatically—and perhaps imitatively—be attributed to collective organizations not forming part of industrial relations prac-

[50] The deliberation in question is that of 15 June 1995, no. 3.1. After one year, referring to the Constitutional Court's decision, the Commission intervened again, requiring the termination of a very long protest 'in compliance with the law as modified by the Constitutional Court' (deliberation of 13 June 1996, published, together with other documents of organizations active in the protest, in [1997] *Argomenti di diritto del lavoro* 338 ff.). It is interesting to stress that the Commission, despite its weak institutional role, went as far as interpreting extensively a decision of the Constitutional Court which has not as such modified the law. This caused a lively reaction from a national association of solicitors and barristers, disagreeing with the interpretation of the decision, which had not, in its view, 'added' anything to the law.

tices. Organizations of professionals may have a political role and leave members of the profession free to join or not; they may have an institutional relevance, as in professional 'orders' which are empowered to co-opt members on the basis of specific requirements and of which membership is compulsory. The effort to gain recognition in the public sphere is linked to the capacity of new collective actors to prove that they obey the rules of the game and are able to be representative of their members, namely in enforcing rules and exhibiting credibility to consumers.

The easiest way to gain visibility, while lacking an established representativeness, was to start political negotiation with the legislature, trying to influence the making of the law through lobbying. This is still an open forum, while many questions have remained unanswered. In particular the Commission continues to fight its fierce battle: not to be interpreted as a sign of arrogance, its determination not to abandon the scene must be seen as a commitment towards consumers, perhaps a way to help them develop trust towards a body with limited binding powers, and yet with a special capacity to act as an effective protagonist.

What is being achieved, through acts of a symbolic rather than a binding nature, is forcing the media to report on suggestions and evaluations given by the Commission, thus making ideas circulate on how consumers' rights could be better protected in an area which is not yet clearly covered by the law. Furthermore, the Commission is obliged to keep Parliament informed of its activity: deliberations addressed to the professional lawyers' organizations, regardless of their willingness to obey them, thus become part of a discursive body of law, open to constant changes and available for observers of the political and legislative process.

9. The Role of Collective Agreements in the Privatization of Public Employment—Are Consumers' Rights Relevant?

The Italian decree which has privatized the legal regime of employment contracts in what was once described as the public sector would merit a very long and detailed presentation. For the purposes of this chapter, only a few remarks will be offered, as a further confirmation of the arguments developed above. It must first be recalled that the decree regulating this matter finds its origins in a statute[51] empowering the Government to issue legislation on various matters, ranging from health and social security to local finances and public-sector reform. It was the Legislature's intention to prove that there is an interdependence of all such measures, relevant for intervention both in modernizing and in rationalizing important state

[51] D. Legislativo, 3 Feb. 1993, no. 29, amended by D. Legislativo 4 Nov. 1997, no. 396. The statute delegating to intervention by decree is L. 23 Oct. 1992, no. 421.

functions. This is yet another way of achieving the general aims inherent in public services, pointing to the necessity of adopting an overall view of them, whenever a legislative reform is being conceived. The intention of the Legislature in 1992 was in fact to begin a long-lasting review of existing laws in strategic areas, aimed at increasing efficiency and cutting expenditure, in order to improve the public budget.

Citizenship rights should inspire the whole reform of the former public sector, although it is no easy task to extrapolate them from the intricacies of this very complex piece of legislation. The much stronger position acquired by collective bargaining, especially after the reform of 1997, is in itself an indication of the new functions that such a consolidated form of private governance is capable of performing, even in the arena of public administration. The idea of privatizing contracts of employment implies that the same tools as those used in the private sector must be made available; although adaptation is required, given the different aims inherent in the running of a public apparatus, the dominant intention of the Legislature is to narrow the gap between the two sectors and to favour co-ordination of bargaining activities.

The changes in the law brought about by the 1997 Decree are a significant confirmation of the fact that straightforward transplants between different spheres of economic activity are neither productive nor possible. The current state of affairs is that collective bargaining in the former public sector is acquiring its own identity and is shaping the relationship between centralized and decentralized agreements in an original way, different from the rigid hierarchy of sources indicated in the 1993 Decree. One of the crucial elements is establishing procedures and principles of representation in negotiations. Previous provisions on binding governmental guidelines, which were aimed at encapsulating the whole bargaining process, soon proved incompatible with the very notion of collective bargaining; they have now been replaced by more flexible regulations which enable the administration to relate more closely to its bargaining agent.

Nevertheless, procedures are lengthy and detailed. An 'agency'[52] stands as a representative of the public in the negotiations; its members are appointed by the Prime Minister; its functions are specified in the decree and result in more limited autonomy, if compared with the private sector.

[52] Art. 50 of Decree no. 29 is devoted to the agency's functioning and composition and was amended in 1997. Art. 51, as amended, deals with collective bargaining procedures and with the guidelines the agency receives from sectoral organizations within the administration. This change is a significant one, when compared with previous rules according to which binding guidelines were imposed by Government. The latter must now express its evaluation on the general guidelines suggested by the administration prior to the renewal of national collective agreements. The leading criterion is compatibility between the goals of the negotiation and general economic and financial policies.

Decentralized bargaining takes place as a result of rules agreed at national level and within the budgetary constraints of each government department. This still implies a hierarchy of different bargaining levels, whereby the broader and higher level indicates matters to be dealt with at the lower level, subject to the available financial resources; in a transitional phase, experimental bargaining is favoured even before the signing of national agreements on matters such as the reorganization of the services provided, particularly in relation to personnel training, flexible working time, part-time work, the working environment, and equal opportunities.

If we go back to what we said earlier about public services very often being dependent on a decentralized organization for service provision, and on local users' demands and expectations, we realize how important collective bargaining can be in the definition of citizenship rights. The fact that this particular area of activity is undergoing such significant changes in the regulation of employment contracts, while maintaining the public nature of employers, opens up room for further reflection. Previous references in the Decree to ways of preventing the lowering of standards in the quality of services as an effect of privatization have disappeared in the new amended version. This may be taken as a sign of pragmatism on the part of the Legislature, a way of acknowledging that references to the compatibility of efficiency in the public administration with consumers' demands are often purely nominal and difficult to translate into concrete and actionable rights.

Furthermore, the privatization of employment contracts in the public sector throws a new light on the anomalies of the Italian collective-bargaining system—namely the lack of *erga omnes* enforceability of collective agreements—especially when these voluntary sources attempt to regulate issues of public relevance, including consumers' rights. All this implies that recognition of the general and public interest in a well-run administration does not disappear from the catalogue of constitutional values, but must be constantly confronted with private means, such as collective agreements, for the implementation of employees' rights and, at the same time, for the satisfaction of consumers' demands.

These only seemingly conflicting ambitions harboured by the Legislature reveal that the regulatory technique chosen in such a particular case, similar to that used in the 1990 Statute on the right to strike in public services, consists in the balancing of constitutional rights and bringing them to a new equilibrium. Rather than reducing the scope of separate—but not conflicting—spheres of constitutional values, these new attempts by the Legislature may, in the long run, reveal new dimensions of the values themselves. The right to bargain collectively, as an expression of the right to organize, consolidates its own constitutional relevance, especially when exposed to the regulation of public interests.

In this new legal framework, emphasis must be placed on the strengthened and now very visible quasi-public relevance of employees' organizations, an inevitable consequence of the more institutionalized bargaining procedures laid out in the Decree. The 1997 reform has taken these new union functions into account and opened up the way for future legal intervention in the private sector, introducing for the first time rules aimed at measuring the representativeness of employees' organizations, for the purpose of bargaining collectively.[53] The quasi-public role played by private associations is also a necessary answer to the new model of bargaining agent on the employers' side, introduced by the Decree. The 'agency' is yet another example of a body appointed on the basis of expertise rather than political affiliation; although its tasks were thought of as purely technical ones, they result in very delicate balancing powers extending beyond the compatibility of wage costs with general budget constraints.

Even when the law—such as the decree so far analysed—does not offer any clear ground for citizenship rights, their grant comes as a result of strong constitutional traditions, such as the Italian one. Labour law contributes immensely to building the bridge that first inspired the title of this chapter.

10. Concluding Remarks

One of the threads linking the various chapters of this book is the search for a new paradigm of citizenship rights, in dealing with public services and with the labour law implications in their organization. The centrality of industrial enterprises has been questioned, following the diversification of production techniques and market needs. Yet, the core of constitutional rights and the construction of labour law traditions were built around the enterprise, the place in which opposing powers and interests had to be balanced and measured in concrete terms. The outcome was different in different legal systems, although centred around a small number of principles which also emerge from the present analysis.

Collective bargaining is undoubtedly very central in laying the foundations of constitutional values which may be disseminated in spheres of public relevance. We have underlined the fact that, as a mere expression of private governance, collective bargaining cannot by itself be the only pillar on which rights may be built, nor the only source of regulation. Yet,

[53] Art. 7 of Decree no. 396, now Art. 47 *bis* of D. legislativo 29/1993. Only unions which can show that they represent a minimum of 5% of the workforce, as an average between membership and votes gained in elections of union representatives, may be admitted to the bargaining table.

we have also stressed—particularly in relation to the Italian legal system and the examples taken from it—that there is a tendency to rely on this well established system of interest representation for the solution of problems which are not within its original scope. This leads to the rediscovery of collective bargaining and the placing of it in a new perspective; issues of public relevance are slowly being incorporated into its procedures and tending to be shaped by its inherent normative function.

A different legal discourse is linked to the right to strike. We are aware of the uniqueness of the Italian example in comparative terms, although functional equivalents can be found in other legal systems, whenever the provision of public services is at stake. Despite the specificity of this example, we feel that it is extremely useful in demonstrating the theory of proportionality as between citizenship rights. Whenever we want to make sure that new rights are established, especially in emerging new areas, such as public services, we must also be certain not to destroy previous rights; on the contrary, we must adapt them and revisit their tradition, so as to bring out the full potential of their regulatory scope.

Proving that labour law is a very fertile ground for experimenting with new balances of powers and new relationships between different legal and non-legal sources has been one of the aims of this chapter. Whether it will be possible to favour such an experiment at Community level still remains to be seen. At this stage in legislative and political developments, it may suffice to say that the dissemination of constitutional values, even in the absence of a catalogue of constitutional rights, is essential in creating a favourable environment in which new traditions may develop and new liberties may be granted. The lesson taught by labour law, as indicated earlier, in the first chapter of this book, should be that, in overcoming the historical divide between public and private spheres of regulation, individuals become citizens both within the place of work and outside it, and establish their own rights as full members of the working environment as well as of the community of consumers.

Index